Coming Again

Coming Again

by Jerry Newcombe

Chariot Victor Publishing
A Division of Cook Communications

Chariot Victor Publishing
a division of Cook Communications, Colorado Springs, Colorado 80918
Cook Communications, Paris, Ontario
Kingsway Communications, Eastbourne, England

COMING AGAIN

Published in association with the literary agency of Alive Communicaitons, Inc., 1465 Kelly Johnson Blvd., Suite 320, Colorado Springs, CO 80920

Printed in the United States of America.

1 2 3 4 5 6 7 8 9 10 Printing/Year 03 02 01 00 99

Editor: Jerry Yamamoto, Julie Smith
Design: Jeffrey P. Barnes

Library of Congress Cataloging-in-Publication Data

Newcombe, Jerry.
Coming again/by Jerry Newcombe.
p. cm.
Includes bibliographical references and index.
ISBN 1-56476-769-8
1. Second Advent. I. Title.
BT886.N48 1999 99-15575
236'.9--dc21 CIP

CONTENTS

Dedication

To Dr. Ron Kilpatrick, librarian of Knox Theological Seminary, whose help with the research for this book was invaluable.

Preface

The predictions about Christ's first and second coming is one of the most important parts of the Bible.[1]

—T. Norton Sterrett

Ben Franklin once said, "Many a long dispute among divines may be thus abridg'd, It is so, It is not so; It is so, It is not so."[2] Don't let the old-American English get in the way of appreciating what he's saying. His observation would seem to apply quite well to the end-times disputes between theologians, writers, and speakers: "Yes, it is." "No, it's not." "Yes, it is." "No, it's not."

Anybody familiar with the subject of Bible prophecies and the end times knows that there's quite a bit of the Ben Franklin-type disputes: Yes, it is! No, it isn't! There are all sorts of opinions out there, and they all claim to base their version of the last days on what the Bible says.

The questions at hand for this book deal with end-times prophecies.

- When and how is Christ coming again?
- Is there a literal millennium to look forward to?
- Is the Antichrist alive and well and awaiting his turn to take center stage?
- Are these the last days? Are we the generation that will see the Second Coming?
- Are these and similar questions theologically on target?

Views differ on eschatology, even among scholarly, Bible-centered Christians. How can we get through the maze of all these different opinions? It is my goal to simplify much of the controversy and be your objective—hopefully—guide through this labyrinth of some two thousand years of views. I say two thousand years, but in reality the controversy has heated up since the rebirth of the great interest in prophecy beginning in the 1830s.

What can we know for sure about His return? Is there common ground between the various views of the return of Christ?

While we don't have time for every pet theory of every obscure group, we do want to look at some of the *major* opinions on some of the key issues of the last days. Here's a quick overview of where we're headed in our journey:

Part 1 is "What's the Difference?" The goal will be to form a clear idea of some of the major theories about the Second Coming and to see what they're based on. Included in this section will be a briefing on key terms helpful to our journey, a chapter on how the premillennialists envision the end time, and also a look at what the amillennialists and postmillennialists think will happen.

I should point out that when I quote a premillennialist, he or she is not necessarily speaking for all premillennialists. Nor is each nonmillenarian speaking for all amillennialists or postmillennialists. But often they are.

As we progress to Part 2, we enter what I call "The Heart of the Controversy." On the subject of the end times, Charles Ryrie points out, "the disagreement is in the interpretation of prophecy."[3] That is absolutely correct, and it's helpful to back up and examine the underlying assumptions.

Then we head to Part 3, "Is the Great Tribulation a Past or Future Event?" The primary goal will be to look at what Jesus said on the subject. Then we'll explore two key questions in depth: Is the great tribulation a past event? That may sound like heresy to modern ears, but some leading theologians through the ages would basically answer that question yes. Then we'll look at the counterpoint: Is the great tribulation a future event?

We'll move on from there to Part 4, a section I call "Issue by Issue." Here, we'll go through some of the controversial subjects surrounding the end times chapter by chapter, such as the Rapture, the Antichrist, the Millennium, the role of Israel in the last days, and Daniel's Seventieth Week.

Finally, we'll progress to Part 5, which is a look at "Practical Applications." With the differing views on Christ's coming, is there some common ground? Then we'll look at ways in which prophets of the Apocalypse have blown it in the past, predicting Christ's sure return by XYZ date even though He told us nobody knows the day or the hour. (I even read one such prophet who essentially said—with a straight face: Christ didn't tell us the day or the hour, but that doesn't mean we can't know the year, the month, or the week![4]) Finally, we'll consider Ezekiel's question that Francis Schaeffer popularized: How should we then live?

As we consider differing opinions on the end times, keep in mind a few points:

(1) It's best to try to keep an open mind and approach this subject with humility. Truly committed Christians take differing sides on this issue.

Thus, though you may have your own opinions and convictions, at least try to understand other opinions. I'm not exploring the views of the cults or other religions—I'm exploring opinions by Bible-believing Christians. Therefore, it behooves us to be humble. Many have been wrong in the past on the end times. How can we think *we're* infallible?

(2) Let's all try to be Bereans. The Berean Jews, we are told in Acts 17:11, were more noble than the Thessalonian Jews because when they heard what Paul had to say about Jesus of Nazareth, they "searched the Scriptures" to determine whether these things were so. Judge the various opinions you encounter here with what God says in His holy Word.

(3) Above all, we need to be ready at all times for His return. He could come tonight. He could come next year. Some people even think He could come tens of thousands of years from now. He could come whenever. It's quite clear that when He does, He wants to find us active in His work, not idly speculating on the minutia of details of the last days.

So with these thoughts in mind, let us humbly cross the threshold into the maze of opinions on the end times. On to Part 1. Let the journey begin.

Part One

What's the Difference?

1

The Return of Christ

Behold, I am coming soon!

—Jesus Christ (Rev. 22:7)

Millennium fever is in the air.

- You can see it in the spate of books coming out.
- You can see it in the apocalyptic movies that Hollywood churns out.
- You can see it in the kind of dire predictions related to Y2K (the computer problem) with many messages along the lines of "Y2K and the Rise of Antichrist."

Already, millions in our culture, Christian and nonChristian, are curious as to what the dawn of the new millennium means. Is the end of the world at hand? Are these the last days, as we hear quite often? Are we the generation that will finally see the Second Coming?

Millennium fever is in the air.

Writer Richard Erdoes points out:

> It is no longer only the sandal-clad hermits and oddballs walking the streets with placards proclaiming "the end of the world" who think that this puny planet of ours might not survive the twentieth century. Perfectly sane people, among them scientists and Nobel laureates, predict humankind's demise due to overpopulation, famines, deforestation, pollution, depletion of the earth's ozone layer, errors in human engineering, or simply the collapse of civilization due to the exhaustion of essential, nonrenewable raw materials. The end of Christianity's second millennium is near, and A.D. 2000 is just a few years away. Today, as a thousand years ago, fears of the future are submerged, pushed into the background by the minifears of daily life, which, as Mark Twain pointed out, "is one d— thing after another."[1]

That's an amazing statement—especially when you consider Erdoes wrote that ten years ago.

Is the end of the world at hand? Based on all that you hear and all the hype, you would certainly think so. Many people think that *this* is it, that *ours* is the final generation, that in *our* lifetime Christ will finally return.

Consider just a few examples:

- Hal Lindsey: "We are the generation that will see the end times . . . and the return of Jesus."[2]
- William T. James: ". . . the indicators strongly suggest that we stand at the very precipice of that horrific period that Jesus called the great tribulation . . ."[3]
- Salem Kirban: ". . . it is my considered opinion, that the time clock is now at 11:59."[4]

The irony is that statements like this can be found throughout church history from virtually any era. And yet, in our day . . .

- With the pallet-loads of books that state or suggest the end of the world is at hand selling like proverbial hotcakes;
- With Christian broadcasters discussing the end times with a Bible in one hand and the newspaper in the other;
- With the explosion of cults, the occult, and spiritual deception seemingly all around us;

. . . interest in eschatology seems to be at an all-time high, especially as we move closer to the turn of the millennium. So are these the last days?

More Than 60 Percent Believe in the Second Coming

Americans by and large believe in the Second Coming. A Gallup poll in 1983 found that 62 percent of Americans "harbor no doubt" that Jesus is coming back.[5] They note: "Among those who say religion is very important in their lives, 79% believe in the second coming of Christ."[6] A decade later, in 1994, a *U.S. News and World Report* survey found that 61 percent believe in the second coming of Jesus. Moreover, 60 percent of Americans believe the world will end; one-third of them believe it will end in the near future.[7] Millennium fever is surely in the air.

Meanwhile, belief in the second coming of Jesus is not just a Christian view. In *The History of Islam*, Robert Payne writes that Muslims . . .

> have roots which are the same as ours; share the same portion of the energy of God. We tend to forget that Jesus is the Messiah of the Muhammadans, as He is ours. According to a famous *hadith*, one of the traditional sayings of Muhammad was: "There is no Mahdi [Messiah] save Jesus son of Mary." And at the coming of the Last Day Jesus will descend triumphantly from the skies, wage war on Antichrist and die for the second time, and His body will be buried in a tomb beside Muhammad before he rises once more to rule over a Paradise of youth and freshness.[8]

It's hard to picture the average Muslim expecting Jesus Christ's return, but it's technically in their own theology. It's also in their own holy book, the Koran.

When you realize there are roughly two billion Christians worldwide and roughly one billion Muslims, that means that three billion people worldwide (more than half) believe, at least *theoretically*, that Jesus is coming back. That means well over half (maybe even two-thirds) of the world's population claim to subscribe to a belief system that includes the second coming of Jesus Christ. And who knows how many non-Christians think that He might come back as well?

Now it would seem that there is a substantial number (though far, far from the majority) who profess to be Christians, but don't necessarily believe in His return. For example, *Time* magazine reports that 78 percent of Americans call themselves Christians,[9] and yet only 61 percent of Americans are expecting the return of Jesus. What do we make of that? I know there are a few "full preterists" out there, people who believe Christ came back in A.D. 70 and won't be coming again at some future time. In the above cited survey, Gallup found that 1 percent believe that "the Second Coming has already taken place or is happening now."[10] Maybe there are a lot of "Christian agnostics"—which is quite an oxymoron. In any event, 61 percent of Americans who believe in the return of Jesus is still a substantial number of Americans who believe the future belongs to Christ.

Unsolved Mysteries?

Reader's Digest once published a large picture book filled with unsolved mysteries. The book listed some of the prophecies about Jesus' first coming, which in fact Jesus fulfilled during His earthly ministry. According to the editors, it was a mystery how these things could have been foretold so accurately. Yet we know that God the Holy Spirit foretold these things. To the believer there's no mystery at all. If anything, they provide strong evidence that God inspired the Scriptures.

Adrian Rogers defines prophecy as "prewritten history."[11] We know that there are 333 prophecies in the Old Testament that Jesus of Nazareth fulfilled. They are not vague fortune cookie–type statements (e.g., "More money will soon come your way"). The Bible's prophecies are very specific messages containing elements that were not fulfilled until hundreds of years later when Jesus first came as a man. For example, this statement was written about 750 B.C.: "We all, like sheep, have gone astray, each of us has turned to his own way; and the Lord has laid on him the iniquity of us all" (Isa. 53:6). Sound familiar?

Prophecies written somewhere between 1500 B.C. and 400 B.C. spell out 456 specific aspects about the coming Messiah.[12] It was written:

- Where He would be born—Bethlehem (Micah 5:2, about 720 B.C.);
- How He would die—"they have pierced my hands and my feet" (Ps. 22:16, about 1000 B.C.);
- That He would bear our sins, and by His stripes we would be healed (Isa. 53:5, about 750 B.C.).

You can read the fifty-third chapter of Isaiah to a non-Christian and ask, "About whom is this written?" and the average person, even many Jewish people, will answer, "Jesus." Yet these things were written more than seven centuries *before* Christ. That would be like predicting something for the year A.D. 2750 and having it turn out exactly as you predicted. The mathematical odds of your prediction occurring are staggering.[13]

Note what former skeptic and journalist Lee Strobel said about the Old Testament prophecies pointing to Christ. He was a Yale-trained lawyer and the legal affairs editor of the *Chicago Tribune*. After his wife's conversion, he decided to use his skills as a journalist to see whether there was possibly any merit to the claims of historic Christianity. He was in for a staggering surprise. Here's what he said about the messianic prophecies of Christ's first coming:

> In all, there are about five dozen major prophecies concerning the Messiah, and the more I studied them,

> the more difficulty I had in trying to explain them away. My first line of defense was that Jesus may have intentionally maneuvered His life to fulfill the prophecies so that He would be mistaken for the long-awaited Messiah. For instance, Zechariah 9:9 foretold that the Messiah would ride a donkey into Jerusalem. Maybe when Jesus was getting ready to enter the town, He told His disciples, "Go fetch Me a donkey. I want to fool these people into thinking I'm the Messiah because I'm really anxious to be tortured to death." But that argument fell apart when I read prophecies about events that Jesus never could have arranged, such as the place of His birth, which the prophet Micah foretold seven hundred years in advance, and His ancestry, how He was born, how He was betrayed for a specific amount of money, how He was put to death, how His bones remained unbroken (unlike the two criminals who were crucified with Him), how the soldiers cast lots for His clothing, and on and on.[14]

We could belabor this point, but we won't because the issue at hand for this book is the prophecies dealing with His coming again. And yet, even that statement is not without controversy. For instance, some theologians interpret the Old Testament prophecies picturing the Messiah as the conquering king as in the process of being fulfilled in Christ and His church today, whereas others interpret them as yet to be fulfilled.

There are two strands of prophecies related to the Christ in the Old Testament. (*Christ* is simply the Greek word for the Hebrew word *Messiah*, which in English means "the Anointed One.") One strand deals with the suffering servant; the other with the vanquishing, victorious deliverer. Clearly, Jesus fulfilled the first strand when He came the first time, but it's a matter of controversy as to whether He (through His church) is in the process of fulfilling such verses as "the earth will be full of the knowledge of the Lord as the waters cover the sea" (Isa. 11:9) or "No longer will a man teach his neighbor, or a man his brother, saying, 'Know the Lord,' because they will all know me, from the least of them to the greatest,' declares the Lord" (Jer. 31:34).

Paul Little points out how Christ fulfilled the suffering servant passages and has begun the process of fulfilling the second strand:

> The first coming of Christ, as the suffering servant, answered the hope for God's coming to redeem his people. The second coming of Christ will bring consummation of that hope when he returns as reigning king.
>
> In the meantime, though, Satan has been conquered by Christ—at the cross and in the resurrection—so that "through death he might destroy him who had the power of death, that is, the devil" (Heb. 2:14). But Satan is temporarily still "the god of this world" (2 Cor. 4:4), and he is actively opposing Christ and his church.[15]

Surprised by Jesus of Nazareth

It's interesting to note that those who were expecting the Messiah the first time were caught off guard by Jesus of Nazareth. He was not expected, not the way He was. In fact, irony of ironies, the Jewish leaders themselves helped fulfill a lot of the prophecies about the Messiah in their acts of judgment against Him—even though they were quite familiar with the Scriptures. Perhaps this is why a large number of the Jews—though certainly not the majority—repented of their sins and came to faith in Him when Peter preached at Pentecost (Acts 2:37-41). Their eyes were opened to the messianic prophecies Jesus of Nazareth had fulfilled.

Why did the scribes and Pharisees blow it? Because of their preconceived notions of His coming. Is it not possible that many of us today might not misunderstand His second coming because of our preconceived notions? This is why I believe there should be great humility in our approach to handling the prophetic portion of the Word of God. I don't see how some writers can be exceedingly dogmatic about it—and they are.

Confessions of a Former "Hodgepodgist"

The labels of end-times positions seem endless. "I'm a premil, pretrib dispensationalist." "I'm an amillennialist." "I'm a posttribulational premillennialist." I must confess that before I began my research on this book, the best label for me on the end times would be a "hodgepodgist"—that is, an eclectic. In fact, I had latched onto bits and pieces from various schools of thought without knowing their origin or without thinking through the ramifications of those beliefs. It gets confusing, and the more you study it, the more confusing it often gets.

When you begin to get bogged down, and when you begin to realize the divergence of strongly held opinions of the end times among well-meaning, Bible-believing Christians, you can easily be baffled. Dr. R. C. Sproul, a respected conservative scholar, wrote *The Last Days According to Jesus*. He points out in his conclusion that ambiguities within the texts of Scripture—not that there's the slightest defect within Scripture—lie at the root of this conflict:

> Debates over eschatology will probably continue until the Lord returns and we have the advantage of hindsight rather than the disadvantage of foresight. The divisions that exist within the Christian community are understandable, considering that both the subject matter and the literary genre of future prophecy are exceedingly difficult. This does not mean that we may push the Bible aside or neglect its eschatological sections. On the contrary the interpretive difficulties presented by eschatological matters simply call us to a greater diligence and persistence in seeking their solution.[16]

We are called to be Bereans, rather than Hodgepodgists

Thus we are called to be Bereans, rather than Hodgepodgists.

Why would God give us ambiguities so that many scholars are divided in this area? Could it be that He wants a few things from us? Such as:

(1) Each generation to live in tension with the understanding that Christ could come at any minute, but He might not. As a result, we need to engage in long-term planning and strategy for the kingdom, while never getting too settled on this earth, which is not our ultimate home. Like the cliché that we should pray as if it all depends on God and work as if it all depends on us, we should live each day as if He's coming any second and plan ahead as if He were to come a thousand years from now.

(2) For us to avoid the "dating game." There's a whole chapter on that very issue ("Failed Predictions of Christ's Return"), where we see how misguided believers have falsely predicted Christ's return, and not just

the lunatic fringe. Even such stalwart believers as St. Martin of Tours, Martin Luther, Christopher Columbus, and Isaac Newton got it wrong.

(3) That we might have a test of our faith and of our love for each other. It is not clearly revealed by God (although some claim that it is) as to when Jesus is coming back. Yet it *is* clearly revealed that we are to love our Christian brother and sister. Therefore, because our master is away on a long journey (a very long one), He expects to find us busy about our Father's business upon His return. "Occupy until I come." He doesn't want us to sit lazily, reviewing our latest end-times charts to dazzle and tickle our curiosity. The secret things belong to God, but that which is revealed clearly is revealed for our obedience (Deut. 29:29).

Several years ago my younger brother and some of his friends used to sit around in what they called "the Box." It was a small room in the basement of one his friends. This small coterie of companions would meet quite often and chew the latest theory. (They were just like the Athenians Paul encountered in Acts 17, who would spend all their time discussing the latest theory to come down the pike.) The friends in the Box were decidedly anti-Christian in their bias. They quickly dismissed the idea of the church or the Bible as providing the answers to the solutions to life's riddles. My brother quit attending the discussions in the Box when they began to receive answers to life's questions from a Ouija board. He knew enough about satanic deception to discontinue attending.

Sometimes evangelical Christians have their own version of the Box when they sit around speculating on the details of Christ's return. Meanwhile, our nation continues its downward plunge into moral darkness. Some people dogmatically assert that they *know* when Jesus is going to come back. They claim to know more about the subject than Jesus when He was on earth. It's tragic too because they gain many followers and then shipwreck their faith when their predictions inevitably turn out to be untrue.

In an essay on the Second Coming, Chuck Swindoll writes, "The ultimate extremists would be those who set specific dates, then quit their jobs and mooch off others as they wait for the Lord's return."[17] Yes, we have our own version of the Box. The New Testament teaches the return of Christ so that we may be busy working and watching for His return—not that we sit around and speculate about His coming again.

The Last Days Versus the Last, Last Days

Are we living in the last days?

In our day, particularly with the new millennium upon us, focus on the Second Coming looms large. One well-known author (still making the circuit) had the audacity to declare on Christian television that if Jesus doesn't come back by a certain date, then Jesus is a liar. The date in question was 1988. But Jesus didn't lie. The fault lay with the interpreter.

Do you remember the small book making the rounds several years ago entitled *88 Reasons Why the Rapture Is in 1988*? Dr. D. James Kennedy, pastor of Coral Ridge Presbyterian Church in Fort Lauderdale, mentioned that booklet a few days before the alleged target date in September. As I recall, the Rapture was supposedly going to take place on Tuesday. Dr. Kennedy asked, "What do I think of that booklet? Well, let's have breakfast on Wednesday and discuss it." This was not the first time, nor will it be the last, that someone tries to nail down the exact time of Christ's return. One minister told me recently that one of the first things he learned in seminary was that virtually every generation of Christians thought that theirs was the last.

Do you realize it is possible Jesus will come back before this day is out?

My thirteen-year-old son said he has figured out when Christ is coming back. It's when no one in the world will be expecting it. So it wouldn't be January 1, 2000, or some other high-profile date. (Not bad for a teenager.)

Are we living in the last days?

Do you realize that it is possible that Jesus will come back before this year is out? Before this week is out? Before this day is out? But it's also true that Jesus may come back five thousand years from now. You may say there's no way that could be because the signs of His coming have all aligned themselves in our day with such incredible precision. Yet that interpretation is based on some assumptions, which, if incorrect, make the whole scenario irrelevant.

Furthermore, remember: To God, a day is like a thousand years and a thousand years like a day. If Christ came back in five thousand years, that would be like five days from now. What were you doing five days ago? That wasn't that long ago, was it? Yet even this application of Scripture is questionable. In fact, when Peter said that to the Lord, a day is like a thousand years and a thousand years a day (2 Pet. 3:8), isn't it likely he means long eons of time, not just strictly one thousand literal years? The point is God is outside of time.

So back to my question. Are we living in the last days?

J. Marcellus Kik points out in his book *An Eschatology of Victory*:

> A general impression prevails that the term, "last days," has reference to a short period just before the second coming of Christ, but that term is not so defined in Scriptures. The "last days" began with the first advent of Christ and will continue until his second advent.[18]

When did it start? At the establishment of the church at Pentecost, which occurred shortly after Christ's ascension. The writer of Hebrews notes, "In the past God spoke to our forefathers through the prophets at many times and in various ways, but in these *last days* he has spoken to us by his Son" (1:1-2, emphasis mine). The past was past, but now these are the last days. But they've been the last days since the time of the New Testament. Thus the question becomes: Are these "the *last*, last days?"

How and When?

There have been endless books dealing with Christ's second coming (most often from a premillennial dispensational viewpoint). As I set out to see what has been said on this topic *through the ages*—on the Second Coming, the Millennium, the Rapture, the Antichrist, and so on—I discovered that while the early Christians (first two to three centuries) thought in terms of a literal Millennium to come, the church for the most part adopted the amillennial position (especially through St. Augustine's influence) for some fourteen centuries. Not until the 1830s did there arise serious questioning of the amillennial position.

Consider for a moment what St. Augustine said. He was surely one of the greatest theologians in the history of the church. In his monumental work, *The City of God*, he highlighted the key events of the last times:

> In connection with the last judgment, therefore, we who believe can be sure of the following truths: Elias [Elijah] the Thesbite will return; the Jews will believe;

> Antichrist will persecute the Church; Christ will be the Judge; the dead will rise; the good will be separated from the wicked; the world will suffer from fire, but will be renewed. Of course, what we believe is the simple fact that all these things are to be; but how and in what sequence the events are to occur we must leave to future experience, which alone can teach these truths so much better than human intelligence can at present understand. My own view is that they will occur in the order I have just mentioned.[19]

Let me repeat and emphasize one part of his quote, which is so relevant to our time: "... **what we believe is the simple fact that all these things are to be; but how and in what sequence the events are to occur we must leave to future experience, which alone can teach these truths so much better than human intelligence can at present understand.**" Amen. Hindsight is always 20/20.

How and when will the details of the Second Coming be? We don't know.

In All Things Charity

One conviction I hold on this issue is that it's not right for Christians to be dogmatic about the end times. It's not right for Christians to stop loving one another because of divisions over the end times. We know for a fact that we are called to be a part of the same body. How can members of the same body divert time and energy to fight over details about which we can't be fully sure this side of paradise? Meanwhile, we know for a fact that Jesus wants us to be united, inasmuch as it is up to us. But we don't know for sure all the details nor the chronology of each event tied to the return of Christ. Those who think they know will in all likelihood soon join the ranks of those who thought they knew in times past and led others down that same misguided path. History is strewn with false prophesies made by false prophets concerning the end times, even some well-meaning ones.

I subscribe to the statement attributed to the Christian philosopher Blaise Pascal: "In essentials, unity. In nonessentials, liberty. And in all things, charity." Christians who are committed to the lordship of Christ and the inerrancy of the Bible can and do disagree with each other on the specific details pertaining to the return of Jesus. The important thing is to retain the firm conviction that Jesus is coming back and to living life in such a way that we're ready for His return. Speaking of the return of Christ, Dr. Kennedy once said:

> How will it be? How will He come? Unfortunately, it is true many fanatics have labored over their charts to set their dates and hours and seasons for Christ's return. Others have divided the people of God endlessly on all the minutiae connected to the second coming. And often they are woefully wrong in these details.[20]

I once heard about a woman whom a minister called upon for an evangelism visit. She was already saved, and she excitedly pulled out a few spiral notebooks filled with her notations taken at various prophecy seminars. She had all sorts of details and charts to consult. He gently asked her if she had led anyone to the Lord within the last year. She sheepishly replied in the negative.

"The last two years?"

"No."

"Well, have you shared the Gospel with anybody in the last five years?"

Looking down, she shook her head. The pastor then said that he didn't have the heart to go any further, but his point was clear. Some people spend all their time focusing on the details of their particular interpretation related to the Second Coming. Meanwhile, they miss the things God has clearly commanded us to do. They are guilty of what Christ accused the Pharisees of: They nullify the Word of God by their own traditions.

Do Differing Views on Christ's Return Really Matter Anyway?

Is this really that important an issue? So what if there are different camps on this, as well as other theological interpretations? Who cares?

When it's all said and done, does it really matter what our view of the end times is? Does it really matter whether we think Christ will come back within our lifetime or that He may tarry another one hundred years or more? It's easy to think that it doesn't matter, as long as we believe Jesus is truly coming back. However, I do think there are natural implications that flow from one's view of eschatology—the study of the end times. Indeed, this question is not merely a theoretical one. It has numerous implications and applications that can't be dismissed.

For example, as a young Christian, I heard a taped message from a key evangelical leader on how Christ was about to return virtually any day now. When I heard that tape as a freshman in college, I walked out in a daze. This teaching was all new to me, and it struck me powerfully. I felt like dropping out of school and never getting married, since it didn't matter—ours were the very last, last days. Thankfully, I didn't hear more tapes like that one. I might easily have done something foolish—like dropping out of college. That was in 1975, and it would have greatly limited my future. Would the Puritans have founded Harvard, Yale, and other great institutions that were established for the advancement of the kingdom of Christ if they thought theirs was the very last generation? On the other hand, all Christians of all generations need to be ready for Christ and live as if He could return at any moment. After all, He might. This held true for the Christians of Jesus' day as well as our own.

Today, however, it would seem that many evangelicals have abandoned their role as salt and light in society because they *know* Christ is coming back in their lifetime. They are sure that ours is the generation that will see the return of Jesus. Listen to what Pastor David Moore, pastor of Southwest Community Church and author of *Five Lies of the Century* says about the Second Coming *and* our nation's future if the present trends continue. During one of the Reclaiming America for Christ conferences, I interviewed him for *The Coral Ridge Hour*. Here's what he said when I asked him, "Can we reclaim America for Christ?":

> I certainly hope so. The reason that I invest some of my time and energy in this arena is because I believe it's a winnable battle, and I wouldn't give a chunk of my life to something that's over. I'm always concerned about the pastors who will preach with the spirit of, "Well, you know, we're the last faithful twelve, and it's over, and we've given away the country. And we just have to wait for Jesus to come and rescue us." Well, He's going to return, and He will rescue us *in His time*. But what if it's a hundred years [from now]? What if it's five hundred years? What kind of world do I want my children in?

> What kind of world do I want my grandchildren raised in? And if I don't get involved to tell the truth and be involved and to impact politics and use the little sphere of influence that I have for something that's wholesome, my grandkids may wonder why I gave away the farm.[21]

Amen. Whether Jesus is coming today, tomorrow, or a thousand years from now, let us "occupy" ourselves until He comes (Luke 19:13).

Obviously not everybody feels this way. I read about a prominent preacher who said this about getting involved in anything political and cultural: "You don't polish brass on a sinking ship."[22] Who says it's a sinking ship? Things may look bad. They may look hopeless, but even after the darkest of times, God's light breaks through.

Consider this one example. Put yourself in the shoes (or sandals) of a beleaguered Christian in the early fourth century. The Emperor Diocletian is in the process of a fierce persecution against people of your faith. People you know personally have been maimed, tortured, and killed—just for the "crime" of believing in Jesus and not worshiping the emperor, who you know is merely a man. You are encouraged greatly by rereading the tiny fragment of a portion of the Scriptures, one of your few prized possessions. You exchange that periodically with your catacomb friends for other fragments. No one you know has a complete copy of the scrolls that comprise what we know today as the Old and New Testaments, for the emperor has decreed that any and all copies of the Scriptures should be burned. You then hear, to your relief, that Diocletian is no longer in power. Suddenly you think, now what? The oppressed Christian church has now undergone ten waves of diabolical persecution for nearly three hundred years. What's coming next? Then you hear a rumor that the new emperor, Constantine, has supposedly embraced your religion. That he is a believer in Jesus. Can it be true?

Can you imagine how Christians in those days felt? It is reported that at the time of the Nicene Council—the first overground council (apart from the Council of Jerusalem we read about in Acts 15) of the church—virtually every Christian leader present had been injured in the previous persecution(s). Some were missing eyes; others teeth. Others walked with a limp. Virtually each of them bore on his body some sort of mark of torture for having been a Christian. Many of them had friends or loved ones who had been killed for their faith. When it may have seemed as if there was no hope for the world, God changed history through the professed conversion of Constantine. Suddenly, overnight, God turned everything around.

I like the quote attributed to Mother Teresa: "God doesn't necessarily call us to be successful. He calls us to be faithful."

The point of all this? Our time looks dark from a spiritual and moral perspective. The signs of the time on the world scene, according to many interpreters, look as if the Rapture will take place any minute now. But we don't know. The end of the world might not be at hand. Even if it is, let Jesus find us busy about our Father's business.

One Downside to Keep in Mind

It's important not to neglect the subject of Bible prophecy, including the end times, but it's important to keep such studies in balance. There is far too much out-of-balance thinking and teaching in this area. John Calvin wrote commentaries on almost every book of the Bible, but he intentionally declined to write one on Revelation. He declared, "The study of prophecy either finds a man crazy, or it leaves him so."[23] (Another variation of the same quote is "The study of Revelation either finds a man mad or leaves him that way.") After much bleary-eyed research on this subject, I would tend to agree. Look at how many of the cults get off track because of overemphasis on and false reading of end-times prophecies. The Jehovah Witnesses and David Koresh's Branch Davidians are two prominent examples that come to mind. Chuck Swindoll points out, "Never once in Scripture is irresponsibility excused on the basis of one's confidence in Christ's return. Anticipation is one thing. Blind fanaticism is quite another."[24]

Through the centuries, the church assigned one Sunday of the year to end-times teaching—the last Sunday of the church year (the church year starts the first Sunday of Advent). This provided a built-in balance and prevented any of the clergy from focusing too much on the last days.

Conclusion

Although the chasm of the differing visions of the end times often seems wide and deep, keep in mind a few basics, lest you lose perspective. Those who believe in Jesus and the reliability of His Word can *all* agree on a few basics:

(1) Christ *is* coming back. Therefore, the future belongs to Him.

(2) Until He returns, let us be busy "about our Father's business."

(3) The details of His return are not fully clear in Scripture, but the command to love our Christian brother and sister—whether premil, posttrib, amil, postmil, preterist, and so on—is crystal clear.

Even so, come quickly, Lord Jesus.

2

A Few Key Definitions

A definition is that which so describes its object as to distinguish it from all others.[1]

Edgar Allan Poe

Have you ever read a book on the end times only to say to yourself after a while, "Huh? What is this guy talking about?" Part of the reason is that so many confusing words are tossed about. Alas, the issue of eschatology has a vocabulary all its own, and even the word "eschatology" is part of that vocabulary. **Eschatology** is the study of end times. It comes from the Greek word *eschaton*, meaning "the end."

Because my goal is to simplify and clarify differing opinions on the end times, it's important to understand key words that will be used repeatedly throughout the book. Certain words and phrases are unavoidable. Terms like the Olivet Discourse, postmillennialism, and pretribulational premillennialism.

Therefore, it's imperative to familiarize you with pertinent terms before we begin our discussion of this issue. For those who are already familiar with these terms, feel free to quickly skim through this chapter or just jump to the next chapter and refer to this list when you need to. In either case, it will be helpful to have these definitions available to us up front.

Millennialism

The **Millennium** is a thousand-year period referred to directly in only one passage of the Bible, Revelation 20:1-6, which begins when Satan is bound so he can no longer deceive the nations. Some argue that it is referred to in many other places in the Bible, albeit indirectly. Representative of this view, for example, is this statement of Donald Grey Barnhouse in his book *Revelation*: "So we come back to the fact that there are hundreds of promises in the Old Testament which concern a literal kingdom."[2]

The Millennium issue is hotly disputed. Often, how it's defined depends on where you stand on the issue. The word "millennium" comes from the Latin words *mille* for "a thousand" and *anno* meaning "years." Noah

Webster, who provides a neutral perspective in the Christian version of his dictionary, defines millennium (n.) as "a word used to denote the thousand years mentioned in Revelation XX during which period Satan shall be bound and restrained from seducing men to sin, and Christ shall reign on earth with his saints."[3]

Note: How millenarians and nonmillenarians *define* the Millennium is different. In another context, C. S. Lewis once observed, "*Mere* [i.e., neutral] description is impossible. Language forces you to an implicit comment."[4] This is a good caveat to keep in mind throughout this chapter. Meanwhile, in this context, when premillennialists talk about the Millennium, what they have in mind is quite different from what amillennialists or postmillennialists have in mind. In a nutshell:

- The Millennium of the premillennialists is a literal reign of Christ on earth yet to happen. Satan will be bound during that time for the entire period. Christ will rule the earth with "a rod of iron." Overall, life will be wonderful.
- The Millennium of the amillennialist and postmillennialist is not literal. To most of them it refers to the Church Age in general. Satan is bound in the sense that the Gospel can go forth and the nations are no longer deceived by him when the Gospel is proclaimed.
- **Millenarianism** is the view that there is a *literal* Millennium to come. Millenarians are premillennialists. The reason for even using the term is because in one word you describe all the various premillennial positions at once (pretrib, midtrib, posttrib, historic, etc.).

Nonmillenarians, encompassing nonmillenarians and postmillennialitsts, do not believe in a literal Millennium; nonmillenarians are the same as **amillenarians**. Basically, nonmillenarianism can be used interchangeably with the terms nonchiliasm, antichiliasm, or amillenarianism.

- **Chiliasm** is an old-fashioned term that communicates the same idea as millenarianism—belief in a *literal* Millennium. Chiliasm comes from the Greek word meaning "thousand." Generally, if the term is used, it is applied to early Christians of the first few centuries. Modern-day "chiliasts" are generally called premillennialists or millenarians. **Antichiliasts** don't hold to a literal thousand-year period (see Rev. 20:1-6).

The three most common millennial views are premillennial, postmillennial, and amillennial:

- **Premillennialism** is the view that Christ will come back before (*pre*) the Millennium, a literal thousand-year reign on earth. There are two basic types of premillennialism:

  Historical premillennialism asserts that the church will go through the great tribulation before Christ returns and ushers in the Millennium. Many of the early Christians held this view, including Tertullian, Justin Martyr, and Irenaeus. Sometimes this position is also called classic premillennialism. (By and large, Webster's definition above would fit closer to the historical premillennial view than any other view.)

  Dispensational premillennialism (we'll discuss this position in greater detail shortly). Among other beliefs, this maintains that Christ will secretly rapture the church before the time of great judgment on earth (the Great Tribulation) and then He'll return to establish His kingdom, thus ushering in the Millennium.

- Since the secret **Rapture** is one of the hallmarks of dispensationalism, we will define it here. The Rapture is the "blessed hope" looked forward to by Christians. It is described best in 1 Thessalonians 4 where Paul talks about how believers who are still alive when Christ comes back will be caught up in the air with Him. Premillennialists Thomas Ice and Timothy Demy liken it to the experience of Philip when he was translated in the air from one place to another locale miles away in order that he might share the Gospel with the Ethiopian eunuch (Acts 8:39). They write, "Similarly, the church will, in a moment of time, be taken from earth to heaven."[5] The idea of a secret Rapture for the church, separated (by seven years or three and a half years) from the Last Day, is less than two hundred years old; premillennial dispensationalists introduced this view starting in the early 1830s, which has gained wide acceptance within today's evangelical circles.

Some critics charge that it is "splitting the Second Coming." Nonmillenarians tend to think of the passage concerning the Rapture as primarily dealing with the resurrection of the dead. In the context of the passage (1 Thess. 4), Paul was writing to those whose loved ones had died so that they would be comforted knowing that those who had died in Christ before His return won't miss out on His Second Coming. In any event, Christians of all eschatological stripes can look forward to being caught up in the clouds with Christ and finally meeting Him face to face.

There are at least five different types of premillennialist positions today, all depending on when they think the Rapture will occur—before the Tribulation (held by **pretribulational premillennialists**), during the Tribulation (held by **midtribulational premillennialists**), or after the Tribulation (held by **posttribulational premillennialists**). (Some people define "historical premillennialism" as essentially being posttribulational premillennialism.) Premillennialist M. R. DeHaan notes that there are also "**partial rapturists**," those who hold to the teaching "that only those who attain a certain degree of holiness will be taken up at the coming of Christ and the rest will have to endure the fires of the judgment of the Tribulation."[6] There's a relatively new position (just a couple decades old) that holds the **"prewrath" Rapture** position. (I would say it's a variation of the midtrib premil view in that it believes in a Rapture that will come sometime during the tribulation).

The vast majority of premillennialists tend to be in the pretribulational camp. Moreover, premillennialism would seem to be the most popular view of end times in evangelical circles today. It's certainly the view we hear about the most in Christian broadcasting and in best-selling books.

Premillennialism would seem to be the most popular view of end times in evangelical circles

- **Postmillennialism** believes Christ will come after *(post)* the Millennium. This view does not believe the Millennium is necessarily an era yet to come; we're in it now. They believe Christ is coming after the Millennium (thus, the word "post" or "after"). They believe the world will eventually become more Christianized, not perfect, but much better than what it was when Jesus first came.

Some millenarians have written off postmillennialism as if it was no longer held, but that's inaccurate. Today, there is a rare strand of postmillennialism that does seem to be dormant that believes the Millennium (golden age) will indeed be a literal thousand years.

- **Amillennialism** could easily be confused with the term amillenarianism. Amillennialists, however, are a subset of amillenarians (postmillennialists would supply the other major subset). Amillennialism—coming from the Greek word *a*, meaning "no," and the English word millennium, meaning "one thousand years"—technically means "no millennium." It holds that the millennium was not intended to be taken as a literal thousand-year period. It views the number 1,000 as symbolic of "completeness" (1,000 is the number 10 cubed).

The world may get both better and/or worse before the end comes. To the amillennialists it may get better and worse simultaneously. The Catholic and Protestant churches held to the amillennial position for more than 1400 years. The Roman Catholic Church still holds it, and it is still widely held in many academic and theological circles of Protestantism.

Dispensationalism

Dispensationalism pertains to more than just one's position on the Rapture or the Millennium. It also deals with some fundamental theological questions, such as what is the kingdom of God? Has it come to earth yet, or, as some dispensationalists hold, was it put on hold when the Jews rejected Jesus?

The amillennial position is widely held in many academic and theological circles of Protestantism

Dispensationalism is certainly a popular school of theology in our time. They are best known for their view that there is a secret Rapture, followed by the Great Tribulation and Armageddon, followed by the return of Christ and the Millennium, and so on. All pretribulational premillenialists are dispensationalists.

The name comes from the view that God has dealt with separate groups differently according to their dispensation. C. I. Scofield, who greatly popularized this view through his Bible study notes, defined a dispensation as "a period of time during which man is tested in respect of obedience to some specific revelation to the will of God."[7] The old covenant was a dispensation of law; the new covenant is a dispensation of grace. (Note that orthodox dispensationalists would be quick to add that only through the blood of Christ is anyone saved, including those who were looking forward by faith to the promised Messiah before He came.)

Some of the best-known proponents of dispensationalism include some of today's leading writers and speakers, including Hal Lindsey, Chuck Swindoll, Tim LaHaye, and John Hagee. *The Scofield Reference Bible* (first published in 1909) helped widely promote dispensationalism. All dispensationalists are premillennialists, but not all premillennialists are dispensationalists. Premillennial dispensationalist Lewis Sherry Chafer—

founder of the leading dispensationalist school, Dallas Theological Seminary—argues that if you're an evangelical, you're a dispensationalist. How's that? He says, "Any person is a dispensationalist who trusts the blood of Christ rather than bringing an animal sacrifice, . . . who observes the first day of the week rather than the seventh."[8] That statement, however, doesn't necessarily give the total picture, because usually dispensationalism involves a rather elaborate view of the end times.

One of the leading dispensationalists, Charles Ryrie, provides a more accurate picture on that branch of theology:

> The essence of dispensationalism . . . is the distinction between Israel and the Church. This grows out of the dispensationalists' consistent employment of normal or plain interpretation, and it reflects an understanding of the basic purpose of God in all His dealings with mankind as that of glorifying Himself through salvation and other purposes as well.[9]

When it comes to understanding the prophetic passages of the Bible, the dispensationalist would tend to interpret these literally. As Moody Bible Institute professor C. Marvin Pate puts it: "The hallmark of dispensationalism has been its commitment to a literal interpretation of prophetic Scripture."[10]

Preterism Versus Futurism

Before we define these two words (one referring to things already fulfilled, and the other to things yet to take place), we must define at least one term:

- The **Olivet Discourse** refers to a lengthy talk Jesus gave to His disciples in answer to their questions about when the temple would be destroyed (He has just told them that bad news) and about the signs of His coming and of the end of the age. The Olivet Discourse is found in Matthew 24 and 25, Mark 13, and Luke 19. When the term "the Olivet Discourse" is used in this book, I am referring to those four chapters in the Bible. It is so named because the disciples were perched on the Mount of Olives when it took place.
- **Preterism** is the view that some of the things prophesied about the

end times have already taken place. Preterism (meaning "past tense" in Greek) is in contrast with **futurism**, which holds they will happen sometime in the future. A significant conflict between preterists and futurists is over the tribulation described in the Olivet Discourse; to the preterist, it already happened in the destruction of Jerusalem in A.D. 70. Preterist R. C. Sproul writes, ". . . the coming of Christ in A.D. 70 was a coming in judgment on the Jewish nation, indicating the end of the Jewish age and the fulfillment of a day of the Lord. Jesus really did come in judgment at this time, fulfilling his prophecy in the Olivet Discourse. But this was not the final or ultimate coming of Christ."[11]

Sproul calls himself a partial or moderate preterist; he is in contrast to full preterists who take preterism to the nth degree and deny a future coming of Christ at all. Obviously, such a position as full preterism is beyond the scope of orthodox Christianity. The controversy between Christians over end times relates to the *details* of His return, not to whether or not He *will* return. When the word "preterist" is used in this book, I am suggesting a partial or moderate preterist.

Some partial preterists see much of the Olivet Discourse as having been fulfilled, but not necessarily the Book of Revelation. The Reformers, such as Martin Luther and John Calvin, held such a view.

- The **Tribulation** (sometimes referred to as the **Great Tribulation**) is a disturbing period of time yet to be if you're a futurist, or which already took place if you're a preterist. To the preterist, what Jesus described in the Olivet Discourse occurred when the Jews rebelled against Rome, who crushed the Jews in A.D. 70 and destroyed their temple. To the futurist, the Tribulation is yet to happen (even if A.D. 70 was a foreshadow of such events). The Great Tribulation is believed to last seven years because of the Seventieth Week of Daniel (see below).

During the Great Tribulation of the futurist—for example, the premillennial dispensationalist—many of the things listed in Revelation will take place. The Tribulation will be divided into two main sections—the first and second halves. The Tribulation will include in the first half the seal and trumpet judgments; the ministry of Elijah and the two witnesses; the rise of the Antichrist, a world ruler who makes a covenant with Israel; 144,000 Jewish believers in Jesus who will preach the Gospel. Then in the middle, the death and resurrection of the Antichrist; the death and resurrection of the two witnesses; the mark of the beast: 666; the Antichrist breaks his covenant with Israel; the Abomination of Desolation; the Jews are persecuted. In the second half of the Tribulation will come the bowl judgments; Armageddon; the conversion of all Israel.[12] Some preterists hold that all these things will yet happen but not necessarily in a seven-year time frame.

- **Signs of the Times** generally refers to all sorts of warning signs discussed in the Olivet Discourse, such as:
    - Wars and rumors of war
    - Earthquakes and famines
    - The rise of false christs and so on.

To the futurist, these signs are yet to come. To the preterist, they are not significant to us today.

The Antichrist

The **Antichrist** is an evil world ruler who is believed to come at the end of time. He will demand to be worshiped; he will wage war against the saints. Paul talked about "the man of lawlessness," which many believe to be the Antichrist: "He will oppose and will exalt himself over everything that is called God or is worshiped, so that he sets himself up in God's temple, proclaiming himself to be God" (2 Thess. 2:4). Some preterists believe he already came, and it was Nero. Others believe Nero may have been a type of the real one to come. The book of the Bible that gives us the word "antichrist" (1 John 2:22) says there are "many antichrists"—referring to those that deny that Jesus is the Christ. The spirit of Antichrist is that which sets itself up against God and His Son, Jesus Christ.

The **Beast** of Revelation 13 is widely believed to be the Antichrist.

Other Definitions

- **Exegesis** refers to the process of explaining the meaning of biblical verses. It is akin to mining the shaft of Scripture to bring out the treasures of God's Word. Exegesis simply means interpretation.
- **Parousia** is a Greek word meaning "coming." As in other areas of the end times, scholars often disagree whether this refers to the final second coming of Christ or to His return in other ways (at His resurrec-

tion, at His enthronement, at His coming in judgment against Jerusalem in A.D. 70, and so on).

- The **Seventy Weeks of Daniel** refers to a period of 490 "days" (held by virtually all to mean years). Each week means a seven-year period. To some (preterists), all the seventy weeks have taken place; to others (futurists), there is one left to take place. The reason dispensationalists believe the Great Tribulation will last seven years is because of Daniel's Seventy Weeks (Dan. 9:24-27). We have an entire chapter dealing with Daniel's hotly contested seventy weeks. (Actually, it's only the last week that is passionately disputed.)
    - The **Divine Parenthesis** is a view held by premillennial dispensationalists that the first sixty-nine weeks of Daniel's Seventy Weeks have been fulfilled, but the last week is yet to occur. It will be the time of the Great Tribulation. (For that reason, they believe the Great Tribulation will last seven years.) We are currently living in the Divine Parenthesis, ie., the Church Age.

Conclusion

Note that all these eschatological words are not always used with pinpoint accuracy. For example, I have often seen some writers use amillennial and amillenarian virtually interchangeably. The problem with that is that one group (amillennialists) is a subset of the other (amillenarianists). This is part of the reason that throughout the book, I generally refer to *non*millenarians (amillennialists and postmillennialists) as opposed to *a*millenarians.

Hopefully, we've added a few words to your vocabulary or clarified a few points in the maze of opinions on the Second Coming. Now that we have some working definitions, let's explore a little further some of differences of opinion on the end times and what it means for our lives today.

3

So What's the Difference?

***With all these various views and able teachers to champion them, it is no wonder that confusion has resulted.*[1]**

—M. R. DeHaan

Did you know that before World War II, there were twenty-three Hitlers in the New York City phone book? After the war, there were none. Presumably, they all changed their name to something else. If I were in their shoes, I certainly would have.

Names are important.

Labels are important.

Words are important.

Unless your goal is to obfuscate—that is, to hide the truth in a barrage of rhetoric—you want to use language to clarify things. When it comes to the end times, there are so many terms to describe the various positions that it gets quite confusing. How confusing? Well, just consider, there are . . .

- Premillennialists. And in this category, there are:
    - Classical or historic premillennialists
    - Historically known as "chiliasts"
    - Dispensationalist premillennialists
    - Pretribulational dispensationalist premillennialists
    - Posttribulational dispensationalist premillennialists
    - Midtribulational dispensationalist premillennialists
    - Partial Rapture dispensationalist premillennialists
    - Prewrath dispensationalist premillennialists
- Amillennialists, including
    - Radical preterists
    - Moderate preterists
- Postmillennialists, including
    - Radical preterists
    - Moderate preterists

And among preterists, we can find the following types:

- Moderate preterists
- Orthodox preterists[2]
- Exegetical preterists
- Comprehensive preterists
- Theological preterists[3]
- Radical preterists, sometimes known as:
    - Hyperpreterists
    - Consistent preterists
    - Full preterists[4]

Have you heard about the *pan*millennialists? They think it'll all just pan out in the end.

Some of these names overlap or are just other names to describe the same phenomenon. But, as I see it, those would be the major categories.

Two key issues divide theologians on the end times

Boil it all down, there are two basic issues that divide well-meaning, learned Christians on the end times. They are:

- Whether or not there is a *literal* thousand-year reign of Christ on earth yet to come.
- Whether or not many of the end-time prophecies were fulfilled in A.D. 70 or whether they are yet to come. Or whether they were partially fulfilled then and will be fulfilled in a more complete way at a future time.

Thus there are two key issues that divide theologians on the end times. One issue deals with the Millennium; the other issue deals with how much, if anything, of the last days prophecies have *already* been fulfilled. That's the controversy in a nutshell.

Yet I think it's safe to add that the controversy goes well beyond that. It gets to the heart of questions such as:

- What do we mean by the kingdom of God? Has it come—even partially—or is it a completely future event to begin with the Millennium?
- Is the church the new Israel? Does God have one program for the church and another for Israel? Is the modern state of Israel the fulfillment of Bible prophecy? Are the rebirth of Israel as a nation in 1948 and the recapture of Jerusalem in 1967 surefire signs that we are living in the last, last days?
- Will there be some sort of revised temple worship in Jerusalem, and if so, will God be pleased with such animal sacrifices, even in remem-

brance of Christ's death on the cross?

- Are the messianic prophecies of the Old Testament (for example, the knowledge of the Lord shall fill the whole world—Isa. 11:9) being spiritually fulfilled right now through the worldwide spread of the Gospel, or is it all yet to happen with Christ's literal reign from Jerusalem during the Millennium?
- Is prophecy to be taken symbolically? If so, then when, if ever, are we to take the Bible literally?
- How many judgments will there be and when?
- Is there hope for our world in its present state? Is it a matter of destiny, of fulfilled prophecy, that the world will just get worse and worse and then the end will come?
- Is the enthronement of Jesus something to happen later or did it happen in the first century?

Richard Kyle says of the various end-times views, "These positions differ as to when Christ will return. But their differences go well beyond the timing of Christ's return. They touch upon attitudes toward life, the way in which Scripture is interpreted, the number of resurrections, and the nature of the millennium itself."[5]

Thus end-times disputes go far beyond end-times issues. They seemingly touch on just about every aspect of theology.

What Is Prophecy?

In the beginning of the Book of Revelation, it is stated that the purpose is to "show his servants what must soon take place" (Rev. 1:1). Several of the world religions have a fatalistic view of history. What is to be will be. It is all set in stone, and nothing can change what is supposed to happen. This view makes prayer a futile exercise. It makes prophecy only a lifting of the veil to peak into a future already determined in every detail. This, however, is not the biblical view of history and therefore not the correct view of prophecy either.

Kismet?

Bible prophecy is not the same as kismet, as some sort of fate that ignores human response. Joel Green observes, "Predictive prophecy is by nature conditional."[6] Biblical prophecy is not fatalistic. If doom is decreed for a people and they repent—for example, Jonah and Nineveh—then the doom predicted is withheld. Green adds, "Because of human infidelity, some promises may have been nullified or amended."[7]

A biblical prophet is not merely someone whom God has allowed a peek behind the curtain. No, it's a person God has taken into His confidence to let him or her know His plans. God sometimes changes His mind according to the way His people respond. Consider the Jeremiah 18:7-10 passage:

> If at any time I announce that a nation or kingdom is to be uprooted, torn down and destroyed, and if that nation I warned repents of its evil, then I will relent and not inflict on it the disaster I had planned. And if at another time I announce that a nation or kingdom is to be built up and planted, and if it does evil in my sight and does not obey me, then I will reconsider the good I had intended to do for it.

Thus people are not puppets in the hands of God. He sometimes changes what He has planned. For example, God gave King Hezekiah fifteen more years to live just because he asked for it even though the prophet Isaiah had already told him to put his house in order for he was going to die and not recover from his illness. Did God lie? Of course not. He just listened to Hezekiah's prayer and changed His mind (see 2 Kings 20:1-7).

Another example of this is found in the Book of Jeremiah beginning with 26:16. Jeremiah has predicted the fall of Jerusalem and the destruction of the temple, and the leaders of the people consider charging him with treason. Then they remember that the prophet Micah had made similar predictions about a hundred years earlier. At that time the king didn't kill the prophet but repented and asked God's forgiveness, and God spared the people. Micah wasn't wrong, nor had he misunderstood God. The message was that unless you repent, destruction will come. Now Jeremiah was preaching the same message, but this time the destruction of Jerusalem did happen. There was no more grace.

Multiple Fulfillments

Something else to consider with regard to biblical prophecy is multiple fulfillments—that is, one passage being fulfilled at least two or more times. When David wrote, "They have pierced my hands and my feet" (Ps. 22:16), who knows what David was talking about with this incident? Meanwhile, scholars see this description as applying to the crucifixion of Christ, which occurred some one thousand years later. Thus the passage has had a dual fulfillment.

Let's look at an example where it would seem there has been *partial* fulfillment of prophecy with *partial* fulfillment of the rest yet to come. Consider the promises of salvation, peace, joy, and everlasting bliss that we find in Isaiah 51:11:

> The ransomed of the Lord will return. They will enter Zion with singing; everlasting joy will crown their heads. Gladness and joy will overtake them, and sorrow and sighing will flee away.

When Israel returned home from exile (c.516 B.C.), this passage was fulfilled (at least partially) the first time. Yet the everlasting joy and the absence of sorrow did not happen at that time. Presumably it still has not happened.

The promise of Isaiah 51:11 is echoed in Revelation 21:4, "He [God] will wipe every tear from their eyes." Many scholars tend to look at that promise as a future event. If that's the proper interpretation, then at some future point there will come a time when there will be no sorrow and no pain. Some see this as applying to heaven. Others see it as applying to both a literal Millennium to come and to heaven. Thus multiple fulfillments of the same prophecy.

During Jesus' earthly ministry, He sometimes fulfilled parts of a verse while the rest of the verse will be completely fulfilled at the end of time when his eternal kingdom is complete. This is true of the well-known passage of Isaiah 9:6-7:

> For to us a child is born, to us a son is given, and the government will be on his shoulders. And he will be called

> Wonderful Counselor, Mighty God, Everlasting Father, Prince of Peace. Of the increase of his government and peace there will be no end. He will reign on David's throne and over his kingdom, establishing and upholding it with justice and righteousness from that time on and forever.

Dispensational premillennialists would say that His kingdom has not yet been established. Historical premillennialists would likely say that it began, but has not yet been fulfilled. Even a postmillennialist would generally agree that at the present time this verse has not yet been *completely* fulfilled. That person might argue that while Christ reigns in His kingdom now, that kingdom has yet to penetrate completely throughout the whole world. Therefore, in Bible prophecy there can be the *then*, the *now*, and the *not yet*.

We can understand from this passage why many Jews did not think Jesus was the Messiah, because He did not come as the expected ruler. He did come and fulfilled part of the prophecy. He also established His kingdom according to many interpreters. Yet as for the sovereign ruler who rules forever, this reign is yet to come. Time seems to be of little importance in God's kingdom. This reminds me of what the Heidelberg Catechism says on the petition "Thy kingdom come" in the Lord's prayer: "until the perfection of Thy kingdom arrive wherein Thou shalt be all in all"[8]

The New Testament Interpretation of Old Testament Prophecy

Critics charge that so many of the modern-day "prophets" leapfrog over the New Testament and apply Old Testament passages directly to today's events. Indeed, when we ask about the meaning of an Old Testament text, we cannot walk around the New Testament. We have to ask ourselves: How is this prophecy dealt with in the New Testament? Many Old Testament prophecies have gotten, or will get, their fulfillment *in Christ*. Christ is the central figure of the Bible. All promises of salvation and heaven and all the questions of when and how have to be seen in light of Jesus Christ and His work. Furthermore, many of the major Old Testament prophetic texts are dealt with in the New Testament.

Seemingly Major Divisions

There is a significant division in the opinions between the two major camps—millenarians and nonmillenarians. (Generally, futurists would tend to be millenarians, and preterists nonmillenarians.) And within those two basic camps (millenarians and nonmillenarians), there are subdivisions and subdivisions within those subdivisions. And on it goes. No wonder we have some 23,500 different Christian denominations in the world today![9]

Can there be some common points to consider?

In light of this large chasm between the differing views on the end times among well-meaning Christians, can there be some common points to consider? Certainly. By thinking of the big picture:

(1) There is good news in the long run for the believer in Jesus.

(2) There is bad news in the long run for the nonbeliever.

(3) We should be busy about our Father's business. We should lead people to Christ and disciple them, teaching them the whole counsel of God. We should be occupied until He comes—whether that may be in the next hour or in the next millennium.

Above all, we can agree on this: Jesus is coming back one day. That will be the climax of history as we know it.

Although the division between Bible-believing Christians on eschatology may seem quite large, consider the fact that we have far more in common with each other than we have with nonbelievers, who are not awaiting His return, even if those nonbelievers are priests or pastors in the official church. Postmillennialist Loraine Boettner writes:

> Christ's return is taught so clearly and so repeatedly in Scripture that there can be no question in this regard for those who accept the Bible as the word of God. They also agree that at His coming He will raise the dead, execute judgment, and eventually institute the eternal state. No one of these views has an inherent liberalizing tendency. Hence the matters on which they agree are much more important than those on which they differ. This fact should enable them to cooperate as evangelicals and to present a united front against Modernists and Liberals who more or less consistently deny the supernatural throughout the whole range of Bible truth.[10]

Divisions Need Not Divide Us As Much As We Let Them

There's a hilarious skit from comedian Emo Philips that shows how goofy extreme denominationalism can become. Sometimes we divide over things that will be trivial only from the eternal perspective, but we take them quite seriously.

Here's Emo's routine, in which he describes an encounter between two men on a bridge. One (described as "he" in this story) was about to jump; the other (the narrator) was attempting to talk him out of it. We pick up where their conversation turns to the subject of religion:

> I said, "Are you a Christian or a Jew or a Hindu or what?"
>
> He said, "A Christian."
>
> I said, "Small world! Me, too. Protestant or Catholic or Greek Orthodox?"
>
> He said, "Protestant."
>
> I said, "Me, too! What franchise?"
>
> He said, "Baptist."
>
> I said, "Me, too! Northern Baptist or Southern Baptist?"
>
> He said, "Northern Baptist."
>
> I said, "Me, too! Northern Conservative Baptist or Northern Liberal Baptist?"
>
> He said, "Northern Conservative Baptist."
>
> I said, "Me, too! Northern Conservative Fundamentalist Baptist or Northern Conservative Reformed Baptist?"
>
> He said, "Northern Conservative Fundamentalist Baptist."
>
> I said, "Me, too! Northern Conservative Fundamentalist Baptist, Great Lakes region, or Northern Conservative Fundamentalist Baptist, Eastern Region?"
>
> He said, "Northern Conservative Fundamentalist Baptist, Great Lakes Region."
>
> I said, "Me, too! Northern Conservative Fundamentalist Baptist Great Lakes Region Council of 1879 or Northern Conservative Fundamentalist Baptist Great Lakes Region Council of 1912?"
>
> He said, "Northern Conservative Fundamentalist Baptist Great Lakes Region Council of 1912."
>
> I screamed, "DIE HERETIC!" And I pushed him over.[11]

4

The Second Coming According to Premillennialists

The details of His next appearance are interesting and important to study, but differences in interpreting these details should never obscure the central fact of His coming.[1]

—Paul Little

"There is no question we are living in the end times."

"This is the generation that will see Armageddon."

"The Antichrist is probably alive at this very moment and soon will be ready to move center stage onto the world scene."

We've heard these statements many times in the last few decades. They reflect the most popular view of the end times of our day—premillennialism. It's the most popular view, that is, based on book sales and radio and television broadcasts. How *will* the end times play out, according to premillennialists and dispensationalists? First, we'll look at what dispensationalists believe. Then, we'll briefly touch on historical premillennialists, because the beliefs of both groups overlap considerably.

Here's a rough overview of how premillennial dispensationalists view the end times. Yet before we get into the Second Coming, we have to back up to Jesus' first coming. Keep in mind that many of these beliefs are similar to other views as well.

Jesus Offers the Jews the Kingdom; They Reject It

Jesus of Nazareth was predicted in the Old Testament in two types of prophecies—the suffering servant and the conquering king. The Jews misread the prophecies, considering only the latter.

He came to earth among His own people, the Jews, announcing that the kingdom of heaven was at hand. But they blew it; they rejected their Messiah. Consequently, God went to Plan B. (At this point, dispensationalists would disagree with more traditional theologians, including covenantal theologians.)

Therefore, according to dispensationalists, Jesus postponed the establishment of the kingdom (which has to do only with Israel), and He revealed a mystery: He created the church—something not foretold in the Old Testament. C. I. Scofield wrote, "That the Gentiles were to be *saved* was no mystery . . . The mystery 'hid in God' was the divine purpose to make of Jew and Gentile a wholly new thing—'the church, which is his [Christ's] body.'"[2]

Because the Jews rejected Christ's kingdom, all the predictive statements in the Old Testament about the messianic kingdom were postponed. They were put on hold. They will not be fulfilled until Christ later returns to earth. One of those is the final "week" or seven-year period described in Daniel 9. Daniel talked about a very specific period of seventy weeks (seven plus sixty-two plus one). Virtually all commentators hold that when Daniel talked about weeks, he was talking about seven-year periods. Some scholars, however, maintain that all that he wrote about was literally fulfilled at the time Hanukkah was born. Others believe it was fulfilled when Jerusalem was destroyed. Meanwhile, dispensationalists believe the last week is *yet* to be fulfilled. It's been nearly two thousand years since this delay in fulfillment, which some people call "the Divine Parenthesis." (Later we'll devote an entire chapter to Daniel's Seventieth Week.)

God Has Two Programs: One for Israel, One for the Church

Dispensationalists do not believe the theory that the church is "the new Israel." Even before the modern state of Israel was created, dispensationalists were anticipating its return as a nation (new Israel). Hal Lindsey maintains that Lord Balfour (as in the Balfour Declaration) was influenced by dispensational beliefs. Therefore, dispensationalism helped pave the way to the birth of modern Israel in 1948.[3]

In any event, to dispensationalists God's dealings with Israel are one way; His dealings with the church are another. As M. R. DeHaan puts it: "God has a program for the world, the Church, the nations and for His people Israel."[4]

Because of their belief that the kingdom has been postponed, dispensationalists interpret passages like the Sermon on the Mount as not binding for today. They believe we can glean principles from it, but on the whole it's not applicable. Nor are the kingdom parables for today. Nor is the parable of the sheep and the goats; instead that parable applies only to the saints during the Millennium.

Scofield, whose Bible notes did a great deal to popularize dispensationalist ideas, wrote, "The Sermon on the Mount is law, not grace, for it demands as the condition of blessing (Matt. 5:3-9) that perfect character which grace, through divine power, creates (Gal. 5:22, 23)."[5]

In the context of comments on the Sermon on the Mount, Scofield adds:

> Whenever the kingdom of heaven is established on earth it will be according to that constitution, which may be regarded as an explanation of the word "righteousness" as used by the prophets in describing the kingdom (e.g. Isa. 11:4, 5; 32:1; Dan. 9:24). In this sense the Sermon on the Mount is pure law, and transfers the offence from the overt act to the motive (Matt. 5:21, 22, 27, 28). Here lies the deeper reason why the Jews rejected the kingdom. They had reduced "righteousness" to mere outward splendour and power. They were never rebuked for expecting a visible and powerful kingdom, but the words of the prophets should have prepared them to expect also that only the poor in spirit and the meek could share in it (e.g. Isa. 11:4). . . . For these reasons the Sermon on the Mount in its primary application gives neither the privilege nor the duty of the Church. These are found in the Epistles.[6]

Scofield went on to say that the Sermon on the Mount provides "beautiful moral application" for the Christian, but essentially it's not for today. Scofield's above-cited passage is illuminating because it shows how dispensationalism touches more than just the end times. It relates to how we view God's kingdom at this time.

The Blessed Hope: The Rapture

At any moment now, according to dispensationalists, Jesus could come for His own, the church. In the Rapture, He will take us out of the world and leave all the unbelievers behind. We'll be up in heaven with Him for seven years, while they experience hell down on earth. Some writers say we'll be literally "in the air,"[7] that is, in the clouds with Him for those seven years.

As we've already seen, other dispensationalists hold different views on whether Christians are taken out of the world *before* the Tribulation, *during* it, or *after* it. In any event, the pretribulational premillennialists (dispensationalists) believe the Rapture could be imminent. Indeed, at any moment the "blessed hope" can occur. The believers' judgment will then take place at this time.[8] Because salvation is not by works but by faith, it will essentially be an examination of what our rewards should be and the degree to which we will be rewarded for all eternity.

The dispensationalists who don't believe the Rapture could be any day now include the midtribulational, posttribulational, partial Rapture, and prewrath rapturists. They believe the Great Tribulation will already have to be in progress before the Rapture can take place. Therefore, it would be safe to say pretribulational premillennialists believe in the imminent return of our Lord (through the Rapture), but other types of premillennialists do not.

The Rapture, of course, is the belief that Christians will one day be flown up to heaven to be with Jesus. He will shout, "Come up here!" and those who are in their graves will instantly be changed, and they'll fly up. Believers alive at that time will also be flown up. The belief in a *secret* Rapture is one of the hallmarks of dispensationalism. M. R. DeHaan defines the Rapture as "the secret sudden coming of Christ for His own."[9]

Picture this scenario: The unbelieving husband wakes up to find his wife is gone. No note. No good-bye. Nothing. That's not like her. He walks outside in his T-shirt and pajama bottoms only to find his neighbor complaining that his brother is reported missing. Yeah, the goody two-shoes Sunday School teacher. Meanwhile, a dozen sirens pierce the morning sky, while police cars all around the city attempt to attend to the innumerable accidents caused by the drivers who have mysteriously disappeared into thin air. There is chaos everywhere. All the true Christians have flown up to be with the Lord.

It's important to make a distinction here between the Rapture and what premillennialists call "the Revelation." M. R. DeHaan describes the Rapture as the before and revelation as the after: "There are two phases of His coming again. The one is *before* the Tribulation, when Christ comes *for* His Church, to take her *out* of the earth so that she will escape the awful blood bath of the day of the Lord."[10] The Rapture is when Christ comes back secretly for His church, but when Christ comes back in visible glory to usher in the Millennium, that will be the revelation.

After the Rapture, Christians then experience the Bema seat (or believers') judgment. They give an account of their lives.

Meanwhile, after the Rapture life on earth goes on, and nonbelievers receive another chance to repent according to this belief system. Historically, there is greater affirmation by theologians for the belief that the resurrection (including the Rapture of the saints who are still alive) occurs on the Last Day—at the end of the world. Those left behind will be judged that very day. In other words, if the postmillennialists or amillennialists are right, it will be too late for those "left behind" when Christ returns. In any event, we can all agree, whatever our view of the end times, *no one* should put off salvation. "Today, if you hear his voice, do not harden your hearts" (Heb. 4:7).

The true church of Jesus Christ will be caught up in the air

The true church of Jesus Christ—those who are truly His—will be caught up in the air. Subsequently, Christians will be up in the clouds with Jesus (or in heaven) for seven years. Meanwhile, terrible things will take place on earth. All the horrible plagues described in Revelation 6 through 16 will terrorize the inhabitants of the earth during that time.

The Great Tribulation

According to the dispensationalists, the Great Tribulation will last seven years. It will not start off as a tribulation, but virtually no time in history (including the Nazi Holocaust) will rival the horrors of the last three and a half years.

Scofield says of the Great Tribulation that it "involves the people of God [i.e., Israel] who will have returned to Palestine in unbelief."[11] During the Great Tribulation, the only people left on earth initially will be nonbelievers (because the church will have been raptured). During this time, many Jews will accept Jesus as their Messiah. They will then witness to their friends and neighbors and lead great multitudes to Jesus, proportionately more than the church ever did in some twenty centuries of Christian history. As Hal Lindsey puts it, "They are going to be 144,000 Jewish Billy Grahams turned loose on this earth—the earth will never know a period of evangelism like this period."[12]

At the outset of the Tribulation, the Jews will make a deal with the ruler who comes to reign over the earth at that time. Likely to be a European, this man is the long-expected Antichrist. He is the beast of Revelation. His number is 666. He will reign over a revised version of the Roman Empire (since Rome is the city with the seven hills). This foxy dictator, however, will double-cross the Jews and break whatever agreement he has made with them. He will then desecrate the temple and put on the altar "the abomination that causes desolation." In the first half of the Tribulation, the Jews are protected; in the second half, they are persecuted.

During this time, the general population will worship the Antichrist. He will make things impossible to buy or sell unless you have his mark on your right hand or forehead. Yet if you bear his mark, you show yourself to be at enmity with God. During this reign, true Christians (those who have come to faith since the beginning of the Great Tribulation—known as "Tribulation saints") will not have that mark, and they will likely perish unless they have some food stored somewhere. (I have read about some people, holding this view of the end times and thinking the Tribulation is near. They have stored food in caves in Israel to be prepared.)

The Antichrist will commence to slay the Tribulation saints. He will wage war against them and martyr many of them. Then God will pour out His wrath on all the people in many stages in a series of judgments against the wicked.

- There will be seven *seal* judgments. Revelation 6 through 8 describes all of them. These judgments will occur during the first half of the Great Tribulation.
- Next will come the divine wrath of the trumpet judgments (Rev. 8-11).
- Seven angels then will bring seven plagues on the earth (Rev. 15).
- And the bowl judgments will follow (Rev. 16).

These judgments will decimate the earth, killing tens of millions. It will make World War II look like a veritable Boy Scout picnic.

Armageddon

Then comes Armageddon! The showdown of the ages. The Antichrist makes a deal with some of the world leaders ("the kings of the north") in which they mobilize to attack Jerusalem, but God intervenes just in time. Jesus Christ comes down and destroys the enemies of God. Thomas Ice and Timothy Demy provide more details on Armageddon:

> According to the Bible, great armies from the east and the west will gather and assemble on this plain [the Plain of Esdraelon, about twenty miles southwest of Haifa in Israel]. There will be threats to the power of the Antichrist from the south, and he will also move to destroy a revived Babylon in the east before finally turning his forces toward Jerusalem to subdue and destroy it. As he and his armies move on Jerusalem, God will intervene and Jesus Christ will return to rescue His chosen people, Israel.[13]

Ice and Demy even provide battle maps for the Battle of Armageddon. When they say "according to the Bible" in the above passage, they combine what is said in Revelation 16 about Armageddon with Daniel 11:40-45, Joel 3:9-17, and Zechariah 14:1-3. Other commentators agree. For instance, *The NIV Study Bible* says in a footnote on Daniel 11:40-45 that the events in that passage are "doubtless in connection with the battle of Armageddon."[14]

A few chapters later (Rev. 20), the Devil is then leashed. He is bound and cast into the pit, unable to bother humanity on earth for a thousand years.

The Millennium

Jesus subsequently sets up His kingdom, prophesied in the Old Testament. Thus the Millennium will finally have arrived. His messianic reign will finally start. He will rule the whole world from Jerusalem. He will rule from a revived throne of David. Here is a vivid description of the Millennium from dispensationalist writers Ice and Demy:

> The millennium will be a time in which the Adamic curse will be rolled back (except for death) and people will live for 1,000 years. Sickness and infirmity will be

> virtually removed; no one will live in poverty or lack food to eat. Christ, sitting on the throne of David, will ensure equity and justice for all. However, many tasks will be delegated and mediated through a hierarchy of redeemed individuals as rewards for faithfulness in this present life.[15]

This description reminds me of one of the verses from the great Christmas carol "Joy to the World" (lyrics by Isaac Watts). The third stanza rings out:

> No more let sins and sorrows grow,
> Nor thorns infest the ground;
> He comes to make His blessings flow
> Far as the curse is found . . . [16]

The Millennium will thus be the undoing of the curse Adam's sin caused.

Scofield says of the Millennium: "Upon His return the King will restore the Davidic monarchy in His own person, re-gather dispersed Israel, establish His power over all the earth, and reign one thousand years."[17]

During the millennium, people will enjoy unparalleled prosperity. For the most part, Jesus' subjects will pay Him at least outward homage. Seething under the surface, however, there are some whose hearts are in unconscious rebellion toward the Great King. He rules with "a rod of iron," and these people would break free from his rule if given the chance.

At the end of the thousand years, Satan is finally released. Taking advantage of those unrealized, rebellious wishes of some of the unbelievers in the Millennium, Satan wages war once more against Christ and is utterly defeated and all those with him. And that's it. Satan can never bother humanity again.

The Great White Throne Judgment

Then comes the Great White Throne judgment. Unbelievers—all the wicked and unrepentant unbelievers from the very beginning of time—will be gathered before Christ's throne of judgment, even if they have to

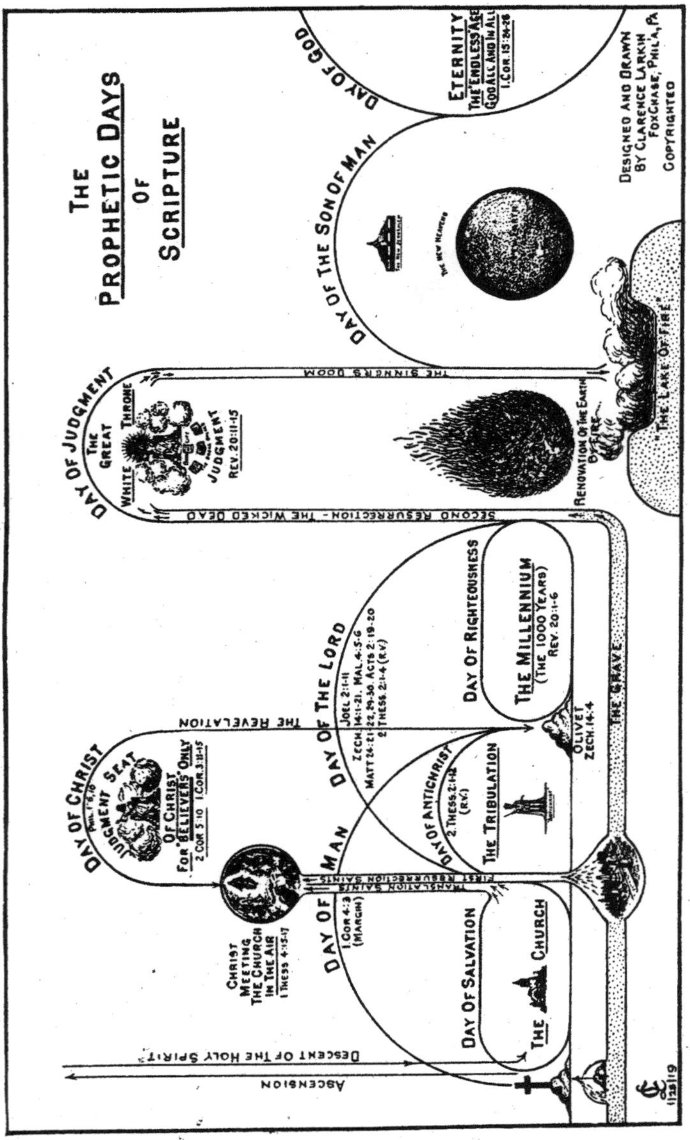

A premillennial chart highlighting the present and future dispensations.

be raised from the dead for the occasion. Having no savior for their sins, they bear the penalty for themselves. Thus they will be cast into hell.

Meanwhile, true believers will enjoy an eternity of bliss with their Savior, who ushers in the new heaven and new earth. While believers enjoy Christ's presence in heaven forever, all the rebellious, wicked unbelievers suffer eternal torment with Satan and his minions in hell forever.

That's It in a Nutshell

This is a broad overview of the things to come according to most premillennialists. To my knowledge it is an elaborate framework that can't be found in this form prior to 1830. As was mentioned earlier, millenarians of the early centuries believed in a literal Millennium to come, but not with all these details.

All of the above comes from the Bible in one passage or another. Some of them have multiple verses or passages to support them.

When Israel became a nation again in 1948, the prophetic clock began to tick

Other-Trib Premillennial Dispensationalists

The elaborate picture we've painted would also hold for most midtrib, partial-trib, and prewrath premillennialists. As dispensationalists, they, too, believe the kingdom was postponed when Israel rejected their Messiah, but it will come when He returns in the flesh. Their main dispute with the above would be the timing of the Rapture vis-à-vis the Great Tribulation.

How Soon Could These Things Take Place?

In their own words . . .

- Dave Hunt wrote in 1990: "Somewhere, at this very moment, on planet Earth, the Antichrist is almost certainly alive—biding his time, awaiting his cue. Banal sensationalism? Far from it! That likelihood is based upon a sober evaluation of current events in relation to Bible prophecy. Already a mature man, he is probably active in politics, perhaps even an admired world leader whose name is almost daily on everyone's lips."[18]

- Grant Jeffrey did several calculations involving the Jubilee years. His conclusions are "that the year A.D. 2000 is probably a termination date for the 'last days.'"[19]
- The late Lester Summrall, who founded LeSea Broadcasting, said, "I predict the absolute fullness of man's operation on planet Earth by the year 2000 A.D."[20]

Many, if not most premillennialists, believe we are living in the end times. These are the last days. Christ could come any moment. When Jerusalem was destroyed in A.D. 70, the prophetic clock was put on hold. When Israel became a nation again in 1948, the prophetic clock began to tick again. Thus it can occur any day now, at any moment, according to the pretribulational premillennialist view.

Common Ground for All Premillennial Dispensationalists

Despite the differences between the various types of premillennialists, Dr. Loraine Boettner has pinpointed the common, primary elements within the premillennial dispensational system at large (which does not necessarily apply to historic premillennialists). Here is what Dr. Boettner says in his book *The Millennium*:

> The premillennial system is considerably more complicated than either the post- or amillennial system and, consequently, it has also been attended with greater diversity of opinion among its advocates. But despite these differences it has been characteristic of both [pretrib and posttrib] schools of Premillennialism to hold:
>
> 1. That the Kingdom of God is not now in the world, and that it will not be instituted until Christ returns.
>
> 2. That it is not the purpose of the present gospel age to convert the world to Christianity, but rather to preach the gospel as a witness to the nations and so to warn them of and make them justly subject to judgment; also to gather out of all nations God's elect, the Church saints.
>
> 3. That the world is growing worse and will continue to grow worse until Christ comes to establish His Kingdom.

4. That immediately preceding the return of Christ there is to be a period of general apostasy and wickedness.

5. That we are now in the latter stages of the Church age and that the return of Christ is near, probably to occur within the lifetime of the present generation. [Note: the copyright date on this book is 1957.]

6. That at Christ's coming the righteous dead of all ages are to be raised in the "first resurrection."

7. That the resurrected dead together with the transfigured living saints who are then on the earth are to be caught up to meet the Lord in the air.

8. That the judgment of all the righteous then takes place, which judgment consists primarily in the assignment of rewards.

9. That before and during the tribulation period the Jews are to be restored to the land of Palestine.

10. That at the mere sight of their Messiah the Jews are to turn to Him in a national conversion and true repentance.

11. That Christ at His coming destroys the Antichrist and all his forces in the battle of Armageddon.

12. That after the battle of Armageddon Christ establishes a world-wide Kingdom with Jerusalem as its capital, in which He and the resurrected and transfigured saints rule for a thousand years in righteousness, peace and prosperity.

13. That during this reign the city of Jerusalem and the temple are to be rebuilt, the feasts and fasts and the priesthood, ritual and sacrificial system reinstituted, though performed in a Christian spirit and by Christian worshippers.

14. That the golden age also is to be characterized by the removal of the curse from nature so that the desert shall blossom as the rose and the wild ferocious nature of the beasts shall be changed.

15. That during the Millennium great numbers of the Gentiles will turn to God and be incorporated into the Kingdom.

16. That while many remain unconverted and rebellious at heart they are not destroyed, but are held in check by the rod-of-iron rule of Christ.

17. That during the Millennium Satan is to be bound, cast into the abyss, and so shut away from the earth.

18. That at the close of the Millennium Satan is to be loosed for a short time.

19. That the Millennium is to be followed by a short but violent outbreak of wickedness and rebellion headed by Satan which all but overwhelms the saints and the holy city of Jerusalem.

20. That the forces of wickedness are to be destroyed by fire which is cast down upon them from heaven.

21. That the wicked dead of all ages are then to be raised in the "second resurrection," judged, and with the Devil and the wicked angels cast into hell.

22. That heaven and hell are then introduced in their fullness, with the new heavens and the new earth as the future home of the redeemed, which will constitute the eternal state.[21]

Historic Premillennialism

Historic premillennialism is a very different version of premillennialism from dispensational premillennialism. Although it holds to a literal thousand-year reign of Christ on earth, it dismisses all the programs for Israel and the church listed by Boettner. Above all, historic premillennialists would dispute the idea that the kingdom was put on hold until Christ's return. J. Barton Payne, author of the massive *Encyclopedia of Biblical Prophecy*, believed the Tribulation has already taken place (in A.D. 70 when Jerusalem was destroyed), but he also believed at some future time Christ will set up a literal Millennium on earth. This view makes him both a preterist and a millenarian. (The two do not often go hand in hand.) I'm not sure how popular historic premillennialism is today among premillennial scholars and writers, but no polling data has ever determined correctness in theological matters.

Historic premillennialism would view the kingdom of God as having begun with Christ's first coming, only to be consummated with His second coming. George Ladd, author of *The Presence of the Future*, is a well-known scholar (in theological circles) who holds this view. He talks about the kingdom that began but which will not be completed until Christ's return:

> . . . *history cannot save itself*. However, God has not abandoned history to self-destruction. God has entered into history in the person of his Son to redeem history. The eschatological redemption will be the glorious, public manifestation of what God has already done in veiled form in Jesus of Nazareth. In him, the Word became flesh. In his ministry, the Kingdom of God was like a seed, a handful of dough. However, God's redemptive acting in Jesus will yet be clearly displayed for what it is: the victory of God over evil. This victory of God's Kingdom was a real victory not seen by the world. The presence of the Kingdom in Jesus was not a worldly phenomenon . . . but a hidden presence which must one day be made public. Therefore what God did in history in Jesus and what he will do at the end of history by the Parousia [i.e., Second Coming] are two forms of the same redemptive rule of God; and the former demands the latter. . . . even though the goal of history is beyond history, it nevertheless means the redemption of history, when history is transformed into a new and glorious mode of existence.[22]

Why is Christ taking so long in His return?

The kingdom has begun. It is growing throughout the world. One day it will be completed in toto. There are some nonmillenarians who say roughly the same thing (obviously without the literal Millennium part). Elsewhere Dr. Ladd answers the question: Why is Christ taking so long (in His return)?: "Christ is tarrying until the Church has completed its task. When Matthew 24:14 has been fulfilled, then Christ will come. . . . *Any generation which is really dedicated to the task can complete the mission*. The Lord can come in our own generation, in our life-time—if we stir ourselves and finish our task."[23]

The late Donald Grey Barnhouse, pastor of Tenth Presbyterian Church of Philadelphia, also held to the historic premillennial view. In his commentary on Revelation, he argued for a literal Millennium to come. Then he added a rather interesting argument:

> There is one further item in the argument for the necessity of the literal kingdom of Christ on earth that grows out of all of the utopian literature that has been created by unbelieving man. From Thomas More's "Utopia," there has been a stream of literary dreamings—Butler's "Erewhon," Bellamy's "Looking Backward," Hilton's "Lost Horizon." There has been a whole gamut of socialistic and communistic writings—Marx, Engels, Lenin and the lesser satellites. There have been serious efforts to establish utopian colonies, such as those of Hopedale, Mass., Economy, Penna., Utopia, Ohio, the more pretentious effort of Robert Owen from England to New Harmony, Ind., and Dana's effort at Brook Farm [a communistic experiment led by transcendentalists in West Roxbury, Mass., 1841–47], as well as the gigantic effort of Tolstoy in Russia. Many theological modernists have adopted these various dreams and speak of a classless society without violence and ultimately without a state.[24]

This reminds me of St. Anselm's argument for the existence of God: I believe in God because God put it into my mind to believe that He exists. What Barnhouse is saying is that God has put the idea of the Millennium even in the minds of secular people. Continuing further, Dr. Barnhouse sums up:

> We believe that it can be demonstrated that everything ever imagined by man as a possible solution of the world's problems will be brought into the conditions set up at that time, and that the millennium will be the perfect trial period for every device which the natural heart has imagined as a possible cure for the ills of mankind.[25]

Here is an excellent summary of the key points of the historic premillennial position . . . prior to the Darbyite influence. This is by Alexander Reese, from his *The Approaching Advent of Christ*:

> Until the second quarter of the nineteenth century general agreement existed among pre-millennial advocates of our Lord's Coming concerning the main outlines of the prophetic future: amidst differences of opinion on the interpretation of the Apocalypse and other portions of Scripture, the following scheme stood out as fairly representative of the school:—
>
> (1) The approaching Advent of Christ to this world will be visible, personal, and glorious.
>
> (2) The Advent, though in itself a single crisis, will be accompanied and followed by a variety of phenomena bearing upon the history of the Church, of Israel, and the world. Believers who survive till the Advent will be transfigured and translated to meet the approaching Lord, together with the saints raised and changed at the first resurrection. Immediately following this, Antichrist and his allies will be slain, and Israel, the covenant people, will repent and be saved, by looking upon Him whom they pierced.
>
> (3) Thereupon the Messianic Kingdom of prophecy, which, as the Apocalypse informs us, will last for a thousand years, will be established in power and great glory in a transfigured world. The nations will turn to God, war and oppression cease, and righteousness and peace will cover the earth.
>
> (4) At the conclusion of the kingly rule of Christ and His saints, the rest of the dead will be raised, the Last Judgement ensue, and a new and eternal world be created.
>
> (5) No distinction was made between the *Coming* of our Lord, and His *Appearing*, *Revelation* and *Day*, because these were all held to be synonymous, or at least related terms, signifying always the one Advent in glory at the beginning of the Messianic Kingdom.
>
> (6) While the Coming of Christ, no matter how long the present dispensation may last, is the true and proper

> hope of the Church in every generation, it is nevertheless conditioned by the prior fulfillment of certain signs or events in the history of the Kingdom of God: the Gospel has first to be preached to all nations; the Apostasy and the Man of Sin be revealed, and the Great Tribulation come to pass. Then shall the Lord come.
>
> (7) The Church of Christ will not be removed from the earth until the Advent of Christ at the very end of the present Age: the Rapture and the Appearing take place at the same crisis; hence Christians of that generation will be exposed to the final affliction under Antichrist.
>
> Such is a fair statement of the fundamentals of Premillennialism as it has obtained since the close of the Apostolic Age. There have been difference of opinion on details and subsidiary points, but the main outline is as I have given it.[26]

Reese further says:

> Yet the undeniable fact is that this "any-moment" view of Christ's Return only originated about 1830, when Darby gave forth at the same time the mistaken theory of the Secret Coming and Rapture; but all down the centuries there had existed Christians who longed for the Revelation of Christ, whilst expecting that Antichrist would come first.[27]

Thus we see that though both are premillennialists, the historical and the dispensationalist have some major differences.

Conclusion

We now have a preview of coming attractions—that is, if the premillennialists have it right. Before equal time is given to the nonmillenarians—both amillennialists and postmillennialists, let's read about the excitement and anticipation for what is to come described in Hal Lindsey's premil classic, *The Late Great Planet Earth*:

> We have seen how current events are fitting together simultaneously into the precise pattern of predicted events. Israel has returned to Palestine and revived the nation. Jerusalem is under Israeli control. Russia has emerged as a great northern power and is the avowed enemy of revived Israel. The Arabs are joining in a concerted effort to liberate Palestine under Egyptian leadership. The black African nations are beginning to move from sympathy toward the Arabs to an open alliance in their "liberation" cause.
>
> It's happening. God is putting it all together. God may have His meaning for the "now generation" which will have a greater effect on mankind than anything since Genesis 1.
>
> Will you be ready if we are to be a part of the prophetic "now generation?"[28]

Regardless of your views on the end times, what Lindsey asks is *the* most important question: Will *you* be ready for when Christ returns?

5

The Second Coming According to Nonmillenarians

As someone has stated: "if Satan is bound he must have a long tether." All appearances seem to be against the view that we are in the millennium now.[1]

—J. Marcellus Kik

This chapter title is wrong from the start. There is no *one* picture of *the* Second Coming from the amillennialist or postmillennialist perspective. There would seem to be much greater unanimity on the premil front—despite some divergence on the relationship of the Rapture to the Tribulation—than there is on the nonmillenarian front *when it comes to spelling out specific events of the end times*. The postmil and amil views of the end times are much more difficult to peg than the premil view because prophecies aren't taken literally. In fact, many nonmillenarians believe the Book of Revelation sometimes describes the same things in different ways while not approaching the subject chronologically. In addition, many of them believe much of what was written has already been fulfilled.

Nevertheless, we can observe some things from their various interpretations, and we can point to some significant events as we try to understand their varied opinions on the Second Coming. The following is a thumbnail sketch of some of the nonmillenarian views of the Second Coming.

The Kingdom of God Has Begun but Has Not Been Completed

Nonmillenarians believe the kingdom of God began with the first coming of Jesus even though the Jewish establishment rejected the kingdom when they rejected Jesus, the rightful king. Although Jesus inaugurated the kingdom, it is not yet consummated. It will be, however, one day on earth or on the new earth.

The author of *How to Read Prophecy*, Joel Green (whose *exact* position on end times is unknown to me), writes, "The kingdom is God's reign, already begun."[2] G. C. Berkouwer, author of *The Return of Christ*, puts it this way: "The Kingdom has already come; and the believers must see, discover, and recognize that."[3] Although not necessarily a nonmillenarian, Martin Lloyd-Jones says this about the kingdom: "What is the kingdom of God? Well, it is best defined as the *rule* of God. The kingdom of God is present wherever God is reigning."[4]

Christians pray, "Thy kingdom come, Thy will be done in earth as it is in heaven." This certainly implies that the kingdom hasn't come in its fulness. Yet nonmillenarians believe it *has begun* with the first coming of the Lord. It was not put on hold. During this—the Church Age—we're between the "already" and the "not yet."

Green comments, "The Lord's present reign is most visible in the church. Nonetheless, it must be stated emphatically: the church is *not* the kingdom. The kingdom is the universal, final, eternal, perfect, transcendent and definitive reign of God."[5]

In fact, nondispensationalists view Christianity as like the seed in the parable of the mustard seed. The seed—that is, the church—started out small and has grown immensely. The kingdom reigns in people's hearts, and one day it will reign on earth, even "as it is in heaven." The Sermon on the Mount applies to today, as well as the parables, including the kingdom parables.

Jesus is Lord, not just in heaven, but over earth as well. Amillennialist Jay Adams says, "Christ now rules over all things as Messiah from the right hand of God—a place of power and majesty in heaven—and will continue to do so until all his enemies are destroyed."[6]

Therefore, nonmillenarians hold that the kingdom was not postponed. It has begun, but it certainly has not seen its complete fulfillment.

The New Testament Age Is "The Last Days"

Nonmillenarians also maintain that we are living in the last days, and we have been since the day of Pentecost. On that day, Peter quoted the Book of Joel (2:28-32), which talks about how God will pour out His Spirit during "the last days." Peter applied that phrase to his day. Now, nearly two thousand years later, ask the nonmillenarians, how much more does the phrase apply to our day?

The Stone Becoming a Mountain

While the premillennialist believes the Millennium, the literal reign of Jesus Christ—on the throne of David in Jerusalem on this earth—is yet to come, the nonmillenarian believes the Millennium is a spiritual phenomenon, and we're experiencing it right now. Nonmillenarians believe the Church Age was not Plan B. They believe God knew the Jews would reject their own Messiah, and thus He made provision to spread His kingdom throughout the earth through the church. To the nonmillenarian, we are now experiencing the messianic age predicted in the Old Testament. Jesus the Messiah is ruling in the hearts of His people. His kingdom is spreading from shore to shore; it is filling all the earth.

The prophet Daniel interpreted King Nebuchadnezzar's dream, which dealt with a four-part statue that represented different kingdoms to come. (I discuss this dream briefly in the chapter on Daniel's Seventieth Week.) In the context of talking about the Roman Empire, he said:

> In the time of those kings, the God of heaven will set up a kingdom that will never be destroyed, nor will it be left to another people. It will crush all those kingdoms [Babylon, Medo-Persia, Greece, and Rome] and bring them to an end, but it will itself endure forever. This is the meaning of the vision of the rock cut out of a mountain, but not by human hands—a rock that broke the iron, the bronze [Greece], the clay [Rome], the silver [Medo-Persia] and the gold [Babylon] to pieces (Dan. 2:44-45).

Nonmillenarians see this description as a beautiful picture of how the kingdom of God has come into our world and superseded all other kingdoms.

On the other hand, dispensationalists insist this has not yet occurred. *The Scofield Reference Bible* notes:

> The smiting Stone (2:34, 35) destroys the Gentile world-system (in its final form) by a sudden and irremediable blow, not by the gradual processes of conversion and assimilation; and then, and not before, does the Stone become a mountain which fills "the whole earth."

> (Cf. Dan. 7:26, 27.) Such a destruction of the Gentile monarchy-system did not occur at the first advent of Christ. On the contrary, He was put to death by the sentence of an officer of the fourth empire, which was then at the zenith of its power. Since the crucifixion the Roman empire has followed the course marked out in the vision, but Gentile world-dominion still continues, and the crushing blow is still suspended. . . . The God of the heavens does not set up His kingdom till after the destruction of the Gentile world-system. It is noteworthy that Gentile world-dominion begins and ends with a great image.[7]

Nonmillenarians, on the other hand, believe this has already been fulfilled and is in the process of being fulfilled. The kingdom of Christ played a role in destroying ancient Rome, which now lies in the dust. Meanwhile, Christ's reign is spreading throughout the world. It's interesting to note that the secular historian Edward Gibbons once sneered that it was the Christian religion that ultimately caused the downfall of ancient Rome—mainly because its acceptance weakened the Roman army and restrained its former policies of cruelty during military conquest. I remember a vocal anti-Christian professor at Tulane University gleefully stress this point to his class on ancient history. Little did he or Gibbons (or I at the time) consider the possibility that these secular historians might well have been confirming biblical truths.

Incidentally, the eminent secular historian Will Durant wrote a definitive, multivolume set on the history of the world, entitled *The Story of Civilization*. Here's what he said about the contest between the mighty Roman Empire and the infant Christian church:

> There is no greater drama in human record than the sight of a few Christians, scorned or oppressed by a succession of emperors, bearing all trials with a fiery tenacity, multiplying quietly, building order while their enemies generated chaos, fighting the sword with the word, brutality with hope, and at last defeating the strongest state that history has ever known. Caesar and Christ had met in the arena, and Christ had won.[8]

Joseph Mede, a premillennial dispensationalist of the last century, noted to interpret this passage properly we must first differentiate between the kingdom of the stone versus the kingdom of the mountain: "The *interval* between these two—from the time the stone was first hewn out, that is, the kingdom of Christ was first advanced, until the time it becomes a mountain, that is, when 'the mystery of God shall be finished' (Rev. 10:7)—is the subject of the *Apocalyptical visions*."[9]

Postmillennialist David Brown, however, counters Mede's view: "The kingdom of Christ, instead of commencing with the millennium, will, it seems, have run one entire stage of its career before that era arrives. There are not two kingdoms [but] one. . . . There is but *one kingdom* of Christ in 'two states,' commencing during the existence of the last of the four monarchies; that is, on the Redeemer's exaltation to the right hand of power, stretching across the era of the latter day, and losing itself in the final state. However different its *aspects* as 'the stone,' and as 'the mountain,' *it is the stone that becomes the mountain*."[10]

That mountain in Daniel's vision goes on to fill the whole earth. Interestingly, Brown's book was written in 1849. Today, after more than a hundred years of incredible progress in world missions, we can see far better how much more of the earth is hearing the Gospel than ever before. Understandably the nonmillenarians insist that the stone that smote the Roman Empire is at this present time in the process of becoming a mountain.

The Church Age Is the Messianic Age

The nonmillenarians contend that the messianic prophecies of the Old Testament are being fulfilled now. As Christ's kingdom spreads from nation to nation, the reign of God's Messiah is also spreading. For example, Psalm 72 is a messianic psalm written by Solomon. Here are selected verses (arranged in paragraph form):

> Endow the king with your justice, O God, the royal son with your righteousness. He will judge your people in righteousness, your afflicted ones with justice. . . . He will endure as long as the sun, as long as the moon,

> through all generations. . . . He will rule from sea to sea and from the River to the ends of the earth. The desert tribes will bow before him and his enemies will lick the dust. The kings of Tarshish and of distant shores will bring tribute to him; the kings of Sheba and Seba will present him gifts. All kings will bow down to him and all nations will serve him. For he will deliver the needy who cry out, the afflicted who have no one to help. He will take pity on the weak and the needy and save the needy from death. He will rescue them from oppression and violence, for precious is their blood in his sight. . . . All nations will be blessed through him, and they will call him blessed (Ps. 72:1-2, 5, 8-14, 17).

Recall that the dispensationalists interpret such messianic prophecies as not being fulfilled until Israel is restored and after the Jews have accepted Jesus as the Messiah. In commenting on this psalm, Scofield wrote, "It is through restored Israel that the kingdom is to be extended over the earth."[11] On the other hand, the nonmillenarians interpret such Old Testament pictures of the messianic reign as being fulfilled during the Church Age with the worldwide spread of the Gospel.

The Rapture and the resurrection occur on the last day of history

No Secret Rapture Before the Seven-Year Tribulation

Nonmillenarians believe the proof text of the Rapture refers more to the resurrection of believers than to a secret escape from the troubles of the world. Historically, the passage that teaches the Rapture—1 Thessalonians 4—was one of two key resurrection passages in the New Testament; the other being 1 Corinthians 15. The 1 Thessalonians 4 passage was written primarily to comfort and encourage believers who faced death and were grieving over the death of loved ones in the faith. The Rapture and the resurrection occur at the same time—the last day of history. Then comes the judgment for everybody—the quick and the dead.

The Tribulation of the Olivet Discourse Has Already Taken Place

Many, if not most, nonmillenarians say the Great Tribulation has already taken place. In fact, nonmillenarians maintain they can produce considerable evidence for their view that the words of Christ in Matthew 24, Mark 13, and Luke 21—wherein He spoke about the abomination that causes desolation, the signs in the heavens, in short, the Great Tribulation—were fulfilled when Jerusalem fell in A.D. 70.

No Signs of the Times

Some nonmillenarians believe the "signs of the times" Jesus described in the Olivet Discourse have already been fulfilled. Accordingly, these signs have had no significance to the church since A.D. 70. There were signs that warned of His return in A.D. 70—wars and rumors of wars, the worldwide spread of the Gospel (Col. 1:23), false christs, and so on, but there are not necessarily signs for today to look for in His second coming. This present period is one of working toward spreading the Gospel and discipling the nations. In fact, one postmil view is that He won't return until God the Father puts all His enemies at Jesus' feet. Not all nonmillenarians would necessarily agree with that last point. Christ may return at any moment in their view—not just when His enemies are vanquished.

No Literal Millennium

Nonmillenarians believe the passage describing the Millennium (only found directly in Rev. 20) is in a book filled with symbols, and the best approach to interpret this passage is to do so figuratively, not literally. They believe Satan is bound now—albeit with a long leash! They also maintain that the only reason Satan is victorious in any way today is because the church is disobedient and lazy.

According to Revelation 20:1-6, John spoke of two resurrections—the first is the new birth (to nonmillenarians); the second is heaven. Jesus had earlier explained this to His disciples: "I tell you the truth, whoever hears my word and believes him who sent me has eternal life and will not be condemned; he has crossed over from death to life. I tell you the truth, a time is coming and *has now come* when the dead will hear the voice of the Son of God and those who hear will live" (John 5:24-25, italics mine). The nonmillenarians hold that this passing over from death to life is the first resurrection.

John further wrote in his vision of the end times, "They came to life and reigned with Christ a thousand years. . . . This is the first resurrection. Blessed and holy are those who have part in the first resurrection. The second death has no power over them" (Rev. 20:4-6). Who are "they" in this passage? In the beginning of verse 4, we see that they are the souls of faithful Christians who have been martyred for their faith. Then we see later that the second death is the lake of fire (Rev. 20:14), that is, hell.

Thus the nonmillenarians argue that the first resurrection is the life Christ gives to the spiritually dead; it is the "kingdom of God within you" (Luke 17:21). It is being born again. It is the partial establishment of the kingdom on earth. The "first resurrection," writes nonmillenarian Jay Adams, "must be understood spiritually, not physically. The 'second death' is not physical. Why must the 'first resurrection' be?"[12]

Jesus further said about his second coming, "Do not be amazed at this, for a time is coming when all who are in the graves will hear his voice and come out—those who have done good will rise to live, and those who have done evil will rise to be condemned" (John 5:28-30). The condemnation of the unbelievers is the second death. This difficult concept has been made easy by this phrase: "Born once, die twice. Born twice, die once." (Those who are never born again will die twice; those who are born again will die only once.)

Yet what about the thousand-year aspect of the Millennium? How do nonmillenarians view that? Amillennialist Jay Adams comments:

> A word should be said about the millennium as a length of time. The 1000 years is an "ideal" period meaning a long time. It is set in contrast to the shorter designations (three and a half years, 42 months, etc.) which describe the time of intense suffering of the saints. In contrast to these, it embraces the period of ascendancy for the church, or kingdom of God. It is no more to be taken literally (i.e., as an exact period) than the "ten days" of persecution predicted in Revelation 2:10 or the "144,000" sealed ones. These are numbers which create a picture rather than give an exact sum. Already the

"millennium" has lasted almost two thousand years.[13]

In short, this view contends that the Millennium is occurring *at this very moment*. It is the reign of Christ from heaven. Adam adds, "Will anyone still inquire, 'How can we be sure that the millennial rule and the present reign of Christ are one and the same?' . . . A final comparison of crucial Scripture passages should forever remove any remaining doubt."[14] He employs the following verses to support his statement:

- Psalm 110:1: "The Lord says to my Lord: 'Sit at my right hand until I make your enemies a footstool for your feet,'" which is quoted in Acts 2:34-35 as well and applies to Jesus.
- Ephesians 1:20-22: God the Father "raised [Jesus] from the dead and seated him at his right hand in the heavenly realms, far above all rule and authority, power and dominion, and every title that can be given, not only in the present age but also in the one to come. And God placed all things under his feet and appointed him to be head over everything for the church."
- 1 Peter 3:22: Jesus "has gone into heaven and is at God's right hand—with angels, authorities and powers in submission to him."
- Luke 22:69: "But from now on, the Son of Man will be seated at the right hand of the mighty God."
- Hebrews 10:12-14: "But when this priest [Jesus] had offered for all time one sacrifice for sins, he sat down at the right hand of God. Since that time he waits for his enemies to be made his footstool, because by one sacrifice he has made perfect forever those who are being made holy."

From their understanding of these verses it is clear that the nonmillenarians regard the Millennium as not being a literal, future event. It's taking place now on earth. Jesus' reign has begun in the hearts of men and women, and one day that reign will be complete.

The Second Coming Could Be Today—or a Thousand Years from Now

The nonmillenarians further hold that it could be a long time before Jesus returns again. The parable of the talents was told in the context of the Olivet Discourse (remember that the whole discussion in Matthew's version is found in Matt. 24 *and* 25). In that parable, when did the master return to hold his subjects accountable? Right away? After a short time? No, after "a long time" (Matt. 25:19).

Jesus' return may be two hours from now. It may be two days from now. Then again, it might be twenty years from now, or why not two hundred years? two thousand years? twenty thousand years? This is a great contrast with the pretribulational premillennialist view, which insists that it would be inconceivable that Jesus could tarry for another hundred years or longer.

On the other hand, the nonmillenarian view holds that Christ could wait for His return for a *long, long* time. Dr. Loraine Boettner, an eminent Presbyterian scholar, wrote an interesting and helpful book on the post-millennial perspective of the end times, *The Millennium*. This is what he wrote in 1957 on how long the planet earth could still last before Jesus' return:

> It may, for all we know, continue another 2,000 or 200,000 years. One thing that the Bible makes clear is that we do not know even approximately when the end is to come. Let us remember that in every generation there have been those who thought they saw signs which indicated that the end was near, signs which to them were just as convincing as any that are seen today. But they have all been mistaken.[15]

Boettner's words sound like such heresy to some modern ears, conditioned as some are by modern dispensationalism. Yet remember, a day is like a thousand years to the Lord and a thousand years is like a day. Besides, if the key "signs of the times" had already been fulfilled in A.D. 70, as Boettner believes them to be, then we wouldn't know when Christ will come.

There's Only a One-Time Judgment of the Quick and the Dead

Premillennialists believe there will be more than one judgment to come. Interestingly, *The Scofield Reference Bible* lists seven judgments, including that of believers (the Bema seat), the living nations, Israel, and the Great White Throne Judgment.[16] In contrast to this view, nonmillenarians subscribe to a one-time, once-and-for-all judgment of all human beings—believers and nonbelievers alike. The just and the unjust. The quick and the dead. This judgment will take place at the end of time.

At this point, the sheep and the goats passage, which comes at the end of the Olivet Discourse, demands comment. Jay Adams makes this observation about the passage:

> There is no place allowed in the sequence for a millennium *following* the coming of Christ. Consequently, the thousand years must *precede* the advent. Matthew 25 is in full accord with the united testimony of Revelation and the rest of the Bible. When Christ comes, there will be a last judgment and the eternal state will immediately begin.[17]

The nonmillenarians asks us to look at Matthew's version of the Olivet Discourse, not just chapter 24 but chapter 25 as well, which contains the sheep and the goats passage. From this passage they contend that *the* judgment occurs at the end of time on earth.

The World Will End with a Bang (Held by Some Nonmillenarians)

The world will end with a bang. Just as it was destroyed at one time by a flood, so one day it will be destroyed by fire, just as Peter described in his second letter in the Bible (2 Pet. 3:10). The new heaven and the new earth (described figuratively in Rev. 21) will then be ushered in. Literally or nonliterally. In either event, believers will enjoy eternal bliss with the triune God, while those who have followed Satan in this life (whether they know that fact or not) will suffer eternal torment with him in hell.

The Growth of the Mustard Seed

How do we properly understand the differences between the two major camps within nonmillenarianism—postmillennialism and amillennialism? Postmils and amils could be separated in this fashion: The mustard seed parable summarizes the postmillennial view while the parable of the wheat and tares summarizes the amillennial view.

By and large, postmillennialists believe the world will likely get better and better by the hand of Christ in heaven working through His church on earth. Although this may seem radical, consider how life on earth has *already* improved through the Christian influence. For example, when Jesus came the first time, He came into a world that was half-slave, half-free. Slavery and many evils have largely been done away with in those parts of the world where Christianity has had strong influence. Christ unlocked the forces of charity in the world; because of Him hospitals have been built throughout the world. To promote the reading of the Bible, literacy has spread all over; in fact, hundreds of languages have been set to writing for the first time in order to translate the Bible or Christian liturgy.[18] There are still many other evils in the world yet to vanquish, but there has been considerable progress over the centuries.

The postmillennialists point to Jesus' parable of the mustard seed, which reads:

> The kingdom of heaven is like a mustard seed, which a man took and planted in his field. Though it is the smallest of all your seeds, yet when it grows, it is the largest of garden plants and becomes a tree, so that the birds of the air come and perch in its branches (Matt. 13:31-32).

Jesus Christ has exerted a greater influence on human history than any other person who has ever lived. From very humble roots, a traveling rabbi wandered a country under the thumb of Roman conquest and started a faith that has grown to the world's largest religion bar none. Approximately, two billion souls the world over claim to be Christians.[19] Even if the number of true Christians is a mere percentage, we are still talking about a sizeable portion of humanity.

The sun never sets on the Christian church. All over the world, there are hundreds of millions of people whose life aim is to serve Jesus Christ first and foremost. Napoleon, who was well aware of political power, once said this about the Lord: "I search in vain in history to find the similar to Jesus Christ, or anything which can approach the gospel . . . nations pass away, thrones crumble, but the Church remains."[20]

The famous poem "One Solitary Life" by Dr. James Allan Francis puts the growth of the mustard seed into perspective: "All the armies that ever marched, all the navies that ever sailed, all the parliaments that ever sat, all the kings that ever reigned, put together, have not affected the life of man on this earth as much as that one solitary life."[21] In short, the mustard seed has yielded great fruit.

Amillennialists: Things Are Getting Better and Worse Simultaneously

The amillennialists, however, do not see the world as necessarily becoming better, nor do they see it becoming worse. In fact, it's doing both at the same time.

Before we explore their position further, it's important to understand the meaning of the word "amillennialist." On the one hand, I think the terms "premillennialist," "premillennialism," or even its old-fashioned variant "premillenerianism" are basically fine. The terms premillennialists call themselves do not trouble them. However, I sometimes find discomfort on the other side for the term "amillennialist" from amillennialists themselves. For example, Jay Adams (better known for his contribution to Christian counseling than his eschatology) wrote a short book, *The Time Is at Hand*, that explains well the amillennial position. Yet even though Adams is an amillennialist, he doesn't like the term. Instead, he thinks a better term might be a "realized millennialist." He writes, "The unhappy term *amillennialism*, which has become attached to the biblical eschatology, has been the cause of unfortunate misunderstanding among its friends and enemies alike. . . . he task of amillennialism is not to 'explain away' the millennium, but to explain it!"[22]

Perhaps the parable of the wheat and tares can best summarize amillennialism. Jesus told this parable showing both good and evil flourishing at the same time:

> The kingdom of heaven is like a man who sowed good seed in his field; but while men slept, his enemy came and sowed tares among the wheat and went his way. But when the grain had sprouted and produced a crop, then the tares also appeared. So the servants of the owner came and said to him, "Sir, did you not sow good seed in your field? How then does it have tares?" He said to them, "An enemy has done this." The servants said to him, "Do you want us then to go and gather them up?"

> But he said, "No, lest while you gather up the tares you also uproot the wheat with them. Let both grow together until the harvest, and at the time of harvest I will say to the reapers, 'First gather together the tares and bind them in bundles to burn them, but gather the wheat into my barn'" . . . "He who sows the good seed is the Son of Man. The field is the world, the good seeds are the sons of the kingdom, but the tares are the sons of the wicked one. The enemy who sowed them is the devil, the harvest is the end of the age." (Matt. 13:24-30, 37-39, NKJV).

Good and evil grow simultaneously, and then comes the judgment.

Christ's Coming Will Be the Climax of All History

When Jesus returns, every eye will see Him, every knee will bow, everybody will hear it, and there will be no doubt about what is happening. The end will certainly not begin with a *secret* Rapture.

Postmillennialist John Jefferson Davis explains the postmillennial position in such a way that it shows how the return of Christ is the climax of all history:

> The main tenets of the postmillennial position as it was generally held during the nineteenth century can be outlined as follows:
> 1. Through the preaching of the gospel and dramatic outpourings of the Holy Spirit Christian missions and evangelism will attain remarkable success, and the church will enjoy an unprecedented period of numerical expansion and spiritual vitality.
> 2. This period of spiritual prosperity, the millennium, understood as a long period of time, is to be characterized by conditions of increasing peace and economic well-being in the world as a result of the growing influence of Christian truth.
> 3. The millennium will also be characterized by the conversion of large numbers of ethnic Jews to the Christian faith (Rom. 11:25-26).

> 4. At the end of the millennial period there will be a brief period of apostasy and sharp conflict between Christian and evil forces (Rev. 20:7-10).
>
> 5. Finally and simultaneously there will occur the visible return of Christ, the resurrection of the righteous and the wicked, the final judgment, and the revelation of the new heavens and the new earth.[23]

Much of Davis' postmillennial description of the return of Christ can apply to the amillennialist view as well, in particular point 5.

Conclusion

As was noted at the beginning of this chapter, not all nonmillenarians would agree entirely with what has been presented in this chapter, but the primary elements of this view have been set forth.

There is a tension between the now and the not yet of the kingdom of God that is to be found in the nonmillenarian school of thought (as well as the historic premillennialist view). The tension is that the kingdom has started, but is by no means complete. There's a great analogy from the Second World War that illustrates this view of the coming of the kingdom, which has gained a major footing in the world. G. C. Berkouwer writes:

> [Oscar] Cullmann illustrates his criticism of consistent eschatology with an oft-quoted example from World War II. The Allied victory was already implicit in the invasion of Normandy heralding the beginning of the decisive battle; the end had only to be *realized*. Similarly, the community of believers, living out of faith in the accomplished work of Jesus Christ, could no longer lapse into a crisis of delay, as was believed by consistent eschatology.[24]

In short, what Jesus began when He came the first time, He will complete upon His return.

So far we've seen some of the major differences between end-times positions. Now we're going to look at the heart and soul of the controversy. We're going to look at the underlying assumptions that often lie at the root of the dispute.

Part Two

The Heart of the Controversy

6

The Heart of the Controversy

It is admitted by both premillennialists and amillennialists that the root of their difference lies in the method of Biblical interpretation. . . .[1]

—Charles Feinberg

There are all sorts of books and speakers today promoting elaborate pictures of the end times. Yet we have to recognize that much of what is said—on *any* side of the issue—depends on their starting point. If the premise is wrong, then the building, no matter how elaborate, comes crashing down. How can we know—with absolute certainty—on this side of paradise, which system is correct? Or can we know?

Where We Start Determines Where We End Up

Perhaps you've heard the illustration of the Great Divide. Erwin Lutzer tells about a certain river in Canada. The idea is very simple: At one point in the mountains, water droplets are together. Later they separate at a fork in the river, and then they eventually end up a continent apart. Lutzer writes:

> In British Columbia, five hundred miles northeast of Vancouver, the Fraser River parts into two streams—one runs east to the Atlantic Ocean, the other west to the Pacific. Once the water has parted, its direction is unchangeably fixed. The fork in the river is known as the Great Divide.[2]

Imagine two little droplets next to each other, freely floating down the Fraser River. Then they get to that fork in the stream . . . one goes east, the other west, and it's "Good-bye!" They end up *hundreds* of miles apart. A little twist or turn and they could have ended up at the other coast. Sometimes it seems a bit like that in our differing views on eschatology, but surely much less so. Nonetheless, where that fork is often determines where we end up. At the base of the controversy is our starting point from that fork, that is, our underlying assumptions about the interpretation of prophecy.

The Purpose of Prophecy

Before we look at the specifics of prophetic interpretation, let's consider the *purpose* of prophecy in the first place. Here are some thoughts from Joel B. Green, author of *How to Read Prophecy*: ". . . prophecy was more *forth*telling than *fore*telling, and this distinction can hardly be overemphasized when dealing with the issue of fulfilled prophecy."[3] Green adds, "Hence, to treat the biblical texts in general, and the apocalyptic writings in particular, as a beachhead from which to launch eschatological timetables is to do them violence. . . . To seek out correspondences between their symbolism and our newspapers' front pages is to miss the point entirely."[4] Therefore, Green concludes, "The prophetic Scriptures are misused when treated as a grab bag of end-time predictions."[5]

Premillennialist John Walvoord certainly wouldn't word it that way. He points out how predictive prophecy, both fulfilled and yet-to-be-fulfilled, is very encouraging:

> Though philosophers and scientists in various fields have attempted to understand and chart the human race, no book ever written has been a prophetic chart of human destiny like the Bible. It explains the nature of God and his purposes, his working among the nations of the world, his special plan for Israel, and his special plan for the church as well as the Consummation. In these God demonstrates his sovereignty and his righteous judgment as well as his marvelous grace in the salvation of those who inherit the new earth and New Jerusalem. A study of this prophetic chart brings awe and wonder to believers as they contemplate the immensity and detail of God's plan and purpose in his sovereign outworking in the human race to the present hour and on to its consummation. The examination of this chart furthers the hope of believers in the future, as well as their confi-

> dence in the God of grace who can meet humans in their present situations.[6]

In short, prophecy encourages us to see the sovereignty of God in history. And it gives us hope for the future.

How Do We Interpret Prophecy?

So how do we interpret prophecy? For example, is prophecy to be taken literally? That's one of the key elements in all these issues. Let's start with a passage with which virtually all sides would agree. In his book *How to Understand Your Bible*, T. Norton Sterrett writes:

> Prophecies have a great many figures of speech, symbols, etc., which we have already considered. They also have literal statements. The problem of interpretation is not just the individual figures but the larger question of whether prophecy is fulfilled literally, or in a figurative or spiritual way. Our approach to this question is based upon the premise that fulfilled prophecy is the key to understanding the unfulfilled. We must see how the New Testament interprets Old Testament prophecies. It will be well to look at several of these.[7]

Literal Language

On the issue of taking prophecy literally, Hal Lindsey, perhaps the best known of the dispensational school, writes in his new book, *Planet Earth: The Final Chapter*:

> At the beginning of the 19th century, theologians began to apply the same principles of literal interpretation to the field of prophecy that the Reformers had applied to the doctrines of Salvation. This caused a kind of "reawakening" to the reality of Bible prophecy and its growing relevance to the time in which they were living. After the close of the 1st century AD, there had developed apathy toward the study of prophecy. By the 4th century,

> prophecy had been written off as a collection of allegories. Such theologians as Origin [sic] and Augustine allegorized prophecy into meaningless non-sense.[8]

Premillennialist Paul Lee Tan adds these two thoughts:
(1) Origen was known as "Mr. Allegorism."[9]
(2) "Augustine modified allegorism by confining it to the prophetic Scriptures."[10]

Furthermore, premillennialist J. Dwight Pentecost observes, ". . . the allegorical method was not born out of the study of the Scriptures, but rather out of a desire to unite Greek philosophy and the Word of God. It did not come out of a desire to present the truths of the Word, but to pervert them. It was not the child of orthodoxy, but heterodoxy."[11]

In contrast to these opinions, however, postmil theologian Dr. Loraine Boettner says:

> Premillennialists place strong emphasis on literal interpretation and pride themselves on taking Scripture just as it is written. Post- and Amillennialists on the other hand, mindful of the fact that much of both the Old and New Testament unquestionably is given in figurative or symbolic language, have no objection on principle against figurative or symbolic language, have no objection on principle against figurative interpretation and readily accept that if the evidence indicates that it is preferable.[12]

Postmillennialist James Snowden also argues, "It was this literalizing of the Jewish prophesies concerning the Messiah and his kingdom that led the Jews off into views and hopes of the Messiah that were false and cruelly disappoint[ing]. . . . It was the literal interpretation of their Scriptures that blinded the Jews to their own Messiah."[13]

All of these writers quoted above—Lindsey, Tan, Pentecost, Boettner, and Snowden—believe the Scriptures to be the inspired, inerrant Word of God. The first three, however, have very different assumptions on how to read the prophetic portions of Scripture from the last two. As a result, their conclusions are quite different.

Here is another thought representative of the prophecy-is-to-be-taken-literally school. Robert Van Kampen approaches the issue this way:

> In my opinion there is only one legitimate hermeneutic we can use if we seek to know the truth of God's Word. *The text must be understood at face value, in its most natural, normal, customary sense, making allowances for obvious figures of speech, its context, and all the other passages of Scripture dealing with the same issue. When in doubt, let Scripture interpret Scripture! Once the common denominator is found that harmonizes all the passages, without contradiction, then we have truth, but not before. And once we have truth, that truth stands in judgment of us; never do we dare stand in judgment of it!*[14]

Nonmillenarians would totally agree we should *never* stand in judgment on the Word of God (as many liberals do today). Remember one of my chief contentions: Those who believe the Bible is the Word of God, who therefore await the return of Christ to earth—whether they have the pre- , a-, or postmillennial perspective—have a lot more in common than those who don't. Amillennialist John Calvin said in the preface to his *Commentary on the Book of Romans*: "It is the first business of an interpreter to let his author say what he does say, instead of attributing to him what we think he ought to say."[15] To rightly divide the word of truth means trying to understand the Scriptures the way God intends us to. If God intended a passage to be understood symbolically, then wouldn't it do more justice to the Scripture to understand it that way? And likewise, if He intended it to be taken literally.

"Let Scripture Interpret Scripture"

There's an old axiom that goes like this: "Let Scripture interpret Scripture." The word of God is its best interpreter.

Let's take a moment to look at one example. Peter quoted the Old Testament (Joel 2:28-32) in his sermon at Pentecost. Addressing a large crowd, he explained to them that those speaking in tongues were not drunk, but were fulfilling prophecy from the Old Testament. He then quotes from Joel:

> In the last days, God says, I will pour out my Spirit on all people. Your sons and daughters will prophesy, your young men will see visions, and your old men will dream dreams. Even on my servants, both men and women, I will pour out my Spirit in those days, and they will prophesy. I will show wonders in the heaven above and signs on the earth below, blood and fire and billows of smoke. The sun will be turned to darkness and the moon to blood before the coming of the great and glorious day of the Lord. And everyone who calls on the name of the Lord will be saved (Acts 2:17-21).

Yet, wait a minute. The nonmillenarian might say in that context:

- Where was the blood and fire and billows of smoke? Or perhaps that referred to the little tongues of fire that rested on the apostles in that day?
- Did the Lord show "wonders in the heaven above"?
- Did the sun become dark (or was that perchance a reference to the crucifixion)?
- Did the moon become as blood?

In short, is Peter interpreting this Old Testament text literally? It would appear not.

Postmillennialist J. Marcellus Kik comments on this passage: "The same type of apocryphal language is employed in the second chapter of Joel and the Apostle Peter quotes the prophecy of Joel on the day of Pentecost as recorded in Acts 2:16-21. This provides us with an infallible interpreter."[16] About the prophecy of Joel, Kik writes, "The Holy Spirit was and continues to be outpoured. That part of the prophecy has been fulfilled. Also, the Jewish nation has received the judgment of God [which took place in A.D. 70]. Its sun, moon, and stars have been darkened and are still obscured."[17]

The Literal Method of Interpretation

How are we to interpret prophecy? Premillennialist Charles Feinberg asserts, "The only way to know how God will fulfill prophecy in the future is to ascertain how He has done it in the past."[18] Premillennialist Sir Robert Anderson of Scotland Yard says, "There is not a single prophecy, of which the fulfillment is recorded in Scripture, that was not realized with absolute accuracy, and in every detail; and it is wholly unjustifiable to assume that a new system of fulfillment was inaugurated after the second canon closed."[19]

"Literal if Possible"

Nonmillenarians think that the dispensationalists are misguided. Postmil J. Marcellus Kik makes this observation: "Too little study of Old Testament ideas of judgment, and apocalyptic language and style, would seem to be the main reason for this one sided exegesis."[20] For example, in the context of a major study on Matthew 24, Christ's Olivet Discourse, Kik argues, "There is not a single figure ["sun, moon, and stars," "the son of man riding on the clouds," "the fig tree"] employed whose use has not been already sanctioned and its meaning determined in the Old Testament. Prophecy has indicated and history has verified that all events mentioned by Christ have found their fulfillment."[21]

Premillennial dispensationalist Paul Lee Tan, however, explains that a "literal" position on the Scriptures does not preclude figurative interpretation if warranted. He writes:

> The word *literal* is often taken to mean that which is nonfigurative. Interpreters often set the literal over against the figurative. This is a serious misapprehension of the method.
>
> Everyone agrees that great literatures properly use both figurative and nonfiguratives languages. Figures of speech are the legitimate, charming ornaments of language. They help to liven writing and conversing. Like all great literatures, the Bible contains both figurative and nonfigurative languages. For instance, Christ describes Himself as "the light of the world" (John 8:12). Figurative language helps make God's Word linguistically more interesting.[22]

Kik counters, "There is just a little misunderstanding in the minds of some people when you state that certain expressions in the Bible are figurative. They feel that it robs them of reality and makes them meaningless.

That is not true. Figurative expressions stand for realities. The 'Lamb' stands for the reality of the sacrificial atonement of Christ."[23]

Yet Tan maintains that "literal" is perhaps an unfortunate choice of words. Better words to communicate the idea would be: "plain, proper, natural, or normal"[24] Premillennialist Horatius Bonar adds this to the debate: "'Literal, if possible,' is, I believe the only maxim that will carry you right through the Word of God from Genesis to Revelation."[25] Thus it's not always an either-or between literal or figurative.

Two Extreme Examples

Are we splitting theological hairs? I think virtually all sides would agree that we can't take either literalism or figurativeness too far—beyond the letter or the spirit of the word.

Here's an example of literalism taken too far. This is a quote from the discredited minibook *88 Reasons Why the Rapture Is in 1988*: "These events [the Tribulation, the Millennium, etc.] were never restricted from our knowledge, but only the day and hour of our Lord's return for the Church, *and that event was limited only to the day and hour, and not the week, month or year.*"[26] I trust we can all agree that sort of wooden literalism does not do justice to the text!

We can't take either literalism or figurativeness too far

At the other extreme, you have some people spiritualizing Scripture to the degree where they miss the point. For example, the plain teaching of the parable of the Good Samaritan is to love our neighbor and help him in his time of trouble. Yet Origen (c. 185-c. 254) so allegorized Scripture that he said each character in the parable symbolizes something:

- Christ is the Good Samaritan.
- The Jewish nation is the priest and the Levite.
- The innkeeper is the church.

And on and on it goes. That's allegorizing Scripture taken to the nth degree. When Origen was a young man, he castrated himself because of his literalistic interpretation of Matthew 19:12.[27] Perhaps this explains why he turned to the other extreme of allegorizing Scripture.

A C. S. Lewis quote is pertinent here: "The devil is always trying to trick us to extremes." That temptation certainly exists in the realm of prophecy. George L. Murray points out, "The plain truth is that there is not one chapter of the prophetic Scripture which can be taken with absolute literalness. . . . the only safe method of interpretation is neither strictly literal, nor strictly spiritual."[28]

Nonmillenarian Philip Edgcumbe Hughes points out that when it comes to Revelation, even the premillennialist cannot consistently take it literally. Hughes states:

> Those who insist on a literalistic principle of interpretation—though it is a principle to which even they find it impossible to adhere with consistency—object that "one thousand years" means what it says. . . . there is a variety of literary genres in the Bible—such as history, poetry, parable, and apocalyptic—and a proper respect for the text must take this consideration into account. *To interpret literalistically what is intended symbolically cannot fail to do violence to the sacred text.*[29]

"The devil is always trying to trick us to extremes" —C.S. Lewis

All these statements remind us of a Ben Franklin-type dispute: It is so. It is not. It is too. No, it isn't.

No Place for Dogmatism

I believe strongly that there is no place for dogmatism in interpretation of prophecy because there are so many differing opinions. Consider this question: When Christ came the first time, did the Jews recognize their own Messiah, foretold in all those Old Testament predictions? No. Why not? Primarily because of their underlying assumption that the Messiah would be a political savior. They weren't expecting a spiritual savior. When Christ came the first time, they blew it. Their underlying assumptions were wrong. As Joel Green remarks of the Messiah, it was believed: "His would be a political *and* religious rule."[30]

At this point some specific examples will show how important it is to recognize the underlying assumptions of the interpreter. In the next chapter, we will apply some principles of what we're talking about to a few hotly contested passages.

7

Your Starting Point Often Determines Where You End Up

Interpret Scripture by Scripture.[1]

—Anonymous

In the last chapter we saw how important it is to recognize the interpretation mode of Bible prophecy. Indeed, how Scriptures are to be interpreted is at the very heart of the controversy. In this chapter, we will walk through some examples demonstrating how the starting point often leads to a particular conclusion.

A Few Examples of Disputes That Hinge on the Interpretation Mode

Among other issues, we will consider the Millennium, Christ on the white horse slaying His enemies with a sword proceeding from His mouth, and the binding of Satan.

Definitions of the Millennium

Some people actually believe we're in the Millennium

As I stated earlier, some people actually believe we're in the Millennium. I say "actually" because the way the Millennium has been defined, how could we *possibly* be currently experiencing it? Yet others think of the Millennium in broader terms by which it could be argued that we *are* in the Millennium. On the other hand, others feel that there never was nor will be a literal Millennium, nor did Scripture intend to teach one. In short, how we *define* what the Millennium is determines what we believe about the Millennium.

Loraine Boettner articulates his own position:

> The Postmillennialist looks for a golden age that will not be essentially different from our own so far as the basic facts are concerned. . . . Sin will not be eliminated but will be reduced to a minimum as the moral and spiritual environment of the earth becomes predominantly Christian. Social, economic and educational problems will remain, but with their unpleasant features greatly eliminated and their desirable features heightened. Christian principles of belief and conduct will be the accepted standards.[2]

Interestingly, Boettner wrote those words in 1957. Today, after the breakdown of morality in the 1960s and 1970s from which we have not yet recovered, we seem to be living in a post-Christian world. America is going to hell in a handbasket, or so it is often stated. How could *this* be the millennium?

Au contraire! cry the postmils: Take the long view. In the grand scheme of things, there is progress, even if sometimes marred by backward steps. (To paraphrase Chuck Swindoll—in a different context: "Three steps forward, two steps backward.")

Premillennialist Donald Grey Barnhouse defines the Millennium differently from the nonmillenarians, which is the heart of the controversy. He writes, "There shall be no more wars. . . . There will be no more economic exploitation. Every man will be a land owner. They shall all sit, every man under his own vine and fig tree (Micah 4:4). Here is the ideal state according to socialistic principles. . . . Every human being upon the earth shall know that the Bible is the Word of God."[3]

Postmillennialist Kik admits, "All appearances seem to be against the view that we are in the Millennium now. The trouble is that we have altogether a too materialistic concept of the millennial blessings. We fail to see that the greatest blessings are spiritual and they are in our midst."[4]

Therefore, the heart of the controversy goes back to the *definition* of "Millennium"; it boils down to how we are to interpret prophetic Scriptures; it goes back to the question of the kingdom of God: Has God's kingdom been postponed until Jesus returns or is it active in the world? Does it exist in the world today in small measure but will be known later (after Christ's return) in a complete way?

The End Battle

Another example of how our mode of interpretation determines our conclusions on prophetic writings can also be found in how we interpret the Book of Revelation. In chapter 19, three chapters after the discussion on Armageddon, there's a description of Jesus—the King of kings and Lord of lords—who thunders out of heaven riding on a white horse to judge and to righteously make war against His foes. "Out of His mouth comes a sharp sword with which to strike down the nations" (Rev. 19:15).

Postmillennialist B. B. Warfield says he sees this passage as applying to the *present time* as the Gospel goes forth:

> We are not to think, as we read, of any literal war or manual fighting, therefore; the conquest is wrought by the spoken word—in short, by the preaching of the Gospel. In fine, we have before us here a picture of the victorious career of the Gospel of Christ in the world. All the imagery of the dread battle and its hideous details are but to give us the impression of the completeness of the victory. Christ's Gospel is to conquer the earth; He is to overcome all His enemies. . . . What we have here, in effect, is a picture of the whole period between the first and second advents, seen from the point of view of heaven. It is the period of advancing victory of the Son of God over the world, emphasizing, in harmony with its place at the end of the book, the completeness of the victory.[5]

The premillennialists, however, hold that this event is yet to happen. In the context of commenting on Revelation 19:15, John Walvoord notes, "Other Scriptures indicate that judgment will extend to the entire living population on the earth. In the second coming Christ will terminate his time of waiting on the throne of God for the future subjugation of his enemies."[6]

Thus one school of thought contends that it is happening now and will continue to happen until its completion with Christ's return, while the other school of thought argues that it won't happen until Christ returns to planet earth. Interestingly, another school of thought says both views are correct: It is happening now symbolically and it will happen later literally. Here again, how we approach the prophetic Scriptures determines what we conclude from them.

Before turning to another disputed passage, consider this point from an historical premillennialist. This statement from George Eldon Ladd shows how nondispensational premillennialists would tend to disagree with their premillennial brethren on the extent to which prophetic passages are to be taken literally:

> The Revelation, describing the second advent of Christ, pictures him riding upon a white horse, crowned with many diadems, garbed in a robe dipped in blood, accompanied by the armies of heaven on white horses, coming to smite the nations with a sword which proceeds out of his mouth. No argument is needed to prove that this is symbolic language.[7]

With all these differences of opinion, I'm reminded again of Ben Franklin's statement. It is so. It is not. Maybe. Maybe not.

The Binding of Satan

Yet another example of a conclusion depending on the starting assumption when it comes to interpreting Bible prophecy is the binding of Satan so that he could no longer deceive the nations (Rev. 20). Postmil Loraine Boettner writes, "The binding of Satan, described in Revelation 20:1-3, we now perceive to be not a sudden event, but a very long, slow process."[8] Nonmillenarian Philip Edgcumbe Hughes adds, "The advent of Christ has brought about a change in the relationship between Satan and the nations."[9] Is Satan at this present time bound? If so, to what degree does it depend on our obedience? Does Satan have to submit to our authority (in Christ)?

By and large postmillennialists believe Satan is bound *now*, during this epoch, the Church Age. Their understanding is that he no longer has the authority he once had when he deceived the nations. Yet, as someone once pointed out, "If Satan is bound he must have a long tether."[10]

This question on the Devil being bound or not is extremely significant because it *can* lead to a theology of victory or a theology of doom.

Postmillenarian Kik sighs, saying:

> Unfortunately the Church of today does not realize the power that Christ has given her. Christ has placed in her hands the chain by which she can bind Satan. She can restrain his influence over the nations. But today the Church bemoans the fact that evil is becoming stronger and stronger. She bemoans the fact that the world is coming more and more under the control of the Devil. Whose fault is that? It is the Church. She has the chain and does not have the faith to bind Satan even more firmly. Satan is bound and the Church knows it not! Satan can be bound more firmly and the Church does it not![11]

Whether he would agree or not with the overall thrust of Kik's point is one thing, but premillennial dispensationalist John Walvoord surely does not accept Kik's premise. Interpreting the verses at hand, he writes:

> This prediction, like many others, has been tampered with by the amillenarians who have attempted to make the binding of Satan begin with the first coming of Christ. This is not supported by either Scripture or experience. Satan is very much alive and well and still going around tempting, destroying, and murdering, as the Scriptures testify. The context here is clearly the second coming of Christ and the series of judgments that will result from it, as itemized in Revelation 19.[12]

The disciples were called to make disciples of all nations. Boettner points out, "It was no doubtful experiment to which they were called, but to a sure triumph."[13] When Satan is bound as described in Revelation 20, he is thrown into the abyss that he might no longer deceive the nations. The nonmillenarian holds that all of the mission work of the church goes forth with the understanding that Satan can no longer deceive the heathen, some of whom will receive the Gospel.

Boettner notes, "Premillennialists have a tendency to underrate the power of God and to overrate the power of the Devil."[14] Kik adds, "Notice that Satan does not break out of the prison by his own power.

He does not break his chains. He is loosed by the Lord."[15]

Historic premillennialist J. Barton Payne counters, "Amillennialist interpreters, following Augustine, generally associate this period of Satan's binding with the present church era."[16] He quotes Beasley-Murray, who says that the amillennial view confuses "the earth with the abyss."[17] Beasley-Murray maintains, "Satan's [present] expulsion from heaven to earth is followed by a more intense activity on his part among the nations . . . but his imprisonment in the abyss renders him helpless with regard to them."[18] Payne argues that all this will be fulfilled during the "temporary restraint of Satan during the future Messianic kingdom."[19]

Finally, amillennialist Jay Adams says this about the binding of Satan, "This partial binding is now in effect. From the beginning of pagan world-empire, until New Testament times, the Gentiles as a whole were under the sway of the deceptive prince of darkness. Who will deny that this universal sway has been shattered? Who will deny that the gospel has now spread to many lands and peoples?"[20]

"Symbolic Language" in the Olivet Discourse

Jesus provided a significant description about the destruction of Jerusalem and the end of the age as recorded in Matthew 24–25, Mark 13, and Luke 21:

> Immediately after the distress of those days
> "the sun will be darkened,
> and the moon will not give its light;
> the stars will fall from the sky,
> and the heavenly bodies will be shaken" (Matt. 24:29).

The millenarian school of thought interprets this passage literally, asserting that this event will be fulfilled one day yet in the future. On the other hand, the nonmillenarian school of thought maintains that Jesus is using figurative language in this passage. They say what is being talked about here is divine judgment against the nation of Israel. It's not the literal sun in the sky in question. To make their point, postmillennialists and amillennialists argue that some of the prophetic passages in the Old Testament, such as the one Jesus quoted, speak in this way when describing divine judgment against the nations.

For example, in discussing God's judgment against Babylon, Isaiah wrote, "The stars of heaven and their constellations will not show their light. The rising sun will be darkened and the moon will not give its light" (Isa. 13:10). It is clear in the context of this chapter that Babylon is being judged. Yet nonmillenarians argue it doesn't mean that the sun in the sky literally would go dark.

Isaiah 34 provides a similar description of the downfall of Edom, which God is about to judge. Isaiah declared that God's wrath will be poured out against the Edomites and then announced, "All the starry host will fall" (Isa. 34:4).

J. Stuart Russell, a preterist and nonmillenarian, makes this observation of that type of language:

> Symbol and metaphor belong to the grammar of prophecy, as every reader of the Old Testament prophets must know. Is it not reasonable that the doom of Jerusalem should be depicted in language as glowing and rhetorical as the destruction of Babylon, or Bozrah, or Tyre? How then does the prophet Isaiah describe the downfall of Babylon?[21]

The millenarian perspective would say not all prophecy *can* be taken literally, nor do they advocate that it should be. (Remember their maxim: "literal if possible.") Premillennialist Charles Feinberg points out:

> It is not true that the premillennialists require every single passage to be interpreted literally without exception. They do hold, on the other hand, that if the language is symbolic, it is to be governed by the laws relating to symbols; if figurative, by the laws dealing with figures; if typical, by the laws connected with types; if literal, by the laws of non-figurative speech.[22]

Some nonmillenarian theologians, however, say the sun, moon, and stars Jesus mentions in the Olivet Discourse refers to the soul of the Jewish nation. In other words, Israel will be judged. God Himself will turn out their lights because they did not recognize Jesus when He came to them.[23] These preterist nonmillenarians maintain that this judgment was fulfilled in A.D. 70 when Israel was destroyed as a nation. Christ was warning His disciples that instead of being delivered from the Romans, as the Jews expected, God will judge Israel.

Gary DeMar, author of *Last Days Madness: The Folly of Trying to Predict When Christ Will Return*, writes, "The Old Testament is filled with solar, lunar, and stellar language depicting great political and social upheaval. The rise of kingdoms is compared to the brightness of the sun, moon, and stars. The brightness of these heavenly bodies means that a nation is in ascendancy. When a nation is described as falling—coming under the judgment of God—it is compared to the sun and moon going dark and stars falling from the sky."[24] (In addition to quoting Isa. 13 and 34, he cites Isa. 8:9 and Ezek. 32.)

Kik adds these points:

- "Jerusalem and its Temple were central in the worship of the Jews, and their destruction meant the end of the world so far as the Jews were concerned."[25]
- "The judgment upon Jerusalem was the sign of the fact that the Son of man was reigning in heaven."[26]
- "The catastrophe of Jerusalem really signalized the beginning of a new and world-wide kingdom, marking the full separation of the Christian Church from legalistic Judaism. The whole system of worship, so closely associated with Jerusalem and the Temple, received, as it were, a death blow from God himself."[27]

Then, Kik concludes, ". . . in the light of well-defined biblical language, the reference is rather to a coming in terms of the events of his providence in judgment against his enemies and in deliverance of his people."[28] John Calvin noted that the disciples would have thought that the end of the Jewish temple and nation would be the same as the end of the world. This is why they were expecting a physical, not a spiritual, kingdom.

The premillennial rebuttal again makes the point that there's ample warrant in the Scripture for interpreting prophecy literally. Premillennialists also argue that since there's parallel phenomena of fireworks in the sky as described in Revelation, then it is *yet* to happen. They point out that Jesus Himself quoted Isaiah 13:10 (again see Matt. 24:29). Furthermore, premillennialist John Walvoord says of Matthew 24:29, "This scene is described in greater detail in the book of Revelation, which pictures disturbances in the heavens occurring throughout the years leading up to the second coming of Christ but especially just before he comes."[29]

Symbols and Numbers in the Book of Revelation

There are many significant symbols and numbers (7, 12, 24, 666, 1,000, 144,000, etc.) in the Book of Revelation. Are they to be taken literally or figuratively? Do they symbolize something, or are they to be understood with mathematical precision?

Joel B. Green makes the point that numbers were not as precisely important when the Bible was written as they are in our computerized day:

> First, we should recall that the ancients were not nearly as concerned with numerical accuracy as we have become. Checking attendance, constructing flow charts, counting change, filling in Internal Revenue Service tax forms—these and many similar exercises have rendered our present society highly sensitive to exactness in figuring. It was not so for people of old. They were much more interested in statistical approximations and the symbolic meanings of numbers.[30]

Postmillennialist Boettner offers this example: "The churches are symbolized by the seven golden candlesticks."[31] He then cites additional instances:

> Twelve is the number of the Church, and wherever the Church is mentioned we have this number or its multiple—twelve apostles, twenty-four elders, or the totality of God's people symbolized by the number 144,000. In the Bible the number stands for rounded totals. . . . A thousand is the cube of ten, and symbolizes vastness of number or time. In Psalm 50:10 the expression "the cattle upon a thousand hills" means God owns it all.[32]

Premillennial dispensationalist Paul Lee Tan rebuts this view in his book *The Interpretation of Prophecy*. He says it is a "selectively inconsistent" approach to the Bible.[33] After citing many of the same examples, such as 144,000 and 1,000, he writes: "The danger in selective inconsistency is that, based neither entirely on the literal method nor entirely on the non-literal, the interpreter finds himself consistently struggling with the question of how far he should go spiritualizing or when he should stop literalizing."[34] Tan's point is that, whether it's numbers or figures of speech, Bible prophecy should be interpreted consistently, and literally if possible.

Tan has another rebuttal to this issue about biblical numbers. He argues that there are so many specific details surrounding the numbers that it would seem unlikely that the whole is to be taken symbolically (including the numbers):

> The prophecy of the 144,000 in Revelation 7 contains so many incidental details, such as the genealogies, tribal names, and subdivided memberships of that group, that it cannot possibly be a symbol. The two witnesses of Revelation 11 must be non-symbolic persons; otherwise the details given concerning their ministries, death, and resurrection, as well as the earthquake which killed 7,000 would be quite superfluous.[35]

Conclusion

In this and the last chapter a lot of meat has been put on the bones of "Yes, it is," "No, it isn't," à la Ben Franklin. Indeed, that meat is substantial. It gets down to some crucial questions about the nature of the kingdom, the potential success or failure of the church, and the future.

Premillennialist Paul Lee Tan has the final word here. It reminds us once more to be cognizant of underlying assumptions.

> Consciously or unconsciously, most interpreters approach prophecy burdened under a load of presuppositions and assumptions. This is not surprising, for it is virtually impossible to be completely neutral towards such a significant, albeit controversial, subject. Even the neglect of Bible prophecy itself represents one view of prophecy.[36]

Again, let's be aware of the underlying starting points of interpretations of prophecy. Yet more importantly, let's cut some slack for our fellow Christians with whom we disagree.

8

How Are We to Read Revelation?

***Though St. John the Evangelist saw many strange monsters in his vision, he saw no creatures so wild as one of his own commentators.*[1]**

—G. K. Chesterton

No single book of the Bible tells us more about the end times than the Book of Revelation. And perhaps no single book of the Bible has stirred up as much controversy among believers than the Book of Revelation. How are we to understand this enigmatic, apocalyptic book?

- Are we to take it literally word-for-word with the understanding that some obvious things are meant to be symbolic? For example, even those who hold to a literalistic interpretation regard Jesus' title as "the Lamb" (who was slain) as figurative language.
- Is the Book of Revelation chronological?
- Have some or virtually all the events prophesied already taken place?
- When was this book written, and what bearing does that have on our understanding of it?

We want to answer these and similar questions in this chapter. How we approach Revelation often boils down to the heart of the controversy: What is the underlying approach to Bible prophecy?

Before we address these issues, a preliminary observation should be noted: The reason Revelation is exceedingly difficult to interpret is that it contains a mixture of different types of literary genre, primarily "apocalyptic, prophetic, and epistolary."[2] We need to keep this in mind as we study this amazing book.

Overview of the Contents of Revelation

Prior to examining the various commentary on Revelation, a quick overview of the Bible's last book will also aid us in our study.[3]

Chapter 1: Prologue, greetings, doxology, and description of Jesus Christ—"One like a Son of man."

Chapter 2: Letters to the churches in Ephesus, Smyrna, Pergamum, and Thyatira.

Chapter 3: Letters to the churches in Sardis, Philadelphia, and Laodicea.

Chapter 4: John's entry into heaven—where the throne is the chief focus. Twenty-four elders worship God.

Chapter 5: Only Jesus, the Lamb who was slain, is worthy to open the scroll sealed with seven seals.

Chapter 6: Jesus opens the first six seals, which are judgments against the inhabitants of the earth. The "four horses of the Apocalypse" comprise four of the seven sealed judgments. These judgments avenge the blood of the martyrs. The sixth seal involves a great earthquake, and the heavens are rolled up like a scroll. People seek refuge from the wrath of the Lamb in caves; they crave death.

Chapter 7: The 144,000 righteous people (12,000 from each of the tribes of Israel) are then "sealed"; that is, they will be protected from future judgment. A great multitude in white robes assembles in heaven and worships the Lamb.

Chapter 8: The Lamb opens the seventh seal. This initiates the seven trumpet judgments, the first four of which are listed in this chapter. A third of the earth, the sea, the sun, the moon, the stars, and the sky are destroyed. Many people die as a result of this judgment.

Chapter 9: The fifth and sixth trumpet judgments. The fifth seal unleashes an army of countless locusts (likely an army of men) that scourge the earth. "On their heads they wore something like crowns of gold, and their faces resembled human faces" (Rev. 9:7). The sixth seal unleashes an army of 200,000,000, which kills a third of humankind.

Chapter 10: The angel with the scroll. Upon instruction, John eats the scroll, which tastes sweet, but later churns his stomach.

Chapter 11: John is told to measure the temple of God. Two witnesses for God prophesy for 1,260 days. The seventh trumpet judgment is sounded. At this, Jesus is enthroned; the twenty-four elders worship God and praise Him because His time of wrath against the nations has now come.

Chapter 12: The woman and the dragon. She gives birth to a son, whom the Devil tries to destroy, but God spares Him.

Chapter 13: The Beast arises out of the sea. People worship the Beast. Meanwhile, he blasphemes God and wages war against the saints, who are told to patiently endure through all their suffering. Another beast (commonly called "the False Prophet") arises out of the earth. He causes people to worship the beast from the sea. The Beast and the False Prophet have control over the inhabitants of the earth, and they force everyone to bear the beast-of-the-sea's mark on their right hand or forehead; otherwise they can't buy or sell anything.

Chapter 14: The 144,000 worship the Lamb. An angel announces that anyone who worships the Beast or bears his mark will be punished by God. The souls of the earth are harvested. God's wrath is unleashed, and blood flows in the streets like a creek.

Chapter 15: Seven angels bring seven plagues.

Chapter 16: God unleashes seven bowls of His wrath. The sea is turned into blood, and all the creatures of the sea perish. The sun scorches men and women; darkness engulfs them; and the great river Euphrates dries up. Demons deceive the world and inspire people to gather for war against God at Armageddon. An unparalleled earthquake rocks the earth.

Chapter 17: The woman on the beast. The prostitute symbolizing Babylon the Great is judged. The woman sits at a place with seven hills (likely Rome).

Chapter 18: Babylon is judged and cast down. This inspires great excitement and praise in heaven.

Chapter 19: Praise and worship continue. The rider on the white horse, who is the King of kings and Lord of lords, enacts divine vengeance against those who have opposed Him. His enemies have gathered together to make war against Jesus, but He slays them with a sword coming out of His mouth. There are two great meals contrasted in this chapter—one in glory for the people of God (the Marriage Feast of the Lamb) and the other in judgment against the enemies of the Lord (the "great supper of God"), where those who hate God are consumed by vultures and other birds of prey. The Beast and the False Prophet are captured and thrown into the lake of fire.

Chapter 20: The Millennium and the binding of the Devil. Satan's doom—his last attempt to oppose God. He deceives the nations and has them gather for battle again, but fire from heaven slays them. The Devil is then cast into hell for all time. The Great White Throne Judgment.

Chapter 21: The new heaven and the new earth. The New Jerusalem.

Chapter 22: The River of Life flows from the throne through heaven. Jesus is coming soon. Final salutations.

That's a quick overview of this hotly contested book.

Now, onto the controversy . . .

Four Major Approaches to Interpreting Revelation

The four most popular views on how to interpret the Book of Revelation are:

(1) Preterist: It was all fulfilled in the first century. The fall of Babylon refers to the fall of Jerusalem.

(2) Historicist: It has been and is being fulfilled in history.

(3) Futurist: The book is describing events yet to happen.

(4) Idealist: This approach focuses on the main points the book teaches but avoids attempting to pin the events down as past, present, or future occurrences.

The Preterist Interpretation

First of all, when was the Book of Revelation written? This question is important to the preterists because they believe Revelation was written prior to A.D. 70 and that it dealt with events that were *soon* to be fulfilled. *The NIV Study Bible* writes this about the dating of the book:

> Revelation was written when Christians were entering a time of persecution. The two periods most often mentioned are the latter part of Nero's reign (A.D. 54-68) and the latter part of Domitian's reign (81-96). Most scholars date the book c. 95. (A few suggest a date during the reign of Vespasian: 69-79.)[4]

Revelation is a message from one persecuted Christian to his fellow believers suffering for Christ

This school of thought supports the earlier date for Revelation. Preterists see it as before the Great Tribulation—the one that took place in A.D. 70. One of the arguments of preterists for the earlier date is that when John measured the Jerusalem temple in chapter 11, it was still standing. How then could he have taken its measurements, they argue, after it had been so utterly destroyed?

Revelation is a message from one persecuted Christian to his fellow believers suffering for Christ. Because of his faith, John had been exiled

Peter Olson

The Pale Horse

"When the Lamb opened the fourth seal, I heard the voice of the fourth living creature say, 'Come!' I looked, and there before me was a pale horse! Its rider was named Death, and Hades was following close behind him. They were given power over a fourth of the earth to kill by sword, famine and plague, and by the wild beasts of the earth" (Rev. 6:7-8).

Fort Lauderdale artist Peter Olsen has been painting through the Book of Revelation since 1974. He has completed seventy-six canvases and envisions a total of two hundred.

"The Pale Horse" represents just one of Olsen's paintings of the Four Horsemen of the Apocalypse. He chooses to make his work available for all to see on the Internet rather than sell it to private collectors. He's been offered eleven million dollars for the whole set, but he won't sell. To view his interpretations of Revelation, go to http://www.peterolsenart.com.

to the island of Patmos. Meanwhile, the various churches he was addressing had suffered, were experiencing hardship, or were about to suffer persecution (that is, the churches of Smyrna, Philadelphia, and Pergamos). David Chilton, author of *Days of Vengeance*, a huge one-volume commentary on Revelation, asserts, "The purpose of the Revelation was to reveal Christ as Lord to a suffering Church."[5] Kenneth Gentry notes that the purpose of Revelation "was designed to steel the first century Church against the gathering storm of persecution."[6]

The purpose of Revelation is an important key to the overall puzzle. Was it written to tell us the future? Was it written to comfort a severely persecuted church? Was it written to reveal Jesus Christ in His exalted state? Or for all these and other reasons? Jay Adams writes:

> The Revelation was written to a persecuted church about to face the most tremendous onslaught it had ever known. It would be absurd (not to say cruel) for John to write a letter to persons in such circumstances which not only ignores their difficulties, but reveals numerous details about events supposed to transpire hundreds of years in the future during a seven year tribulation period at the end of the church age.[7]

Premillennialists who dispute the preterist position argue that this violates the spirit of what Jesus told us to avoid: trying to predict when He will return. Robert Thomas, a premillennial dispensationalist who presents that perspective in a current book on four views of the Book of Revelation, critiques the preterist position this way:

> Preterism uses the "soonness" of Christ's coming to prove a writing of Revelation in the 60s and fulfillment of much of the book's prophecies by A.D. 70. Placing a time limit on "soon" is, however, unwarranted. Jesus taught against pinpointing the time of his return . . . He could have returned by 70, but he did not. God has not been pleased to reveal how long it will be. So far "soon" has extended to over 1900 years, but God's people still must anticipate an any-moment return of Christ. In other words, the "soon" teaches an attitude rather than

> sets a time limit. Nineteen hundred years may not seem to be "soon" for humans, but they must accept God's lesson about expecting Christ's coming to be near.[8]

In the early history of the church it was believed John had written Revelation in the nineties. Arthur Cushman McGiffert, however, writing in 1890, points out that "internal evidence has driven most modern scholars to the conclusion that the Apocalypse must have been written before the destruction of Jerusalem, the banishment therefore . . . taking place under Nero instead of Domitian."[9]

The reason the dating of Revelation is important should be obvious. If it was written before the fall of Jerusalem in A.D. 70, then the preterists at least have their foot in the door. But if it was written after that, they don't have a leg to stand on. As R. C. Sproul points out, "If Revelation was written before A.D. 70 , then a case could be made that it describes chiefly those events leading up to Jerusalem's fall."[10]

Kenneth Gentry is a preterist, who sees an early date for the book. In fact, Gentry wrote his doctoral thesis on the question of the dating of Revelation and specifically the idea that it was before A.D. 70. He writes:

> My confident conviction is that a solid case for a Neronic date for Revelation can be set forth from the available evidences, both internal and external. In fact, I would lean toward a date after the outbreak of the Neronic persecution in late A.D. 64 and before the declaration of the Jewish War in early A.D. 67. A date in either A.D. 65 or early A.D. 66 would seem most suitable. My hope is that the debate will be renewed with vigor and care, for the matter is more than a merely academic or intellectual exercise; it has ramifications in the area of practical Christianity.[11]

Nevertheless, the nonpreterists argue that part of the problem with this view is that Revelation clearly points out that it is dealing with the *end* of time. When the events described therein take place, it will be the end of the world. D. Martyn Lloyd-Jones, who would appear to hold to the historical premillennialist position, disagrees with the idea that Revelation was fulfilled in the first century:

> First, then, let us look at the *preterist view*. . . . It seems to me that the view is clearly impossible in terms of the book of Revelation itself. For the book takes us on to the very end of time and tells us "that there should be time no longer" (Rev. 10:6). It takes us on to the destruction of the devil and all his powers, and the instruments that he uses—the dragon himself and the various beasts. Revelation deals with that final destruction, so, obviously, it cannot be right to say that it only refers to events confronting the early Christian Church and things which would come to an end when the Roman Empire became officially Christian.[12]

Jay Adams, however, gives further evidence for his view that Revelation deals with mostly first-century events: "It is to remain unsealed *because* 'the time is at hand.' That is, its prophecies are about to be fulfilled. The events which it predicts do not pertain to the far distant future, but they are soon to happen. The message is for this generation, not for some future one."[13] He goes on to explain how he believes the entire book of Revelation, *except for the last two chapters*, were essentially fulfilled in the first century. Christ was enthroned, Israel was judged, and the Antichrist (Nero) was revealed.

Preterists believe John was writing this book with his first-century readers in mind. Adams further points out:

> Should there be any question about the contemporary nature of the second section of the book, the seventeenth chapter dispels it. . . . Can the kings [the seven heads] be identified? Yes. Five of them are already dethroned, one is now (that is, was in John's day) reigning, and the seventh hasn't yet begun to reign. Words could not be plainer. Regardless of which Roman emperors one identifies with the head (depending upon the exact year of Revelation's composition, and also which emperor with which the list begins) there can be no doubt that the beast-prophecy pertains to the Caesars who were then (and for the next period of years) in power. The prophecy can refer to nothing but the contemporary

> Roman empire because of the angel's clear-cut identification.[14]

Therefore, Adams concludes, "Christ's coming follows the millennium and immediately precedes the judgment."[15]

The futurist would argue that to believe that Revelation dealt mostly with first-century events (except the last two chapters), then one must believe that Jesus came back at least in a partial second coming in A.D. 70. Premillennialist Robert Thomas rebuts that view:

> Christ never returned to earth in A.D. 70 personally, so explaining the fall of Jerusalem as his coming violates the principle of literal interpretation. All contextual indications point to a literal and personal coming of Christ in that verse [Rev. 1:7]. Gentry calls this a "judgment-coming" of Christ, but the criteria of Revelation also connect a deliverance of the faithful with that coming.[16]

The Historicist Interpretation of Revelation

The historicist view argues that major portions of the Book of Revelation have been fulfilled in history. For example, because Rome, the city on the seven hills, is the focus of much of Revelation, then one school of thought within the historicist camp sees some of the conflicts and judgments in Revelation as dealing with the rise and fall of the Roman Empire. Richard Kyle provides further explanation of this school of interpretation on Revelation:

The historicist view argues that major portions of the Book of Revelation have been fulfilled in history

> The historicist view sees Revelation as an inspired forecast of human history. Its symbols set forth in broad outline the history of Western Europe from the first church to the second coming of Christ. Some interpreters see the whole book as presaging Western history. For example, they believe that the opening of the little scroll in Revelation 10 depicts the Protestant Reformation. Other interpreters

> contend that only the letters to the seven churches (chs. 2-3) portray the history of the Christian church. Whatever the approach, the historicist view is used to make end-time predictions.[17]

There's a variation of the historicist view that contends that Revelation foretells the entire Christian era. D. Martyn Lloyd-Jones explains that perspective: "A second, and more popular, sub-division of historicist teaching is the *continuous historical view*, which teaches that the book of Revelation is a book of history without a break. It is a prophecy of the detailed history of the Christian Church and there is no overlapping between its various visions."[18]

During major conflicts between Catholics and Protestants, the historicist view was often employed—almost like a weapon—by one side against the other. For example, some Reformers viewed the pope as the Antichrist while some Catholics accused Luther of being the Antichrist. Such harsh accusations employ the historicist interpretation of Revelation.

Another example of a historicist interpretation of the Apocalypse includes the belief that the Black Plague of 1347 to 1349 fulfilled those judgments described in Revelation, in which great numbers of people died in Europe. In fact, a greater percent of people died through that epidemic than have died in any other short period of time. It was horrendous. In that brief period, the bubonic plague killed one-third to one-half of the people in Europe. Conditions were so awful that people believed they were experiencing the Apocalypse. In addition, the plague occurred roughly a millennium after the fall of the Roman Empire and the liberation of the Christian church by Constantine, and thus people at that time thought this was further evidence that prophecy was being fulfilled. In fact, many believed the Millennium was ending.

In his *Halley's Bible Handbook*, Henry Halley makes a case for potential historicist interpretation by providing miscellaneous examples of events in history that possibly could have been foreseen by the writer of Revelation. For example, Halley notes that the rise of Islam might be seen in the fifth trumpet judgment in Revelation 9:1-11, wherein are unleashed "Horrible Monsters, with complex appearance of Locusts, Horses, Scorpions, Lions, and Humans."[19]

First, Halley cites Scripture: "Shapes of Locusts like War-Horses, with Scorpion-like Tails, Crowns like Gold, Faces like Men's Faces, Hair like

Women's Hair, Teeth like Lion's Teeth, Breastplates as of Iron, and Wings that sounded like Chariots and Horses rushing to War" (Rev. 9:7-10).[20] Then he comments, "This is indeed a very good description of Mohammedan Armies, composed of Fierce, Relentless Horsemen, famous for their Beards, with Long Hair like Women's Hair, with Yellow Turbans on their Heads that looked like Gold, and they had Iron Coats of Armor."[21]

Moody Bible Institute Professor C. Marvin Pate, the general editor of *Four Views on the Book of Revelation*, believes this once-popular viewpoint is now waning:

> While the historicist approach once was widespread, today, for all practical purposes, it has passed from the scene. Its failed attempts to locate the fulfillment of Revelation in the course of the circumstances of history has doomed it to continual revision as time passed and, ultimately, to obscurity (a situation, one might add, if Jesus tarries, that contemporary doomsday prophets may eventually find themselves in!).[22]

The Futurist Views of Revelation

Premillennialists see the Book of Revelation as yet to be fulfilled. Many of them see modern events coalescing in ways that would indicate these are likely the last days. Premillennialist Tim LaHaye writes, "Over fifty years ago, Dr. C. I. Scofield said in his notes on Revelation in the *Scofield Reference Bible*, 'Doubtless, much which is designedly obscure to us will be clear to those for whom it was written as *the time approaches*.' That time is at hand, and many things are clearer than they were in Scofield's day."[23]

In contrast, D. Martyn Lloyd-Jones makes this comment about the opinions of the church fathers on the Book of Revelation:

> These Early Church Fathers were not futurists in the sense that we use the term today. Some of them certainly believed that the prophecy of the book of Revelation pointed to the future but not one imagined that two thousand years were to elapse before these things would

> take place. Indeed, all these early Fathers taught that some of the things were already happening, and though others were still in the future, that future was at hand and the end was coming very soon. They certainly had no conception of transferring this book far into the future.[24]

Premillennialists, however, argue that you must have a consistent approach to interpreting the prophetic passages of Scripture. They say a literal approach would lead to a futurist interpretation of Revelation. After acknowledging other interpretations of the Apocalypse, LaHaye writes, "The futurist view, which seems to me to be the most satisfactory, accepts the book of Revelation as prophecy that primarily is yet to be fulfilled, particularly from chapter 4 on. This is the interpretation accepted by most premillennial Bible teachers. A safe rule to follow in the study of the book of Revelation is to accept the book as literal unless the facts are obviously to the contrary."[25] Another way of saying this is "Literal if possible."

A literal approach to Revelation naturally leads one to agree with a futurist interpretation. Premillennialist Robert Thomas is one who defends the literal approach:

> A consistent adherence to grammatical-historical principles leads to a dispensationalist understanding of Revelation. . . . A literal understanding of Revelation erases any questions about the book's coherence, organization, and logic. Its straightforward message is the book's best defense against the maligning it has received because of an alleged incomprehensibility. Usual hermeneutical principles bring out God's plan for the future and the eternal state. No need arises to add to or subtract from what a literal interpretation yields.[26]

D. L. Moody puts it this way: "If God did not wish us to understand the Revelation, He would not have given it to us at all."[27]

The difficulty with this view, argue nonfuturists, is that Revelation itself is filled with such vivid pictures and imagery that it's easy to assume that these are not to be taken literally. Postmillennialist Keith Mathison asserts, "The fact is that nobody can be absolutely literal in his interpretation of

Scripture. The Bible itself will not allow it."[28]

Nevertheless, well-known Bible prophecy teacher Jack Van Impe points out how the futurist view makes the most sense: "Simply put, Bible prophecy and Revelation are history written in advance. They form God's description of future facts and events. Such prophecy is completely trustworthy because God is omniscient."[29]

Preterists, however, would rebut that argument because they believe the book was written prior to A.D. 70. Therefore, it naturally follows that God was predicting the immediate future, and now it's past tense. Kenneth L. Gentry Jr. states, "Though the prophecies were in the future when John wrote and when his original audience read them, they are now in *our* past."[30]

The Idealist Interpretation

The idealist view is not widely held. Therefore, we will deal with it only briefly. If you consult various books on Revelation, you may or may not even find the idealist mode of interpretation listed. For instance, D. Martyn Lloyd-Jones distinguishes three main schools of interpreting Revelation: the preterist, the futurist, and the historicist views.[31]

Nevertheless, what is this approach to Revelation? C. Marvin Pate says, "The *idealist* viewpoint, by way of contrast to the previous three theological constructs, is reticent to pinpoint the symbolism of Revelation historically. For this school of thought, Revelation sets forth timeless truths concerning the battle between good and evil that continues throughout the church age."[32]

The idealist approach takes the overall points of Revelation, such as the lordship of Christ, the fact that the slain martyrs will be avenged one day, and the triumph of God over Satan, and focuses on these points. It avoids any attempt to understand the specific working out of events contained in the book and to figure out when they have or when they will be fulfilled.

The idealist approach holds that the Apocalypse provides many comforting words in our trying times—regardless of the controversy. Sam Hamstra Jr., who champions the idealist view in Pate's book, *Four Views on the Book of Revelation*, says of his hermeneutic:

> Finally, the idealist approach avoids the pitfalls that have plagued interpreters of Revelation for centuries.

> The history of the interpretation of Revelation should teach one lesson: Beware of attempting to correlate apocalyptic imagery with actual events in human history. Religious libraries are filled with the books of sincere Christian authors identifying the anti-Christ and predicting the date of the end of the world.[33]

That last point is well taken. In fact, we'll devote an entire chapter to failed predictions of Christ's return. Hamstra concludes, "The idealist, however, cognizant of a long history of disagreement over the meaning of [Revelation], intentionally walks away from a time-bound and event-oriented perspective that, in the past, has only proved to confuse and divide Christians."[34]

Is It Chronological?

Is the Book of Revelation meant to be chronological? Or does it follow the pattern of Middle Eastern literature, in which you have the same events described over and over from different perspectives? Interpreters who argue for the latter would point to the fall of Babylon as an example. It recurs in at least three different passages, separated by other events. For example, in Chapter 14, we read: "A second angel followed and said, 'Fallen! Fallen is Babylon the Great, which made all the nations drink the maddening wine of her adulteries'" (Rev. 14:8).

After this passage, we read of the harvest of the earth, the seven angels with seven plagues, and the seven bowls of the wrath of God. In the context of the seventh bowl judgment, comes this statement: "The great city split into three part, and the cities of the nations collapsed. God remembered Babylon the Great and gave her the cup filled with the wine of the fury of his wrath" (Rev. 16:19).

What follows is the woman riding the beast with the title

MYSTERY
BABYLON THE GREAT
THE MOTHER OF PROSTITUTES
OF THE ABOMINATIONS OF THE EARTH.

Hal Lindsey calls her "Scarlet O'Harlot."[35] She gets drunk on the blood of the saints. Who is this woman? Babylon, the city itself. "The woman you saw is the great city that rules over the kings of the earth" (Rev. 17:18).

Next comes the judgment of Babylon, which is punished double for what she had done (Rev. 18:6). Chapter 18 centers on the destruction of Babylon and shows all heaven rejoicing at her fall. Meanwhile, all the earth bemoans this great loss.

Therefore, we see one theme repeated several times, separated by other incidents in between. Is it possible that we are to read this as apocalyptic literature and not as a newspaper account of future events? Preterist and amillennialist R. C. Sproul observes, "The language employed in biblical prophecy is not always cold and logical as is common in the Western world, but adopts a kind of fervor common to the East. Scripture commonly describes the visitation of God's judgment with images of convulsion and cataclysms."[36] Green adds, "Apocalyptic writers employ visions for much the same reason that Jesus taught in parables—to drive home in a dramatic, memorable fashion one significant point."[37]

It's important not to miss the main point—that is, who wins in the battle of good versus evil

One interesting sidelight is that some interpreters of the historicist school see the fall of the Roman Empire (A.D. 476) as fulfilling the fall of Babylon. In fact, there is evidence that the Babylon of Revelation is actually Rome because it is a city set on seven hills. Thus many scholars argue that Babylon is Rome. That's why futurists (premillennialists for the most part) believe when the Antichrist comes, he will come from Rome (or at least Europe). Some preterists, however, see Babylon as Jerusalem. (The fall depicted in Revelation refers to God's judgment against her in A.D. 70).

The woman and the dragon of chapter 12 provide another example that the book is not necessarily chronological. It talks about Mary (or is it Israel?) that gives birth to Jesus. The fall of Satan is also mentioned here. Yet it would seem to be describing that which occurred *before* the creation of the world; that is, Lucifer's rebellion in heaven, which resulted in him and his minions being cast into hell.

Christ Is Exalted in Heaven

Regardless of your school of interpretation of the Book of Revelation, it's important not to miss the main point—that is, who wins in the battle of good versus evil. Christ is enthroned in heaven, and one day He will convert or destroy His enemies. Those who choose to reject Him are on the wrong side of history, and they will one day endure His wrath.

Echoing the sentiment of theologians through the ages, including Calvin, Jay Adams says Jesus received His kingdom on ascending to heaven:

> This was the time when he received the kingdom. The judgment "was set," and the "books" which "were opened" correspond perfectly to the heavenly court scene in Revelation 4-7. Verses 13 and 14 picture Christ coming *to the Father*, not coming to earth. The kingdom which he receives is everlasting; it will not pass away, neither will it be destroyed. In Peter's sermon (Acts 2:29-36) the resurrection and ascension of Christ are interpreted as the fulfillment of God's promise to place Christ upon the throne of David. . . . This enthronement (also acknowledged in Acts 15) involved receiving the kingdom which Daniel predicted.[38]

A Clear Picture of Jesus as He Is Today

While the Book of Revelation seems to engender numerous theological controversies (not that the fault lies with the book itself, as opposed to the book's interpreters), there is some beautiful and clear teaching from this book we should not lose sight of. Premillennialist Tim LaHaye points out that we learn a great deal about our Lord that we don't see in other parts of the Bible:

> The book of Revelation is the only book in the New Testament that presents Jesus Christ as he really is today. The gospels introduce Him as the "man of sorrows, acquainted with grief" during His incarnation. Revelation presents Him in His true glory and majesty after His resurrection and ascension into heaven, never again to be reviled, rebuked, and spat upon. No wonder John entitled it "The Revelation of Jesus Christ."[39]

LaHaye also adds that we know from the Book of Revelation that good will eventually triumph over evil:

> The book of Revelation makes it clear that Christ and Christians are the ultimate winners in the game of life. In fact, a study of this book is essential for a comprehensive view of the rest of Scripture. It finalizes God's wonderful purposes for His favorite creatures—mankind.[40]

Conclusion

Finally, we ask once again the question contained in this chapter's title: How Are We to Read Revelation? The answer: It depends on who you ask—the futurist, the preterist, the idealist, or the historicist.

Meanwhile, we should approach the Apocalypse with fear, trepidation, and great humility. There is a blessing found at the beginning of the book: "Blessed is the one who reads the words of this prophecy" (Rev. 1:3) and a curse at the end (a severe warning against adding to or subtracting from the prophecy, Rev. 22:18-19). In light of that solemn warning, Dr. Joseph A. Seiss, author of *The Apocalypse*, expresses the kind of humility writers and readers should take when they approach the Book of Revelation:

> If I have read into this Book [Revelation] anything which he has not put there, or read out of it anything which he has put there, with the profoundest sorrow would I recant. . . . If I err, God forgive me! If I am right, God bless my feeble testimony! In either case, God speed His everlasting truth![41]

9

The Battle Put into Perspective

The date of his return is unknown to all except the Father.[1]

—Philip Edgcumbe Hughes

Given the long history of the church, modern debates over the end times are relatively recent, more recent than 1830. When the early church was holding meetings in catacombs, believers weren't sitting around asking whether the Rapture would take place before, during, or after the Tribulation. During the Middle Ages, when theologians were arguing about the primacy of the bishop of Rome over all the other bishops, they weren't necessarily debating whether the Millennium of Revelation 20 was a literal thousand years yet to come. When the outward church was torn in two during the Reformation, the conflict wasn't centered on whether the temple will be rebuilt in Jerusalem some day. In short, our modern debate on the end times is just that—modern, relatively speaking.

Sometimes, the key to understanding the present is to unlock the past. Let's put the conflict over eschatology in its overall context.

The Early Church

Chiliasm has been around virtually from the beginning. Although the highly defined scenario that many premillennialists subscribe to today can be traced back to the early 1830s *in its specific details*, there were chiliasts of sorts in the first few centuries of Christianity. They believed Jesus was coming back to set up a literal kingdom on earth. Dr. Charles Feinberg, a premillennialist, observes, "The entire early Church for the first three centuries was premillennial, almost to a man."[2]

It's uncertain whether Feinberg's statement will lead readers to an accurate conclusion in that the term "premillennial" can conjure up an exceedingly elaborate picture of how the end times will play out. It's probably more accurate to reword Feinberg's statement as: "The entire early Church for the first three centuries was chilian or millenarian, almost to a man." Premillennialist John Walvoord admits, "It must be conceded that the advanced and detailed theology of pretribulationism is not found in the Fathers, but neither is any other detailed and 'established' exposition of premillennialism. The development of most doctrines took centuries."[3]

Here's further support to the view that the early church was by and large premillennial in perspective. Dispensationalist Charles C. Ryrie, author of *The Basis of the Premillennial Faith*, asserts, "Certain refinements may be of recent origin, but premillennialism was certainly the faith of the Church centuries before the Brethren and Darby."[4] George L. Murray adds further weight to this belief: "Students of church history will agree that if any premillennialism existed in the early church it was during the first four centuries of its history."[5]

The great church historian Philip Schaff, Yale professor from the last century, reinforces the point that most of the early Christians looked forward to a literal Millennium on earth:

> The most striking point in the eschatology of the ante-Nicene Age is the prominent chiliasm, or millenarianism, that is the belief of a visible reign of Christ in glory on earth with the risen saints for a thousand years, before the general resurrection and judgment. It was indeed not the doctrine of the church embodied in any creed or form of devotion, but a widely current opinion of distinguished teachers.[6]

Why is it that most of the theological controversy on eschatology can be found only in the last two centuries? To give a simplistic answer, other significant theological controversies took center stage throughout the centuries, and it wasn't until the nineteenth century that the controversy surrounding the end times was to seize major attention. Previous to the nineteenth century, debate and resolution on key doctrines demanded attention within the church.

The Context of the Controversy over Eschatology: A Bird's-Eye View of Theological Disputes Through the Centuries

In the first three centuries of its existence, the church was struggling for its very survival, for it suffered under ten intense waves of persecution from the Roman Empire. Here you have the fledgling Christian church fighting for its survival amid the fiercest opposition imaginable. The fact that Christianity survived and even thrived is an incredible miracle and a testimony to its divine nature.

Nonmillenarian scholars argue that we should not seek doctrinal discernment from most of the church fathers in the first three centuries, except from the apostles who penned portions of the Bible. As a new baby, struggling in the world, the Christian faith was being threatened by all sides. There were no church buildings. There was no Christian broadcasting or publishing. Christianity was completely underground. The only creeds were very general. They summarized only the key doctrines, like the Apostles' Creed of the second century. The canon of the New Testament wasn't even complete.

Then, in 313, when the church was made legal under Emperor Constantine, doctrinal conflicts that had been simmering all along began to come to the forefront. The first key conflict revolved around the deity of Jesus Christ and subsequently the triune nature of God. Was Jesus inferior to the Father? Was He "made" as opposed to "begotten"? That is, was He a *created* being, even if He was in some way divine? Was there "a time when He was not"? Arius (d. 336), presbyter of Alexandria, believed that was the case. We can see the gist of the Arian views of Jesus' inferior divinity in the modern cult of the Jehovah's Witnesses.

Although the understanding of the Trinity and the divine nature of Jesus is universally accepted today by Christians of virtually all denominations (not counting cult groups on the fringe), there was a long period of time when that was not the case. For half a century (from 325 to 381), a strong battle raged back and forth between Athanasius, who championed the Trinity (as we know it), and the followers of Arius, who championed a Jesus who was divine, but created. Although what we understand as the orthodox and the traditional view of the Trinity was finally formalized in the Nicene Creed (325), this issue was still hotly contested. During some dark moments in the fourth century, Athanasius and the Trinity were actually banished from the empire while Arianism was officially adopted.

In the end, however, truth triumphed over error. "Begotten" triumphed over "made." Athanasius triumphed over Arius, who was declared a heretic.

In 381 with the Council of Constantinople, the church settled the matter once and for all. Thus, centuries later, millions of Christians the world over will affirm this Sunday that Jesus was "begotten, not made"; that is to say, tens of millions of people who bear the name of Christ, whether they understand the words they recite or not, will affirm these biblical truths from the Nicene Creed:

> We believe in one Lord, Jesus Christ, the only Son of God, eternally begotten of the Father, God from God, Light from Light, true God from true God, begotten, not made, one in Being with the Father. Through him all things were made.[7]

Those words are very specific. Each phrase was carefully hammered out. Nothing was simply accepted without a fight.

There never was a Nicene Creed on the issue of eschatology

The point of all this is that there never was a Nicene Creed, if you will, on the issue of eschatology. There never was a definitive statement accepted by all orthodox Christians for all times. Christians never hammered out a universally accepted perspective on the Millennium and the Great Tribulation.

After the Trinity and the deity of Christ were affirmed, there were still some differences to be resolved related to the person of Jesus, especially in regard to His humanity. He is fully God and fully man. This is the only time where 100% + 100% = 100%!

The church held the Council of Chalcedon in 451 and affirmed the full humanity of Christ (as well as His deity). They condemned the heresy of Monophysitism, which held that Jesus was only divine.

Meanwhile, Christianity spread throughout various European lands, despite often fierce resistance from pagan tribes. Beginning in the seventh century, the church had to contend with the rise of the rival religion of Islam. Many formerly Christian lands were forcibly taken over; the cross yielded to the crescent—at sword point. Islamic forces essentially blew out the candles of all seven of the churches of Revelation 2 and 3.

During the Middle Ages, many theological controversies arose, centered around such issues as:

- The appropriateness of the writings of the Greek philosophers to Christians. "What had Jerusalem to do with Athens?" The phenomena of colleges and universities was born in the Middle Ages to try to reconcile Christian theology with the writings of Aristotle in particular.

- The use of icons, holy images (paintings, plaques, etc.). Were they an aid to worship or the object of worship? In the eleventh century, this issue caused the first major split between two major segments in the church—the Roman Catholic Church and the Greek Orthodox Church.
- The investiture controversy. Did the bishop of Rome—that is, the pope—have primacy over all the other bishops around the world, and did he even have authority over all kings and princes within Christendom?

Then came the Reformation in the sixteenth century. At that time the chief bones of contention boiled down to two major controversies:

- Religious authority. Is the Bible alone to be our source of authority, or are we to believe the Bible plus church tradition? The Reformers (Martin Luther, John Calvin, and others) affirmed their belief in "Sola Scriptura"—the Scriptures alone.
- Soteriology. The doctrine of salvation. Are we saved by faith alone (which results in good works), or are we saved by a combination of faith plus works? The Reformers believed the Bible taught "Sola Fide"—by faith alone. Man is justified by faith alone and not by works of the law.

Of course, this crash course on church history is rather simplistic. Yet it helps give a thumbnail sketch of some of the key issues the church has dealt with through the centuries. Notice we still haven't gotten to eschatology.

In centuries following the Reformation, some of the controversies fought over included:

- Calvinism versus Arminianism, that is, predestination versus free will.
- Church-states versus separation of the institution of the church from the institution of the state[8]—not to be confused with the ACLU-type vision of separation of God and state.
- Creation versus evolution.
- Modernism versus fundamentalism.
- Eschatology and the rise of dispensationalism.

Finally, in the nineteenth century comes the dispute at hand. *How are we to understand the end times?* As we've seen in the last few chapters, the whole theological debate about eschatology ultimately boils down to how we interpret the prophetic writings of the Scriptures—especially those of Daniel, the Gospels, Paul's epistles, and Revelation.

John Nelson Darby (1800–1882), a British preacher who broke away from the Anglican Church and joined the Plymouth Brethren, championed the cause of interpreting the prophetic passages of the Bible literally. I remember hearing Hal Lindsey crediting John Darby, not so much for inventing the premillennial view, but rather for being the first theologian in relatively recent times to "take the prophetic passages of the Bible literally."[9]

Richard Kyle, author of the recent book *The Last Days Are Here Again*, points out that Darby "systematized dispensationalism and spread its major principles throughout the English-speaking world."[10] He adds:

> Beyond the futuristic approach to prophecy, Darby's eschatology stood on two principles—his doctrine of the church and his method of interpreting the Bible. He sharply separated Israel and the church, insisting that God had a different plan for each. Moreover, Darby interpreted the prophetic passages of the Bible with a rigid literalism. . . . Darby's system was not original. Futurism began with the sixteenth-century Catholics, and elementary forms of dispensationalism go back at least to Joachim of Fiore. Even the rapture doctrine had earlier precedents, including Increase Mather. Still, Darby combined all of these ideas into a coherent system—one that has significantly influenced modern apocalyptic thought.[11]

An interesting footnote to the Plymouth Brethren is that they believed the end was so near that it would likely occur in their day. William Neatby, author of the 1901 book *A History of the Plymouth Brethren*, noted:

> Brethrenism is the child of the study of unfulfilled prophecy, and of the expectation of the immediate return of the Saviour. If any one had told the first Brethren that three quarters of a century might elapse and the Church be still on earth, the answer would prob-

> ably have been a smile, partly of pity, partly of disapproval, wholly of incredulity. Yet so it has proved.[12]

Prophecy Seminars

During the nineteenth century there was great interest in Bible prophecy, especially here in North America and England. Bible prophecy seminars were held, and Bible institutes sprang up. In addition, revival meetings on the American frontier sometimes dealt with prophecy. Interest in the end times grew immensely. Amillennialist Jay Adams confirms that the explosion of interest in the end times has been in the last two centuries:

> During the last 150 years, more books have been published, and more controversy has arisen concerning the secondary phases of eschatology than almost any other theological subject. Stemming from the Irvingite "revivals" of the early 1800's, the doctrines of pretribulation premillennialism have passed successively from J. N. Darby and his segment of the Plymouth Brethren movement to C. I. Scofield and W. E. Blackstone, who, by means of their two volumes, *The Scofield Reference Bible* and *Jesus Is Coming*, probably did more than any others to spread the system throughout America.[13]

Note that Adams wrote those words in a book published in 1970. That same year, Hal Lindsey came out with his premillennial classic, *The Late Great Planet Earth*, which made Christian publishing history. It sold more than thirty million copies.[14] The *New York Times* declared Hal Lindsey the best-selling author of the 1970s because of that book.[15] In my opinion it's safe to put Hal Lindsey up there with C. I. Scofield and W. E. Blackstone as popularizers of premillennial dispensationalism.

Just because the views of the dispensationalists are relatively new doesn't make them wrong. W. E. Blackstone, whom we just mentioned, said as much in his classic *Jesus Is Coming*, which was published in 1878:

> The Church, hand in hand with the world, plunged into the dark ages, until awakened by the great reformers of

> the sixteenth century, who again began to proclaim the comforting hope and blessed promise of the coming of Christ; and since that time the subject so long neglected has been studied and preached with increasing interest. Indeed, in the last two centuries, it seems to have risen (with the doctrine of salvation by simple faith in a crucified Saviour) into somewhat the same prominence which it occupied in the early church. God be praised for it.[16]

Premillennialist Tim LaHaye also sees the relatively new emphasis on the end times as growing out of the Reformation: "The second generation of reformation Bible scholars saw a rise in the literal interpretation of Scripture, which in turn produced a reemphasis on the ancient 'chiliasm,' now given the more modern title of premillennialism."[17]

Gerald Stanton, author of *Kept from the Hour*, concurs:

> If God used Darby and his associates to restore to the Church doctrines long obscure and neglected, his name should be remembered with gratitude and not profaned as the originator of a twentieth century heresy. In this whole matter concerning the history of the imminent, pretribulational return of Jesus Christ, there is little by way of factual support or way of attitudes taken to comment on the writers from the posttribulational school.[18]

Nevertheless, nonmillenarians (and historical premillennialists) might still argue that because a doctrine is relatively new, that may raise some red flags. Postmillennialist Keith Mathison, author of *Dispensationalism: Rightly Dividing the People of God?*, asserts:

> Historical arguments are not the final test for the truthfulness of any doctrine. Scripture is our sole authority for both doctrine and practice. Yet the history of a doctrine can be highly relevant. We have much more reason to be confident of a doctrine such as the Trinity, which has been taught since the first centuries of the church age, than of a doctrine first taught 150 years ago.[19]

Was Augustine Right?

As was stated earlier, there never was a formal, credal statement concerning the issue of the Millennium. That's true. Yet St. Augustine (354-430), Bishop of Hippo, one of the greatest thinkers in Western history, wrote on the issue of the Millennium and ended up solidifying the direction of the church on this issue for the next fourteen centuries. Whether we agree or disagree with him, his incredible influence can't be denied. He thought the prophetic word—that is, the Book of Revelation—was not intended to be interpreted literally. Augustine did not believe in a literal Millennium but rather that he was living in the time when Satan is bound so that he can no longer deceive the nations. He believed that much of what Jesus prophesied in Matthew 24, Luke 21, and Mark 13 was fulfilled with the fall of Jerusalem.

John Walvoord, past president of Dallas Theological Seminary, which is the leading dispensational school of our times, says this about the nineteenth-century dispute over eschatology:

> The major question was whether Augustine was right that prophecy should be interpreted in a nonliteral sense. Premillenarians held that the point of departure that had led to amillennialism and postmillennialism was a faulty system of interpretation in which prophecy was made a special case and interpreted in a nonliteral sense. Accordingly they [nineteenth-century premillennialists] went back to the starting point of the views of the early church fathers, who had been predominantly premillennial, and claimed to be the restorers of the true biblical faith of the early centuries of the church.[20]

In a very real sense, the conflict boils down to which theologian you agree with—Augustine or John Nelson Darby?

Conclusion

Theological conflicts over whether we go through the Tribulation, whether we're raptured before it, or whether the Tribulation already took place when Christ came back in judgment against Jerusalem in A.D. 70

really have not been center stage during most of church history. Incidentally, although the outstanding theologian Thomas Aquinas seemingly addressed everything under the sun in the thirteenth century, you won't find him wrestling with whether the church is to be raptured before, during, or after the Great Tribulation.

Let's now move on to Part 3 where we'll examine what Jesus said about His return. In addition, we'll explore the issue of the Great Tribulation and how some scholars believe it is a future event and others a past event.

Part Three

Is the Great Tribulation a Past or Future Event?

10

Introduction to What Jesus Said about the End Times

Do you see all these things? [referring to the temple and its adjoining buildings.] "I tell you the truth, not one stone here will be left on another; every one will be thrown down.

—Jesus Christ, c. A.D. 30 (Matt. 24:2)

It's strange when skeptics use something that's faith building to try to tear down the faith. Specifically, Jesus' statement in the Olivet Discourse that "this generation will certainly not pass away until all these things have happened" (Matt. 24:34) is to R. C. Sproul (and many theologians throughout the ages) a strong argument to believe in Christ's accuracy. Yet Bertrand Russell and other skeptics view it as an *error* on Jesus' part. In his book *Why I Am Not a Christian*, Russell says of Jesus: "There are a lot of places where it is quite clear that He believed that His second coming would happen during the lifetime of many then living. . . . In that respect, clearly He was not so wise as some other people have been, and He was certainly not superlatively wise."[1]

R. C. Sproul, however, counters:

> There is irony in Russell's negative polemic. One of the most important proofs of Christ's character and the Bible's divine inspiration is Jesus' astonishingly accurate prediction of the destruction of the temple and the fall of Jerusalem, prophecies contained in the Olivet Discourse. There can be little doubt that the biblical record of this prediction antedates the events themselves. It is now almost universally acknowledged that the Gospels of Matthew, Mark, and Luke were written before A.D. 70.[2]

Sproul goes on to point out:

> The main problem with Jesus' predictions in the Olivet Discourse is that they include not only predictions regarding Jerusalem and the temple, which did come to pass with astonishing accuracy, but also predictions of his own coming in glory, or his parousia. It is these predictions regarding Jesus' return on which Russell seized for fodder for his negative *apologia*.[3]

We can see at the outset that a hotly contested passage concerning the end times is the Olivet Discourse in which Jesus gave answers to His disciples while they were seated on the Mount of Olives about the destruction of the temple and the end of the age. The teaching in this passage is so important to an understanding of the end times that we will explore it in the following four chapters (including this one).

Introduction to the Issue

There are basically two schools of thought on the great tribulation: those who see it as a past event and those who see it as a future event. Theologian D. Martyn Lloyd-Jones, however, considers a third possibility, which perhaps could be viewed as a hybrid:

> There have been those who say that in those chapters [the Olivet Discourse] our Lord deals with nothing but the destruction of Jerusalem in A.D. 70 and the spread of the gospel. Then there is a second school which teaches that our Lord certainly did deal with that, and in a sense it was His main concern, but He did not stop there. He made use of that to say that the events of A.D. 70 were also a picture of what would happen on a much bigger scale at the end of the age and on the day of judgment. In other words, what would happen in A.D. 70 was a fact, yes, but also a picture, a parable, of a yet greater event that would happen when the age was summed up and the final judgment pronounced.
>
> But then there is a third school, . . . this holds that in

> those chapters our Lord was deliberately dealing with the two things: that certain of His statements are a literal account of what would happen in A.D. 70 only while other statements refer to literal events at the end of the age and the day of judgment.[4]

Signs of His Coming?

Are there signs of Christ's coming? This is an interesting point. If the preterists (who believe Christ came in judgment in A.D. 70) are right, then the signs listed in the Olivet Discourse were signposts to the destruction of Jerusalem and its temple. Meanwhile, the preterists argue that no one knows the day or hour when Jesus will return. Even Jesus didn't know the time while He was ministering on earth. This preterist school of thought holds then that Jesus:

(1) gave signs of warning applying to the fall of Jerusalem and the destruction of the temple, and

(2) then spoke of His second coming, which will be like the days of Noah or the fall of Sodom and Gomorrah (unexpected for most of the people).

If this teaching is true, then we must consider the many implications concerning the return of Christ. We hear often about various "warning signs" that we are in the last days—or perhaps we should say "the last, last days." Recall that the people in New Testament times were already in the last days. Yet the preterists maintain that those warning signs related to the fall of Jerusalem in A.D. 70.

Jesus knew when that would occur (within the generation of those standing there). Meanwhile, our Lord did not know the hour of His return. That's interesting. He knew what and when (within that generation) the nation of Israel would be destroyed, but He didn't know when He would return.

So what difference does it make? Well, the implications are far-reaching. Let's first look at what He said in His own words.

The Passage Itself

We will study Matthew's version at length, because it is one of the chief passages on the return of Christ, although it can be argued that Matthew dealt with two subjects: the fall of Jerusalem (which occurred in A.D. 70) and the return of Christ. Here's Matthew 24:

> Jesus left the temple and was walking away when his disciples came up to him to call his attention to its buildings. "Do you see all these things?" he asked. "I tell you the truth, not one stone here will be left on another; every one will be thrown down."
>
> As Jesus was sitting on the Mount of Olives, the disciples came to him privately. "Tell us," they said, "when will this happen, and what will be the sign of your coming and of the end of the age?" (Matt. 24:1-3).

Note here that the disciples asked Him two questions:

(1) When will this happen? That is, when will the temple be destroyed?

(2) What will be the sign of your coming and of the end of the age?

> Jesus answered: "Watch out that no one deceives you. For many will come in my name, claiming 'I am the Christ,' and will deceive many. You will hear of wars and rumors of wars, but see to it that you are not alarmed. Such things must happen, but the end is still to come. Nation will rise against nation, and kingdom against kingdom. There will be famines and earthquakes in various places. All these are the beginning of birth pains.
>
> "Then you will be handed over to be persecuted and put to death, and you will be hated by all nations because of me. At that time many will turn away from the faith and will betray and hate each other, and many false prophets will appear and deceive many people. Because of the increase of wickedness, the love of most will grow cold, but he who stands firm to the end will be saved. And this gospel of the kingdom will be preached in the whole world as a testimony to all nations, and then the end will come.
>
> "So when you see standing in the holy place 'the abomination that causes desolation,' spoken of through

> the prophet Daniel—let the reader understand—then let those who are in Judea flee to the mountains. Let no one on the roof of his house go down to take anything out of the house. Let no one in the field go back to get his cloak. How dreadful it will be in those days for pregnant women and nursing mothers! Pray that your flight will not take place in winter or on the Sabbath. For then there will be great distress, unequaled from the beginning of the world until now—and never to be equaled again. If those days had not been cut short, no one would survive, but for the sake of the elect those days will be shortened. At that time if anyone says to you, 'Look, here is the Christ!' or, 'There he is!' do not believe it. For false Christs and false prophets will appear and perform great signs and miracles to deceive even the elect—if that were possible. See, I have told you ahead of time."

Jesus repeats the point three times that deceivers, false christs, false prophets will arise. Continuing . . .

> "So if anyone tells you, 'There he is, out in the desert,' do not go out; or, 'Here he is, in the inner rooms,' do not believe it. For as lightning that comes from the east is visible even in the west, so will be the coming of the Son of Man. Wherever there is a carcass, there the vultures will gather.
>
> "Immediately after the distress of those days
>
> 'the sun will be darkened,
> and the moon will not give its light;
> the stars will fall from the sky,
> and the heavenly bodies will be shaken.'
>
> "At that time the sign of the Son of Man will appear in the sky, and all nations of the earth will mourn. They will see the Son of Man coming on the clouds of the sky, with power and great glory. And he will send his angels with a loud trumpet call, and they will gather his elect from the four winds, from one end of the heavens to the other.

"Now learn this lesson from the fig tree: As soon as its twigs get tender and its leaves come out, you know that summer is near. Even so, when you see all these things, you know that it is near, right at the door. I tell you the truth, this generation will certainly not pass away until all these things have happened. Heaven and earth will pass away, but my words will never pass away.

"No one knows about that day or hour, not even the angels in heaven, nor the Son, but only the Father"

"No one knows about that day or hour, not even the angels in heaven, nor the Son, but only the Father. As it was in the days of Noah, so it will be at the coming of the Son of Man. For in the days before the flood, people were eating and drinking, marrying and giving in marriage, up to the day Noah entered the ark; and they knew nothing about what would happen until the flood came and took them all away. That is how it will be at the coming of the Son of Man. Two men will be in the field; one will be taken and the other left. Two women will be grinding with a hand mill; one will be taken and the other left.

"Therefore keep watch, because you do not know on what day your Lord will come. But understand this: If the owner of the house had known at what time of night the thief was coming, he would have kept watch and would not have let his house be broken into. So you also must be ready, because the Son of Man will come at an hour when you do not expect him.

"Who then is the faithful and wise servant, whom the master has put in charge of the servants in his household to give them their food at the proper time? It will be good for that servant whose master finds him doing so when he returns. I tell you the truth, he will put him in charge of all his possessions. But suppose that servant is wicked and says to himself, 'My master is staying away a long time,' and he then begins to beat his fellow servants and to eat and drink with drunkards. The master of that servant will come on a day when he does not expect him and at an

> hour he is not aware of. He will cut him to pieces and assign him a place with the hypocrites, where there will be weeping and gnashing of teeth" (Matt. 24:4-51).

The Summary of Matthew 25

Chapter 24 ends, but not Jesus' teaching. Jesus went on in this discourse, and He amplified His point that we must be ready for His return. He told the parable of the ten virgins, in which five were ready and five were not. Those who weren't ready for His return missed out.

He next told the parable of the talents, in which three men were entrusted with different amounts of wealth, and each was to put them to good use. When the master returned, he called their stewardship into account. This parable ties into the return of Christ in that His return will involve our accountability to Him.

The next passage is that of the final judgment, in which all nations are brought before Him, and He separates the sheep from the goats. Here again, Jesus makes the point to be ready by right living. You don't know when Jesus is coming again, so be ready at all times; let Jesus find you doing what is right.

Do Mark and Luke Add Anything Significant?

Because Mark 13 and Luke 21 contain the same basic teaching within Matthew 24, those passages won't be examined except for two statements by Luke. Luke mentions there will be "great signs from heaven" (Luke 21:11). He further said of the destruction of Jerusalem and the fall of the Jewish nation, "They will fall by the sword and will be taken as prisoners to all the nations. Jerusalem will be trampled on by the Gentiles *until the times of the Gentiles are fulfilled*" (Luke 21:24, emphasis mine).

In reference to this verse, Hal Lindsey notes that Palestine is in Jewish hands once again. The modern state of Israel was born in 1948. Moreover, because the Jews recovered Jerusalem in 1967, the time of the Gentiles is nearing its very end. Lindsey writes, "The 'times of the Gentiles'—of which the Church Age is a part—is fulfilled with the Rapture of the Church, and sets the stage for the 70th Week of Daniel, or the Tribulation Period."[5]

Major Prophecies of the Olivet Discourse

When Jesus was approaching His final hours before the crucifixion, He grieved over Jerusalem because its citizens had rejected Him. Hence, they had rejected God. What He said in that famous lament was quite prophetic: "O Jerusalem, Jerusalem, you who kill the prophets and stone those sent to you, how often I have longed to gather your children together, as a hen gathers her chicks under her wings, but you were not willing. Look, your house is left to you desolate" (Matt. 23:37-38). That desolation was to come in full force within forty years.

Major Points of the Olivet Discourse: Matthew 24:4-34

Using Matthew 24 as our guide, let's list Jesus' prophecies one by one, from the beginning through His statement that "this generation will certainly not pass away until all these things have happened" (v. 34). These points will be very helpful as we explore the themes in this passage in the next couple chapters.

1. The temple will be demolished so completely that not one stone will be left on another (v. 2).
2. Many false prophets and false christs will arise and deceive people (vv. 4, 11, 23-26). He mentioned such deceivers three times.
3. They will hear of wars and rumors of wars (v. 6).
4. Nation will rise against nation and kingdom against kingdom (v. 7).
5. There will be famines (v. 7).
6. There will be earthquakes in various places (v. 7).
7. All nations will persecute and even hate and martyr Jesus' followers because of Him (v. 9).
8. Many will leave the faith at that time and betray each other—the great apostasy (v. 10).
9. Wickedness will increase, causing the love of most to grow cold (v. 12).
10. The Gospel will be preached in the whole world to all nations, and then the end will come (v. 14).
11. Standing in the holy place will be "the abomination that causes desolation" (v. 15).
12. When they see the abomination, His followers will then flee and not turn back (vv. 16-20).
13. These days will be unparalleled in their level of distress (v. 21). In

our Lord's own words: "How dreadful it will be in those days for pregnant women and nursing mothers! . . . For then there will be great distress, unequaled from the beginning of the world until now—and never be equaled again. If those days had not been cut short, no one would survive" (vv. 19, 21-22).

14. "For as lightning that comes from the east is visible even in the west, so will be the coming of the Son of Man" (v. 27).

15. The vultures gather over a carcass—someone or something has died (v. 28).

16. The sun and moon will be darkened. The stars will fall. The heavenly bodies will be shaken; that is, there will be signs in the heavens (v. 29).

17. The sign of the Son of Man will appear in the sky, and all nations of the earth will mourn (v. 30).

18. They will see the Son of Man coming on the clouds of the sky with great power and great glory (v. 30).

19. He'll send His angels out with a loud trumpet call and will gather His elect from the whole earth (v. 31).

20. Learn a lesson from the fig tree: When its twigs get tender and its leaves come out, then summer is near. Even so, when they see all these things, they'll know Jesus is near, "right at the door" (v. 33).

21. That generation will not pass away until all those things happen (v. 34).

In the next two chapters, we'll look at which of Jesus' predictions could be construed as having taken place when the Romans completely destroyed Jerusalem.

In addition, we'll add five points from the Gospel of Luke:

- "If you, even you, had only known on this day what would bring you peace—but now it is hidden from your eyes. The days will come upon you when your enemies will build an embankment against you and encircle you and hem you in on every side. They will dash you to the ground, you and the children within your walls" (19:41-44).
- "They will not leave one stone on another, because you did not recognize the time of God's coming to you" (v. 44).
- "There will be . . . great signs from heaven" (21:11).
- "When you see Jerusalem being surrounded by armies, you will know that its desolation is near" (v. 20).
- "There will be great distress in the land and wrath against this people.

> They will fall by the sword and will be taken as prisoners to all the nations. Jerusalem will be trampled on by the Gentiles until the times of the Gentiles are fulfilled" (vv. 23-24).

Conclusion

We have just read some of the most important words ever spoken and written on the subject of the end times. Now we want to consider how theologians and writers interpret these vital words.

Our next two chapters will take a look in depth at some of the historical evidence for the preterist position. They will seek to answer the question: Is the Great Tribulation a past event? We hear so much about the Tribulation that it's almost unthinkable. Yet let's read what others have said on the issue, centuries ago. We'll begin by looking at "The Gospel According to Eusebius" because he, along with first-century historian Josephus, has some thought-provoking material on the potential fulfillment of the Olivet Discourse.

11

A Past Event? Part 1: The Gospel According to Eusebius

***No matter what view of eschatology we embrace, we must take seriously the redemptive-historical importance of Jerusalem's destruction in A.D. 70.*[1]**

—R. C. Sproul

Is it possible that the Great Tribulation that we constantly hear is *coming* has already happened? This and the next couple chapters will deal with the issue of whether the Great Tribulation is past or future. Because the idea of it being a *past* event is such a radical thesis in our day, we will devote two chapters to the subject but only one to the widely heard view that it is yet to be.

While the idea that the Great Tribulation has *already* taken place may seem novel in today's milieu, it's an idea that's been around much longer than the currently popular view. For many centuries it was held that the Tribulation Jesus spoke about in Matthew 24, Mark 13, and Luke 21 was fulfilled in the Roman assault on Jerusalem in A.D. 70. Preterists hold this position, and they see it as an example of the deity of Christ in that around A.D. 30, He could see the future with pinpoint accuracy and predict what was about to occur. At the very least, Jesus saved the lives of His followers who heeded His warning when they saw the Roman army surrounding the city because of what He had said in the Olivet Discourse.

To hold the position that the Tribulation is a past event, one must accept the idea that some of the things Jesus said in the Olivet Discourse are not to be taken literally. R. C. Sproul, who believes the Tribulation is a past event, says, "[Preterists J. Stuart] Russell and [John] Calvin agree that the language employed in biblical prophecy is not always cold and logical as is common in the Western world, but adopts a kind of fervor common to the East. Scripture commonly describes the visitation of God's judgment with images of convulsion and cataclysms."[2]

Yet What About Revelation or Daniel's Seventy Weeks?

Some people who are familiar with the modern end-times interpretation often understand the Great Tribulation as it is tied to Daniel's Seventy Weeks and the various judgments of Revelation. This may or may not be valid. Many nonmillenarians would hold it isn't. To them, even if Jesus did come back in A.D. 70 and did fulfill what He said in Matthew 24:4-34, that doesn't necessarily mean that He also fulfilled those judgments described in the Apocalypse. In short, as we're dealing with the Great Tribulation past or future, we are focusing only on the Great Tribulation as described by Jesus in the Synoptic Gospels.

Eusebius and Josephus

We are going to quote *at length* from the eminent church historian of the fourth century, Eusebius of Caesaria, who in turn quotes from first-century historian Josephus. Some scholars hold that the details of what happened in the destruction of Jerusalem and the temple in the first century shed light on the meaning of the Olivet Discourse. Postmillennialist Gary North says, "Modern Christians are almost totally unfamiliar with the events of A.D. 70."[3] A study of Eusebius' and Josephus' materials won't make that true of us.

Eusebius (c. 265–c. 339) is known as "the Father of Church History." He wrote *Historia Ecclesiastica*, which scholars recognize as "the most important church history of ancient times."[4] H. Lietzmann writes that Eusebius "liberated Christian chronography from the bonds of apocalypticism . . . basing it on purely logical foundations."[5]

Eusebius believed events in the first century were precise fulfillments of what Jesus foretold. Meanwhile, Eusebius quoted at length from Josephus, who was a direct witness to the events of A.D. 70. Josephus certainly was not partial to the cause of Christ. Yet the secular history he wrote would seem to verify the authenticity of Jesus' prophetic word with pinpoint accuracy.

Flavius Josephus (c. 37–95) was the son of Mattathias, a priest in Jerusalem. He was a Jew who did not accept Jesus as the Christ. At one point he had fought against the Romans, but they subdued him and forced him to be present at the fall of Jerusalem. Eusebius wrote that Josephus "was the most noted of all the Jews of that day, not only among his own people, but also among the Romans, so that he was honored by the erection of a statue in Rome, and his works were deemed worthy of a place in the [imperial] library."[6] His work as an historian is first-rate. He was an eyewitness to the tragic war on the Jews that culminated in the destruction of Jerusalem and the temple in A.D. 70, and he wrote it all down.

Our Signposts

You will recall that we carefully highlighted the major points in Matthew 24:4-34 in the last chapter and added some verses from Luke. Using these various points of information as our signposts, we will now take the writings of Eusebius and Josephus and determine how and why Eusebius was convinced that many of the prophecies of the Olivet Discourse were fulfilled at the time of the destruction of Jerusalem and the temple. Why are we specifically stopping at Matthew 24:34? Because that's when Jesus said, "This generation will certainly not pass away until all these things have happened." To preterists, this verse is key to understanding the passage (at least, understanding what was spoken up to this point). Even futurists find this verse pivotal for their interpretation of the end times. (For example, Hal Lindsey and others understand it to apply to the generation that sees the restoration of Israel/Jerusalem.)[7]

Some of these points will be repeated. Many will be out of sequence. Eusebius' own writing will dictate the order.

Portions of Eusebius' "Church History"—Which Includes Lengthy Quotes from Josephus' "War on Jerusalem"

- **His followers will be persecuted and even martyred and hated by all nations because of Jesus (Matt. 24:9).**
- **Nation will rise against nation and kingdom against kingdom (Matt. 24:7).**

Eusebius:

> After Nero had held the power thirteen years [from October 16, 54–June 9, 68], and Galba and Otho had ruled a year and six months, Vespasian, who had become distinguished in the campaigns against the Jews, was proclaimed sovereign in Judea and received the title of

> Emperor from the armies there. Setting out immediately, therefore, for Rome, he entrusted the conduct of the war against the Jews to his son Titus. For the Jews after ascension of our Saviour, in addition to their crime against him, had been devising as many plots as they could against his apostles. First Stephen was stoned to death by them, and after him James, the son of Zebedee and the brother of John, was beheaded, and finally James, the first that had obtained the episcopal seat in Jerusalem after the ascension of our Saviour, died.[8]

- **The Gospel will be preached in the whole world to all nations, and the end will come (Matt. 24:14).**

Eusebius:

> But the rest of the apostles, who had been incessantly plotted against with a view to their destruction, and had been driven out of the land of Judea, went unto all nations to preach the Gospel, relying upon the power of Christ, who had said to them, "Go ye and make disciples of all the nations in my name."[9]

- **These days will be unparalleled in their level of distress (Matt. 24:21). In our Lord's own words: "How dreadful it will be in those days for pregnant women and nursing mothers! . . . For then there will be great distress, unequaled from the beginning of the world until now—and never be equaled again. If those days had not been cut short, no one would survive" (vv. 19, 21-22).**
- **There will be famines (Matt. 24:7).**
- **Standing in the holy place will be "the abomination that causes desolation" (Matt. 24:15).**
- **When they see the abomination, His followers should then flee and not turn back (Matt. 24:16-20).**

Eusebius:

> But the people of the church in Jerusalem had been commanded by a revelation, vouchsafed to approved men there before the war, to leave the city and to dwell in a

> certain town of Perea called Pella. And when those that believed in Christ had come thither from Jerusalem, then, as if the royal city of the Jews and the whole land of Judea were entirely destitute of holy men, the judgment of God at length overtook those who had committed such outrages against Christ and his apostles, and totally destroyed that generation of impious men. But the number of calamities which everywhere fell upon the nation at that time, the extreme misfortunes to which the inhabitants of Judea were especially subjected, the thousands of men, as well as women and children, that perished by the sword, by famine, and by other forms of death innumerable,—all these things, as well as the many great sieges which were carried on against the cities of Judea, and the excessive sufferings endured by those that fled to Jerusalem itself, as to a city of perfect safety, and finally the general course of the whole war, as well as its particular occurrences in detail, and how at last the abomination of desolation, proclaimed by the prophets, stood in the very temple of God, so celebrated of old, the temple which was now awaiting its total and final destruction by fire,—all these things any one that wishes may find accurately described in the history written by Josephus.[10]

The irony here is that hundreds of thousands of Jews sought refuge from the Romans within Jerusalem's walls. They were in the city to celebrate the Passover, but the place of refuge became instead a type of prison.

> But it is necessary to state that this writer records that the multitude of those who were assembled from all Judea at the time of the Passover, to the number of three million souls, were shut up in Jerusalem "as in a prison," to use his own words. For it was right that in the very days in which they had inflicted suffering upon the Saviour and the Benefactor of all, the Christ of God, that in those days, shut up "as in a prison," they should meet with destruction at the hands of divine justice.

> But passing by the particular calamities which they suffered from the attempts made upon them by the sword and by other means, I think it necessary to relate only the misfortunes which the famine caused, that those who read this work may have some means of knowing that God was not long in executing vengeance upon them for their wickedness against the Christ of God.[11]

- **There will be famines (Matt. 24:7).**
- **Wickedness will increase, causing the love of most to grow cold (Matt. 24:12).**
- **"If you, even you, had only known on this day what would bring you peace—but now it is hidden from your eyes. The days will come upon you when your enemies will build an embankment against you and encircle you and hem you in on every side. They will dash you to the ground, you and the children within your walls" (Luke 19:42-44).**
- **"When you see Jerusalem being surrounded by armies, you will know that its desolation is near" (Luke 21:20).**
- **Many will leave the faith at that time and betray each other—great apostasy (Matt. 24:10).**

Josephus:

> Nowhere was food to be seen; but, bursting into the houses, men searched them thoroughly, and whenever they found anything to eat they tormented the owners on the ground that they had denied that they had anything; but if they found nothing, they tortured them on the ground that they had more carefully concealed it. The proof of their having or not having food was found in the bodies of the poor wretches. Those of them who were still in good condition they assumed were well supplied with food, while those who were already wasted away passed by, for it seemed absurd to slay those who were on the point of perishing for want. Many, indeed, secretly sold their possessions for one measure of wheat, if they belonged to the wealthier class, of barley if they were poorer. . . . Of all evils, indeed, famine is the worst,

> and it destroys nothing so effectively as shame. For that which under other circumstances is worthy of respect, in the midst of famine is despised. Thus women snatched the food from the very mouths of their husbands and children, from their fathers, and what was most pitiable of all, mothers from their babes. And while their dearest ones were wasting away in their arms, they were not ashamed to take away from them the last drops that supported life.[12]

With these graphic descriptions of the famine, could it not be surmised that this fulfills what Jesus predicted: "the love of most will grow cold"? Preterists think so. Josephus goes on to describe how neither infant nor elder was safe in the famine. But they were beaten by their fellow citizens, even for just tiny morsels of food. Soon corpses were lying everywhere. In fact, many people died trying to bury others.

To make matters worse, looters "were more terrible than these miseries." They broke into houses, which had now become "sepulchres." They robbed the dead, but in the event they came upon a dying person, they thrust in their sword, except in those circumstances where the victim begged for death. In those cases, they laughed and abandoned the victim to let the famine slowly finish its work. Surely, the love of many had grown cold.

Not only were the dead and dying lying about everywhere, survivors managed to heave many corpses over the besieged city walls into the trenches below, which were now filling up. Josephus says, "And as Titus went around and saw the trenches filled with the dead, and the thick blood oozing out of the putrid bodies, he groaned aloud, and, raising his hands, called God to witness this was not his doing."[13]

- **Many false prophets and false christs will deceive many (Matt. 24:4, 11, 23-26).**
- **"If you, even you, had only known on this day what would bring you peace—but now it is hidden from your eyes. The days will come upon you when your enemies will build an embankment against you and encircle you and hem you in on every side. They will dash you to the ground, you and the children within your walls" (Luke 19:42-44).**

Josephus described a horrible incident in which some enraged Roman soldiers slaughtered about six thousand women and children who sought refuge in a secluded part of the outer temple. Why had they fled there in the first place? Because of a deceiving seer.

Josephus:

> The soldiers also came to the rest of the cloisters that were in the outer temple, whither the women and children, and a great mixed multitude of the people, fled, in number about six thousand. But before Caesar had determined anything about these people, or given the Commander any orders relating to them, the soldiers were in such a rage, that they set that cloister on fire; by which means it came to pass that some of those were destroyed by throwing themselves down headlong, and some were burnt in the cloisters themselves. Nor did any one of them escape with his life. **A false prophet** was the occasion of these people's destruction, who had made a public proclamation in the city that very day, that God commanded them to get upon the temple, and that there they should receive miraculous signs of their deliverance. Now there was then a great number of false prophets suborned by the tyrants to impose on the people, who denounced this to them, that they should wait for deliverance from God; and this was in order to keep them from deserting, and that they might be buoyed up above fear and care by such hopes. Now a man that is in adversity does easily comply with such promises; from when such a seducer makes him believe that he shall be delivered from those miseries which oppress him, then it is that the patient is full of hopes of such his deliverance.[14]

Josephus:

> Now as for the affairs of the Jews, they grew worse and worse continually, for the country was again filled with robbers and imposters, who deluded the multitude. Yet did Felix catch and put to death many of those impostors

> every day, together with the robbers.[15]

- **There will be famines (Matt. 24:7).**
- **Wickedness will increase, causing the love of most to grow cold (Matt. 24:12).**

Josephus:

> I cannot hesitate to declare what my feelings compel me to. I suppose, if the Romans had longer delayed in coming against these guilty wretches, the city would have been swallowed up by a chasm, or overwhelmed with a flood, or struck with such thunderbolts as destroyed Sodom. For it had brought forth a generation of men much more godless than were those that suffered such punishment. By their madness indeed was the whole people brought to destruction. . . . Of those that perished by famine in the city the number was countless, and the miseries they underwent unspeakable. For if so much as the shadow of food appeared in any house, there was war, and the dearest friends engaged in hand-to-hand conflict with one another, and snatched from each other the most wretched supports of life. Nor would they believe that even the dying were without food; but the robbers would search them while they were expiring, lest any one should feign death while concealing food in his bosom. With mouths gaping for want of food, they stumbled and staggered along like mad dogs, and beat the doors as if they were drunk, and in their impotence they would rush into the same houses twice or thrice in one hour. Necessity compelled them to eat anything they could find, and they gathered and devoured things that were not fit even for the filthiest of irrational beasts. Finally they did not abstain even from their girdles and shoes, and they stripped the hides off their shields and devoured them. Some used even wisps of old hay for food, and others gathered stubble and sold the smallest weight of it for four Atticdrachmae [a few dollars].[16]

He then goes on to tell a terrible story, the kind not even heard among the "Greeks and Barbarians." This story was so awful that to be sure of its accuracy he inquired of many eyewitnesses who verified its truthfulness.

> There was a certain woman named Mary that dwelt beyond Jordan, whose father was Eleazer, of the village of Bathezor (which signifies the house of hyssop). She was distinguished for her family and her wealth, and had fled with the rest of the multitude to Jerusalem and was shut up there with them during the siege. The tyrants had robbed her of the rest of the property which she had brought with her into the city from Perea. And the remnants of her possessions and whatever food was to be seen the guards rushed in daily and snatched away from her. This made the woman terribly angry, and by her frequent reproaches and implications she aroused the anger of the rapacious villains against herself. But no one either through anger or pity would slay her; and she grew weary of finding food for others to eat. The search, too, was already become everywhere difficult, and the famine was piercing her bowels and marrow, and resentment was raging more violently than famine. Taking, therefore, anger and necessity as her counselors, she proceeded to do a most unnatural thing. Seizing her child, a boy which was sucking at her breast, she said, "Oh, wretched child, in war, in famine, in sedition, for what do I preserve thee? Slaves among the Romans we shall be even if we are allowed to live by them. But even slavery is anticipated by the famine, and the rioters are more cruel than both. Come, be food for me, a fury for these rioters, and a byword to the world, for this is all that is wanting to complete the calamities of the Jews." And when she had said this she slew her son; and having roasted him, she ate one half herself, and covering up the remainder, she kept it.[17]

Thus, the famine was so bad that she did the unthinkable—made a meal of her own son. This act repulsed even the looters, who by now had become extremely hardened having seen and participated in horrible atrocities on a daily basis. Josephus continues with the tragedy:

> Very soon the rioters appeared on the scene, and, smelling the nefarious odor, they threatened to slay her immediately unless she should show them what she had prepared. She replied that she had saved an excellent portion for them, and with that she uncovered the remains of the child. They were immediately seized with horror and amazement, and stood transfixed at the sight. But she said, "This is my own son, and the deed is mine. Eat, for I too have eaten. Be not more merciful than a woman, nor more compassionate than a mother. But if you are too pious and shrink from my sacrifice, I have already eaten of it; let the rest also remain for me." At these words the men went out trembling, in this one case being affrighted; yet with difficulty did they yield that food to the mother. Forthwith the whole city was filled with the awful crime, and as all pictured the terrible deed before their own eyes, they trembled as if they had done it themselves. Those that were suffering from the famine now longed for death; and blessed were they that had died before hearing and seeing miseries like these.[18]

Eusebius adds this commentary to this terrible portion: "Such was the reward which the Jews received for their wickedness and impiety against the Christ of God."[19]

Furthermore, anyone who tried to escape the Romans and was caught died an excruciatingly painful death.

Josephus:

> They were first whipped, and then tormented with all sorts of tortures, before they died, and were then crucified before the walls of the city. So the soldiers, out of the wrath and hatred they bore the Jews, nailed those they caught, one after one way, and another after another, to the crosses, by the way of jest, when their multitude was so great, that room was wanting for the crosses, and crosses wanting for the bodies.[20]

Whether you agree with Eusebius' argument or not that this was *the* Great Tribulation, what the Jews experienced under the Roman conquest of A.D. 70 was indeed a tribulation.

- **These days will be unparalleled in their level of distress (Matt. 24:21).**

Anyone who tried to escape the Romans and was caught died

- **The vultures gather over a carcass—someone or something has died (Matt. 24:28).**
- **"There will be great distress in the land and wrath against this people. They will fall by the sword and will be taken as prisoners to all the nations. Jerusalem will be trampled on by the Gentiles until the times of the Gentiles are fulfilled" (Luke 21:23-24).**

Eusebius:

> The historian [Josephus], reckoning the whole number of the slain, says that eleven hundred thousand [1.1 million] persons perished by famine and sword, and that the rest of the rioters and robbers, being betrayed by each other after the taking of the city, were slain. But the tallest of the youths and those that were distinguished for beauty were preserved for the triumph. Of the rest of the multitude, those that were over seventeen years of age were sent as prisoners to labor in the works of Egypt, while still more were scattered through the provinces to meet their death in the theaters by the sword and by beasts. Those under seventeen years of age were carried away to be sold as slaves, and of these alone the number reached ninety thousand. These things took place in this manner in the second year of Vespasian, in accordance with the prophecies of our Lord and Saviour Jesus Christ, who by divine power saw them beforehand as if they were already present, and wept and mourned according to the statements of the holy evangelists.[21]

- **"There will be . . . great signs from heaven" (Luke 21:11).**
- **The sun and moon will be darkened. The stars will fall. The heavenly bodies will be shaken (Matt. 24:29).**

- **Many false prophets and false christs will deceive many (Matt. 24:4, 11, 23-26).**

Josephus:

> Thus were the miserable people won over at this time by the imposters and false prophets; but they did not heed nor give credit to the visions and signs that foretold the approaching desolation. On the contrary, as if struck by lightning, and as if possessing neither eyes nor understanding, they slighted the proclamations of God. At one time **a star, in form like a sword, stood over the city**, and a **comet, which lasted for a whole year**; and again before the revolt and before the disturbances that led to the war, when the people were gathered for the feast of unleavened bread, on the eighth of the month Xanthicus [roughly corresponds to our April], at the ninth hour of the night, **so great a light shone about the altar and the temple that it seemed to be bright day**; and this continued for half an hour. **This seemed to the unskilled a good sign**, but was interpreted by the sacred scribes as portending those events which very soon took place. And at the same feast a cow, led by the high priest to be sacrificed, brought forth a lamb in the midst of the temple. And the eastern gate of the inner temple, which was bronze and very massive, and which at evening was closed with difficulty by twenty men, and rested upon iron-bound beams, and had bars sunk deep in the ground, was seen at the sixth hour of the night to open of itself. . . . A certain Jesus, the son of Ananias, a common countryman, four years before the war, when the city was particularly prosperous and peaceful, came to the feast, at which it was customary for all to make tents at the temple to the honor of God, and suddenly began to cry out: "A voice from the east, a voice from the west, a voice from the four winds, a voice against Jerusalem and the temple, a voice against bridegrooms and brides, a voice against all the people." Day and night he went through all the alleys crying thus. But certain of the

> more distinguished citizens, vexed at the ominous cry, seized the man and beat him with many stripes. But without uttering a word in his own behalf, or saying anything in particular to those that were present, he continued to cry out in the same words as before. And the rulers, thinking, as was true, that the man was moved by a higher power, brought him before the Roman governor [Albinus]. And then, though he was scourged to the bone, he neither made supplication nor shed tears, but changing his voice to the most lamentable tone possible, he answered each stroke with the words, "Woe, woe unto Jerusalem."[22]

- **The Gospel will be preached in the whole world to all nations, and the end will come (Matt. 24:14).**

Eusebius notes that "the voice of his holy apostles went throughout all the earth, and their words to the end of the world."[23]

- **The sign of the Son of Man will appear in the sky and all nations of the earth will mourn (Matt. 24:30).**
- **They will see the Son of Man coming on the clouds of the sky, with great power and great glory (Matt. 24:30).**

Josephus:

> Then again, not many days after the feast, on the twenty-first of the month of Artemisium [approximately July], a supernatural apparition was seen, too amazing to be believed. What I am now to relate would, I imagine, have been dismissed as imaginary, had this not been vouched for by eyewitnesses, then followed by subsequent disasters that deserved to be thus signalized. For before sunset chariots were seen in the air over the whole country, and armed battalions speeding through the clouds and encircling the cities. Then again, at the feast called Pentecost, when the priests had entered the inner courts of the Temple by night to perform their usual ministrations, they declared that they were aware, first, of a violent commotion and din, then of a voice as of a host crying, "We are departing hence."[24]

Eusebius' Conclusion

Eusebius summed up his main point by saying Jesus, looking into the near future, pronounced judgment on the apostate nation of Israel. They had not recognized God when He came into their midst. Therefore, their whole nation and its temple would be destroyed until "the time of the Gentiles be fulfilled." Not one stone would be left upon another. To anyone who heeded His warnings not to turn back, but to get out of town once the armies surrounded the city, they were spared sure destruction. But to those who didn't listen to the Christ and chose instead to listen to the many false christs arising, they were killed or sold into slavery. Eusebius then pointed to Jesus' amazing ability to foresee the future:

They will see the Son of Man coming on the clouds

> If any one compares the words of our Saviour with the other accounts of the historian [Josephus] concerning the whole war, how can one fail to wonder, and to admit that the foreknowledge and the prophecy of our Saviour were truly divine and marvelously strange. Concerning these calamities, then, that befell the whole Jewish nation after the Saviour's passion and after the words which the multitude of the Jews uttered, when they begged the release of the robber and murderer [Barabbas], but besought that the Prince of Life should be taken from their midst, it is not necessary to add anything to the account of the historian. But it may be proper to mention also those events which exhibited the graciousness of that all-good Providence which held back their destruction full forty years after their crime against Christ,—during which time many of the apostles and disciples, and James himself the first bishop there, the one who is called the brother of the Lord, were still alive, and dwelling in Jerusalem itself, remained the surest bulwark of the place. Divine Providence thus still proved itself long-suffering toward them in order to see whether by repentance for what they had done they might obtain pardon and salvation; and in addition to

> such long-suffering. Providence also furnished wonderful signs of the things which were about to happen to them if they did not repent.[25]

Conclusion

This is an eye-opening history lesson even for those who don't believe the Tribulation was a past event. What a tragedy for the Jews to reject their own Messiah. No wonder Jesus wept over Jerusalem some forty years before all these things happened:

> O Jerusalem, Jerusalem, you who kill the prophets and stone those sent to you, how often I have longed to gather your children together, as a hen gathers her chicks under her wings, but you were not willing. Look, your house is left to you desolate (Matt. 23:37-38).

12

A Past Event? Part 2: Miscellaneous Considerations

Fulfilled prophecy is being interpreted as if it is unfulfilled prophecy.[1]

—Gary DeMar

It's very possible that the last chapter may have raised more questions than it answered. That's all right. Studies on the end times tend to do that.

In this chapter we want to explore this thesis further by going beyond Eusebius and Josephus. First, let's look at the key verse of Matthew 24 according to Preterists: ". . . this generation will certainly not pass away until all these things have happened" (v. 34).

What Is Meant by "This Generation"?

Sometimes it is argued that the word "generation" in Jesus' statement (Matt. 24:34) means "race," not just generation. J. Marcellus Kik, however, disagrees. He wrote *An Eschatology of Victory*, which is an entire book devoted almost exclusively to exegeting Matthew 24, and he says the real solution to understanding this pivotal passage is found in the clear reference of Jesus' statement. He writes, "It is my contention that Matthew 24:34 gives the key to the understanding of the entire chapter. If we accept the ordinary sense of that verse the chapter becomes understandable."[2] R. C. Sproul echoes this sentiment when he writes, "The most critical portion of this text is Jesus' declaration that 'this generation will by no means pass away till all these things take place'"[3]

On the other hand, dispensationalists argue that the word "generation" can have more than one meaning and can refer instead to the Jewish race. Lewis Sperry Chafer states this view in his book *The Kingdom in History and Prophecy*: "Israel, as a nation, not one generation, is to be divinely preserved until all be fulfilled: 'Verily I say unto you, This generation (genea, race, or stock, Israel) shall not pass, till all these things be fulfilled. . . .'"[4] Some nonmillenarians make this same point.

Yet Gary DeMar, in *Last Days* Madness, disputes that view:

> First, "this generation" always means the generation to whom Jesus was speaking. It is the *contemporary generation*, the generation alive at the hearing of Jesus' words. . . . Those who deny that "this generation" refers to the generation to whom Jesus was speaking in the Matthew 24 context must maintain that "this generation" means something different from the way it is used in other places in Matthew and the rest of the New Testament![5]

DeMar cites German scholar Hermann Olshausen, who said *genea* (translated into generation) is never used in the New Testament as "race."[6] But one could point out that is a circular argument. Furthermore, DeMar observes that Jesus said "you" over and over in the Olivet Discourse. They will do this to you; they will do that to you. Then Jesus caps it off by saying, "this generation will certainly not pass away until all these things have happened." In light of all this evidence, DeMar asks, "Now, if you heard Jesus say that all these things would happen to this generation, and in every other instance of its use 'this generation' meant the present generation, and you also heard Him speak of when 'you' see these things, what would you conclude?"[7] R. C. Sproul answers, "When one announces to people that an event will take place within a short time, however, they would hardly understand that to mean a period of millennia."[8]

Hal Lindsey joins in the debate: "What generation? Obviously, in context, the generation that would see the signs—chief among them the rebirth of Israel. A generation in the Bible is something like forty years. If this is a correct deduction, then within forty years or so of 1948, all these things could take place. Many scholars who have studied Bible prophecy all their lives believe that this is so."[9]

Charles Spurgeon says (of this passage and A.D. 70): "It was just about the ordinary limit of a generation when the Roman armies compassed Jerusalem, whose measure of iniquity was then full, and overflowed in misery, agony, distress, and bloodshed such as the world never saw before or since."[10]

Amillennialist John Calvin says, "For within fifty years the city was destroyed and the temple was razed, the whole country was reduced to a hideous desert, and the obstinacy of the world rose up against God."[11] Calvin even paraphrases the meaning of Matthew 24:34: "This prophecy does not relate to evils that are distant, and which posterity will see after the lapse of many centuries, but which are now hanging over you, and ready to fall in one mass, so that there is no part of it which the present *generation* will not experience." He goes on to add a "double fulfillment" type of interpretation to the passage: "So then, while our Lord heaps upon a single *generation* every kind of calamities, he does not by any means exempt future ages from the same kind of sufferings, but only enjoins the disciples to be prepared for enduring them all with firmness."[12]

Logical Alternatives

This passage can be interpreted in the following ways:

Option 1—Jesus initially answered the first question (when will the temple be destroyed?). His answer includes all those points through verse 35. This interpretation maintains that all the events described therein took place through the destruction of Jerusalem in A.D. 70. Jesus then shifted gears and talked about "that day," about which no man knows the hour, that is, His Second Coming. Those statements that follow—Matthew 24:36–25:46—answer the disciples' second question (what are the signs of the end of the age?). If this interpretation of the Olivet Discourse is correct, then many of the specifics in the passage are assumed to be highly symbolic—the Son of Man coming in the clouds; the changes in the sun, moon, stars; and so on.

Option 2—A double fulfillment view. This perspective agrees with Option 1, but it adds that A.D. 70 is the prototype of an additional tribulation in the future.

Option 3—Jesus' answers are not chronological. Some parts fit what happened in A.D. 70 with the destruction of the temple; other parts apply only to His second coming. Thus intermingled is a statement or two on the A.D. 70 judgment, then a statement or two on the Second Coming, then we're back to the A.D. 70 prediction, then back to the Second Coming, and so on. Only when the final chapter of history is written will we know exactly which part applies to which. Defenders of this view argue that Middle Eastern communications are not always as chronological and cut-and-dried as their modern, Western counterparts.

Option 4—It all took place in A.D. 70, and Jesus is not coming back again. Of course, only liberal Bible scholars hold this view. To paraphrase Abraham Kuyper, they are more like "biblical vandals"[13] than they are biblical scholars. I remember when thirty members of the Jesus Seminar[14] made news after they announced their doubt that Jesus ever said He would return.[15] Thankfully, such biblical vandals represent a relatively small number. For example, a Gallup poll found that only 1 percent believe "the Second Coming has already taken place or is happening now."[16]

Option 5—Jesus was mistaken. Jesus thought He was coming back, but He was wrong. This is Bertrand Russell's view. Obviously, Russell was mistaken. On Judgment Day, we won't stand before Russell, but before the Son of God. A variation of this same option is that the Gospel writers were mistaken. There are, however, many volumes that document the complete reliability of the Bible, especially the New Testament.[17]

Option 6—*All* of the things Jesus answered are yet to be. They all apply to "the end times." While there may have been a partial, nascent fulfillment of some of these events when Jerusalem was destroyed in A.D. 70, everything described in the Olivet Discourse will one day literally take place in the *future*.

From all the research I've done on this issue, the most serious options listed here are 1 and 6. Option 1 provides the thrust for this and the previous chapter. Option 6 will provide the emphasis of the next chapter.

Additional Thoughts to Those of Eusebius

The previous chapter drew exclusively from Eusebius and Josephus. I purposefully withheld other evidence from other sources just so that we would hear it from those two historical sources directly. Now, using the same format as the last chapter (with signposts from the Olivet Discourse), let's consider further potential evidences to the idea that the great tribulation of Matthew 24:4-34 may have been fulfilled in A.D. 70.

- **The temple will be demolished so completely that not one stone will be left on another (Matt. 24:2).**

Secular history records that the temple was totally destroyed. Of that there is no doubt. Bible commentator Matthew Henry points out:

> [Jesus] speaks of it as an utter ruin. The temple shall not

> only be stripped, and plundered, and defaced, but utterly demolished and laid waste; *Not one stone shall be left unto another*. Though Titus, when he took the city, did all he could to preserve the temple, yet he could not restrain the enraged soldiers from destroying it utterly; and it was done to that degree, that Turnus Rufus ploughed up the ground on which it had stood.[18]

Remarkably Jesus saw into the future. He knew the temple would not only be razed but also utterly destroyed. Gary DeMar makes another relevant point about the destruction of that holy building:

> The temple that Jesus said would be destroyed is the same temple with the same stones that was pointed out to Jesus by His disciples. No future temple is in view. Jesus gives no indication that He has a future temple in mind. But what if the Jews rebuild the temple? Such a temple will [have] nothing to do with the fulfillment of any part of this prophecy.[19]

Hindsight is always 20/20. Since we know what happened to the temple under the Romans, we often forget how significant it was that Jesus foretold these things. R. C. Sproul observes:

> To first-century Jews it was unthinkable that such catastrophic events as the destruction of the Herodian temple, the devastation of the holy city of Jerusalem, and the dispersion of the Jewish people to the four corners of the earth could take place in the foreseeable future. Such events were eminently not foreseeable, save to one who had information from the omniscient God himself.[20]

- **Many false prophets and false christs will deceive many (Matt. 24:4, 11, 23-26).**

Even in the New Testament, three false messiahs are mentioned by name:

- Theudas (Acts 5:36)
- Judas of Galilee (Acts 5:37)

• Simon Magus (Acts 8:9-11)

St. Jerome wrote that Simon Magus claimed, "I am the Word of God, I am the Comforter, I am Almighty, I am all there is of God"[21] Irenaeus tells us of how Simon claimed to be "the Son of God and the creator of angels."[22] John Calvin notes, "For shortly after Christ's resurrection, there arose imposters, every one of whom professed to be *the Christ*."[23] Another first-century imposter we know of by name is Dositheus, a Samaritan who claimed to be the lawgiver prophesied by Moses.[24]

• **There will be famines (Matt. 24:7).**

In addition to the horrendous famine that took place because of the siege on Jerusalem, we also know of a famine that took place during the reign of Claudius.[25]

• **There will be earthquakes in various places (Matt. 24:7).**

Kik points out that "as to the earthquakes, many are mentioned by writers during a period just previous to 70 A.D. There were earthquakes in Crete, Smyrna, Miletus, Chios, Samos, Laodicea, Hierapolis, Colosse, Campania, Rome, and Judea."[26] Seneca, writing in A.D. 65, complained of the increasing number of earthquakes:

> How often have cities in Asia, how often in Achaia, been laid low by a single shock of earthquake! How many towns in Syria, how many in Macedonia, have been swallowed up! How often has Paphos collapsed! Not infrequently are tidings brought to us of the utter destruction of entire cities.[27]

• **The Gospel will be preached in the whole world to all nations, and then the end will come (Matt. 24:14).**

What about the spread of the Gospel? The spread of the Gospel was phenomenal. Even in the New Testament, we read:

- Acts 2:5: "Now there were staying in Jerusalem God-fearing Jews from every nation under heaven." That chapter goes on to say how a significant number of them accepted the gospel on the day of Pentecost.
- Colossians 1:23: "This is the Gospel that you heard and that has been proclaimed to every creature under heaven, and of which I, Paul, have become a servant."

Gary DeMar concludes that there is "solid Scripture evidence that the words of Jesus were fulfilled in the days of the apostles."[28]

In the first century, the Gospel was preached to the Parthians (an ancient country in West Asia in what is now part of Iran), the Medes (an ancient country in Southwest Asia in the northwest part of modern Iran), the Persians (modern Iran), the Carmanians (Carmania, also spelled as Carmana or Kerman, was an ancient country in what is now part of Iran), the Hyrcanians (an ancient province of Persia), the Bactrians (Bactria was an ancient country of southwest Asia close to the Hindu Kush Mountains), the Magians (a sect of philosophers in Persia), the Scythians, the Sogdians (a province of Persia), the Sacae.

In the first century, the Gospel also spread to India, Egypt, Ethiopia, Mauritania, Britain, Phrygia (an ancient country in west central Asia Minor in what is now Turkey), Armenia,[29] Syria, Spain, Gaul,[30] Pontus, Galatia, Bithynia, Cappadocia, and Asia.[31]

The "end of the ages" is sometimes mentioned in the New Testament. From the perspective of Gary DeMar and others, this means the end of the Jewish age.[32]

Sproul adds this comment about the end: "According to preterists 'the last days' refers to the time between the advent of John the Baptist and the destruction of Jerusalem. This 'eschaton' refers not to a time in the distant future, but to a time that is imminent."[33]

- **"When you see Jerusalem surrounded by armies, you will know that its desolation is near" (Luke 21:20).**
- **When they see the abomination, His followers should then flee and not turn back (Matt. 24:16-20).**

Whether you agree with this Tribulation-as-a-past-event view or not, Jesus played a vital role in saving human lives. He looked into the not-too-distant future and could see what was on the horizon. He told them when they saw the armies surround the city to flee—to get out of town right away. They were not even to go back into their homes to get anything. The Christians took his advice, and thousands of lives were saved. Kik points out, "One of the most remarkable things about the siege of Jerusalem was the miraculous escape of the Christians. It has been estimated that over a million Jews lost their lives in that terrible siege, but not one of them was a Christian."[34]

In his book *Many Infallible Proofs*, A. T. Pierson says this about A.D. 70: "At this crisis, as we learn from church historians of the first century, all the followers of Christ took refuge in the mountains of Pella, beyond the Jordan, and there is no record of one single Christian perishing in the siege!"[35] Posttribulationalist Dave MacPherson adds, "The unbelieving Jews, on the other hand, did not heed the warnings of Matthew 24 or consider themselves the elect but stayed in Jerusalem and were slaughtered by the thousands."[36]

- **"There will be . . . great signs from heaven" (Luke 21:11).**
- **The sun and moon will be darkened. The stars will fall. The heavenly bodies will be shaken (Matt. 24:29).**

As to other signs in the heavens (apart from the unusual ones chronicled by Josephus, which were mentioned in the previous chapter), there were at least two significant comets seen. One appeared in A.D. 60; the other in 66.[37] In his *Asimov's Guide to Halley's Comet*, Isaac Asimov mentions that Halley's Comet flew over Jerusalem in 66. Asimov writes, "The Comet was regarded as an omen predicting the fall of the city to the Romans which actually occurred four years later."[38]

Furthermore, the Jewish nation was destroyed in the last few decades of the first century. Is it possible, asks the preterist, that fact alone could be what Jesus meant in Matthew 24:29?

Immediately after the distress of those days

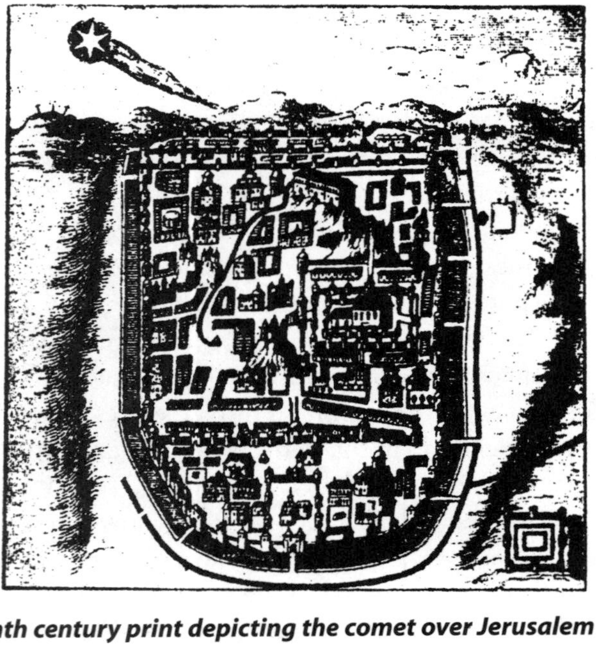

Seventeenth century print depicting the comet over Jerusalem in A.D. 66.

"the sun will be darkened,
and the moon will not give its light;
the stars will fall from the sky,
and the heavenly bodies will be shaken."

The light of the Jewish nation was being extinguished

The light of the Jewish nation was being extinguished at that time (at least for the time being). As we saw in an earlier chapter, Isaiah talks of the sun, moon, stars, and heavenly bodies as being shaken (as a symbol of destruction on the nation of Babylon in Isa. 13:10 and Edom in Isa. 34). The preterist asks, "Is it not possible that Jesus, who was quite familiar with the Old Testament, applied the same imagery to the fall of Jerusalem?"

The Abomination That Causes Desolation

What is the "abomination that causes desolation," which Jesus spoke about? To understand it, some important background information is in order. Daniel had predicted this event. In fact, he spoke of some future evil man who would "pollute the sanctuary of strength, and shall take away the daily sacrifice, and they shall place the abomination that maketh desolate" (Dan. 11:31, KJV). A few centuries after Daniel made this prediction, from 171 to 165 B.C., the Syrian ruler Antiochus Epiphanes took over Israel and stopped the sacrifices in the temple.

Paul Lee Tan writes, "Amidst the carnage created by him and his lieutenant Apollnius in Jerusalem, Antiochus erected the idol Zeus Olympus inside the temple. Hellenization with its concomitant idolatrous worship was foisted on the hapless Jews. A blood bath ensued."[39] It was at that time that Hanukkah was born. The Maccabean family revolted so the Jews could worship again, and they succeeded. They gained their freedom in 142 B.C. and retained it until the Roman conquest of Palestine in 63 B.C.[40]

Less than two centuries later, in A.D. 70, the Roman army devastated Jerusalem and desecrated the temple. The preterists believe the presence of the Roman soldiers in the temple itself was akin to the abomination that causes desolation. Why? J. Marcellus Kik answers, "The Roman Army carried ensigns consisting of eagles and images of the emperor to which divine honors were often paid by the army."[41] The Roman insignia, he points out, was an abomination to the Jews.[42]

First-century historian Josephus writes:

> But now Pilate, the procurator of Judea, removed the army from Caesarea to Jerusalem, to take their winter quarters there, in order to abolish Jewish laws. So he introduced Caesar's effigies, which were upon the ensigns, and brought them into the city; whereas our law forbids us the very making of images; on which account the former procurators were wont to make their entry into the city with such ensigns as had not those ornaments. Pilate was the first who brought those images to Jerusalem, and set them up there.[43]

The protest among the people was so great, however, that ultimately he had to return those abominable signs to Caesarea.

Kik observes, "The word 'abomination' in Daniel has a definite connection with idolatry."[44] When Jesus told His hearers to flee when they hear about "the abomination that causes desolation standing in the holy places," He warned they were to get out of town immediately. They weren't to return for anything. Kik adds, "The housetops of Jerusalem were flat. It was easy to walk from one roof to another."[45]

Premillennialists would obviously not hold to these views. Even if there were foretastes in history of the abomination that causes desolation, such as the evil deeds of Antiochus Epiphanes, they would be just that—*fore*tastes of a *future* event. Thus the premillennialist (especially the dispensational premils) maintain that a future temple needs to be built in order to fulfill prophecy. Premillennialist Robert Van Kampen points out:

> There can be no doubt that the "Abomination of Desolation" is Antichrist, the "beast" of Revelation 12–13, who will have "a mouth speaking arrogant words and blasphemies and authority to act for forty-two months" (Rev. 13:5), the one Paul refers to as the "man of lawlessness," who "takes his seat in the temple of God, displaying himself as being God" (2 Thess. 2:3-4).[46]

"That Day"—A Shift in Thinking at Verse 36?

J. Marcellus Kik and other preterists argue that there's a shift in verse 36 of Matthew 24. Up to this point, they believe Jesus has been talking about His return in A.D. 70 in judgment against Jerusalem. Then He shifts gears to discuss Christ's second coming at the end of time. Spurgeon points out, "There is a manifest change in our Lord's words here, which clearly indicates that they refer to His last great coming to judgment."[47] "That day," argues Kik, refers to the "final day of judgment."[48]

In the first section (Matt. 24:4-35), Jesus gave His followers specific signs to look for:

- When you see the abomination that causes desolation
- When you see signs in the heavens (Luke 21:11)
- When you see the armies surrounding the city, and so on.

Now, however, Jesus talked about how no man knows the hour or the day. Kik believes Jesus shifted His focus by answering the disciples' second question. The first question was about the fall of Jerusalem; the second was about His return and the end of the age. Matthew 24:36–25:46 comprises that second answer.

Contrasting Columns Between the Two Answers

J. Marcellus Kik points out the contrast between what is Christ's answer to the disciples' first question and what is the second. "In the First [Matt. 24:4-35] everything is very specific; in the Second [Matt. 24:36–25:46] everything is general."[49]

To help clarify Kik's point, I have created a graph based largely on his interpretation:

First (Matt. 24:4-35)	Second (Matt. 24:36–25:46)
Specific signs Run away when it happens Christ knows what and when There are warning signs Abnormal times Judgment on earth	Vague signs Be ready at all times Christ did not know the time or hour It will happen unexpectedly Normal times: weddings, buying and selling Judgment in heaven[50]

Preterists believe there are signposts marking the way to A.D. 70, but the Second Coming will occur unexpectedly. Kik writes:

> The unexpectedness and suddenness of the Lord's return are illustrated by a thief coming in the night in Matthew 24:43. The thief gives no sign of his intention to rob. No indication of his coming is given. This exemplifies the coming of the Lord. Unmistakable signs are indicated as to the time of the destruction of Jerusalem but in regard to the second coming of the Lord and the final judgment no definite signs were given.[51]

This view merits further exploration. Obviously, I am greatly in debt to J. Marcellus Kik for his fascinating study on this issue, *An Eschatology of Victory*. The serious scholar of the Second Coming would do well to read this book. Another excellent source providing insight into the preterist view on A.D. 70 is R. C. Sproul's *The Last Days According to Jesus*.

Sproul assembles much of the evidence, primarily from Josephus, of what took place when the Romans destroyed Jerusalem and the temple in A.D. 70. After poring through that history, he concludes:

> Josephus's record of Jerusalem's fall indicates the radical fulfillment of Jesus' prophecy in the Olivet Discourse. As we have seen, preterists see in this event not only the destruction of the temple and its attending circumstances, but also the parousia of Christ in his judgment-coming. Radical preterists see in this even the fulfillment of all New Testament expectations for the return of Christ and for the last things of eschatology. But here we find sharp disagreement among preterists. Moderate preterists, such as those who hold to a postmillennial view of eschatology, insist that though the bulk of the Olivet Discourse was fulfilled in A.D. 70, there still remains a future coming or parousia of Christ.[52]

Problems with the Preterist View

Although many great theologians throughout the history of the

Christian church have held the preterist interpretation, this interpretation obviously leaves many unanswered questions. Some of the obvious questions include:

- How can we say that Jesus returned in the clouds?
- Isn't it a stretch to apply the chariots reportedly seen in the sky (mentioned in the previous chapter) to Christ's return?
- If we say that Jesus came back in A.D. 70, then how do we know He's coming back yet again? The full preterist view takes the position that Christ came back in A.D. 70 and won't come back again. (Surely one can see the consistency of it, but how could that be an orthodox view?)
- Where do we hear about the nation's mourning?
- When are the elect from the four corners called—and what does that mean?

The only way the preterist interpretation could work is if we don't interpret the prophetic language literally. Before Eusebius, Sproul, and others are dismissed, however, keep in mind there are biblical precedents for using symbolic language in prophecy (as was noted in earlier chapters on interpretation and assumptions), especially prophecy dealing with apocalyptic messages, such as the end of the world or the end of the age. Joel Green writes:

> The Hebrew prophets, whether using poetry or not, ordinarily drew images from the real world in their employment of symbolism. Clay in the hand of the potter (Jer. 18:6), the diet of locusts (Joel 2:25), rough country made smooth (Isa. 40:4)—all come from everyday life. The apocalyptic writers, on the other hand, lead us into the realm of fantasy, of images drawn from the creative imagination.[53]

Yet, as we've repeatedly seen, *how* one interprets prophecy is the heart of the controversy. The dispensationalists think the preterist interpretation is flawed because it doesn't take prophecy literally. They ask, Why should Matthew 24:34 (this generation shall not pass away until all these things take place) be taken *literally* by the preterists when that doesn't apply to other verses in the same passage (for example, the Son of Man coming in the clouds, and so on)?

Conclusion

It is important to understand this seemingly radical interpretation. If the Great Tribulation is a *past* event, as preterists maintain, then much of the present-day hype about the end times is off base. It means that arguments about whether Christians will or will not go through the Tribulation are meaningless for the Tribulation has already occurred.

In the next chapter we will examine this issue from the perspective of the futurists. We will look into the question of whether the Great Tribulation will occur in the future.

13

A Future Event?

The Bible clearly warns us that there is coming a time of trouble or tribulation for the whole world.[1]

—Ed Hindson

In the last two chapters, we explored the seemingly radical but centuries-old view that the great tribulation described in the Olivet Discourse already occurred in A.D. 70. Now we want to explore the view that is popular today and that asserts the Great Tribulation is a future event.

Some key elements are believed to herald Christ's imminent return. (Note that these include a few thoughts from other Scriptures as well as the Olivet Discourse because premillennialists will often cross-reference these passages for the combined effect.) Specifically, we will look at such signs as:

- The reestablishment of Israel as a nation
- The worldwide harvest of souls
- The rise of false Christs and cults
- Wars and rumors of wars
- Famines and earthquakes and signs in the sky
- The coming one-world government
- Widespread religious apostasy
- Technological advances that prepare for the mark of the Beast
- Rebellion in the last days

Pick up virtually any popular book on the end times today, and you often find a litany of examples that parallel our present circumstances with the coming Great Tribulation. Is planet earth nearing the end? You'd certainly think so if you were of the premillennial persuasion. According to this perspective, there are many events and trends in our times that seem to be accelerating the end to come. Because of the belief that Christ will return soon, perhaps while *we're* alive, premillennialist William T. James believes, "You and I are privileged to be living at the most exciting time in the history of the human race."[2]

Just to get a clear view of the type of Tribulation period we're talking about, let's look at the statements of dispensationalist Robert Van Kampen:

> Those who hold to the premillennial return of Christ also agree that just prior to the thousand-year reign of Christ there will be a seven-year period of trouble on earth, beginning mildly and increasing in intensity as this period progresses. This period is referred to, in part, by Christ in His Olivet Discourse recorded in the book of Matthew (24:3-31), described in more detail in the final chapters of the prophetic book of Daniel (11:36-12:13), and fleshed out in great detail by John in the book of Revelation. This final, seven-year period of time is normally referred to by teachers of eschatology as the *tribulation period*.[3]

Van Kampen provides the following details of what he believes is the coming tribulation:

> The seven-year tribulation period will begin when this man who becomes Antichrist makes a seven-year treaty with Israel, who will, once again, be living in her own homeland when the treaty is signed (Dan. 9:27). Three-and-a-half years later, those who refuse to worship Antichrist or refuse to take his mark (666) will become the targets of his severe persecution, a persecution unlike any the elect of God has ever known. Antichrist's unprecedented persecution of the elect of God (Matt. 24:21) and the nation of Israel (Dan. 12:1), which initiates the final half of the seven-year tribulation period, is referred to as a time of *great tribulation*, the term Christ specifically gives to this time of intense persecution in His Olivet Discourse to His disciples (Matt. 24:21).[4]

This summary represents well today's popular teaching on the Great Tribulation.

Was A.D. 70 Possibly a Prototype of Things to Come?

Before we delve fully into the Great Tribulation as a future event, let's touch on another view (which is usually presented as a variation of the

Tribulation-as-future view). In addition to the two major views—that the Tribulation is a past event or a future event—is the belief that A.D. 70 was a foreshadow, a foretaste of the really Great Tribulation to come.

This view holds that the things Jesus predicted *began* within their lifetime but were not completely fulfilled. Bible commentators Jamieson, Fausset, and Brown say this about the Olivet Discourse (specifically Matt. 24:34):

> Whether we take this to mean that the whole would be fulfilled within the limits of the generation then current, or, according to a usual way of speaking, that the generation then existing would not pass away without seeing a *begun* fulfillment of this prediction, the facts entirely correspond. For either the whole was fulfilled in the destruction accomplished by Titus, as many think; or, if we stretch it out, according to others, till the thorough dispersion of the Jews, a little later, under Adrian [Hadrian], every requirement of our Lord's words seems to be met.[5]

Even Scofield, who wrote the dispensational Bible, says (in the context of Luke 21):

> Two sieges of Jerusalem are in view in that discourse. Luke 21:20-24 refers to the siege by Titus, A.D. 70, when the city was taken, and verse 24 literally fulfilled. But that siege and its horrors but adumbrate the final siege at the end of the this age, in which the "great tribulation" culminates. At that time the city will be taken, but delivered by the glorious appearing of the Lord.[6]

Even the moderate preterist might partially agree with this position, although none I know of would think that a future temple was to be built, which they certainly wouldn't see the need for.

Israel—God's Timeclock?

Many Christians in our day often view the rebirth of Israel as a nation in 1948 as the most significant event to signal the imminent return of

Christ. For instance, Hal Lindsey writes in *The Late Great Planet Earth*, "Since the restoration of Israel as a nation in 1948, we have lived in the most significant period of prophetic history."[7]

Jesus Himself said, "Jerusalem will be trampled on by the Gentiles until the times of the Gentiles are fulfilled" (Luke 21:24). Because Jerusalem is now finally back in Jewish hands after nearly twenty centuries, the futurists contend the end is near.

In his most recent book, *Planet Earth: The Final Chapter*, Hal Lindsey further writes, "The most certain proof that we are living out the final chapter of human history can be found in the existence of a tiny country in the Middle East."[8] He adds:

> When the six-pointed Star of David ascended for the first time over the Jewish ancestral homeland, the countdown to the end of the present age had begun. "Now learn this parable from the fig tree: When its branch has already become tender and puts forth leaves, you know that summer is near. So you also, when you see all these things [i.e., the predicted signs], know that it is near—at the very doors. Assuredly, I say to you, this generation [that sees the signs] will by no means pass away till all these things are fulfilled. Heaven and earth will pass away, but My words will by no means pass away." . . . There can be no mistake about it, we are now living in the generation of "the fig tree." We are living in the generation that will witness the climactic fulfillment of prophecy—the Rapture of the Church followed by a global holocaust that will be ended by the visible return of Jesus Christ to earth.[9]

Pick up virtually any book on the end times from a premillennial dispensational view, and you will immediately note the conviction that Israel becoming a nation in 1948 is the single most important "sign of the times." Here's another quote reflecting that belief. In the book he edited called *Foreshocks of Antichrist*, William T. James writes:

> God's prophetic clock ticks in time-bomb fashion, counting down to that apocalypse-initiating moment

> when earth's final and most terrible tyrant will give the world the peace that destroys.
>
> Israel, and Jerusalem in particular, which God's prophet foretold will become a "cup of trembling" (Zech. 12:2) for the whole world during the last seven years of this earth age, already command the attention of top-level politicians, military planners, economists, sociologists, and religionists of our time.[10]

The prophetic clock ticks because Israel was restored as a nation.

Premillennialist Tim LaHaye calls Israel's regathering the "Super Sign" of Christ's return.[11] He believes World War I played a critical role in the establishment of Israel as a nation. During that war, in 1917, the Balfour Declaration, which paved the way for Israel's rebirth as a nation, was signed. LaHaye notes:

> The sign was not wars, but a most significant war, which was World War I, with its accompanying phenomena of famines, pestilences, and earthquakes. Out of the fulfillment of this sign, Israel started going back into the land, leading many prophecy scholars to conclude that God's prophetic clock began ticking again. Personally, I look on that period, 1917–1948, as God winding His clock.[12]

They further maintain that the clock began ticking again in 1948 when Israel was reborn. The issue of Israel is so important that we have an entire chapter devoted to it later.

The Worldwide Harvest

Another sign of the times that we are living in the last days is the spread of the Gospel around the globe. Jesus said, "This gospel of the kingdom will be preached in the whole world as a testimony to all nations, and then the end will come" (Matt. 24:14). Did you know that today, like never before, hundreds of thousands of people are being added to Christ's kingdom? Worldwide this is a great time of harvest. More Muslims have come to know Jesus in the last ten years than in the previous ten centuries.[13] In fact, many Muslims are having dreams wherein they see the Lord. Later they hear about Jesus and are converted.

Worldwide this is an *incredible* time of harvest. As Ralph Reed, founding director of the Christian Coalition, once wrote, "How will our times be viewed by history? I believe these days will be remembered as a time of remarkable spiritual awakening. The greatest revival of religion in modern times is breaking out across the globe."[14] We don't often think about this spiritual awakening because so much of this growth is happening in other countries, especially Third World countries, that are not hardened to the Christian message like so many countries in the West today.

Far more human beings have seen the movie Jesus than have seen any other movie

Consider just one movement alone, the Jesus Film Project. Do you realize that far more human beings have seen the movie *Jesus*, which is faithfully based on the Gospel of Luke, than have seen any other movie? Probably three times more than even the most screened movies in history, including *Titanic*, *E.T.*, or *Gone with the Wind*. More than 1.6 billion human beings—that's nearing one-third of the entire population of the world—have now seen this film. As a result of having seen this movie, millions have professed faith in Jesus.

In recent years we've heard about the horrendous persecution of Christians in many lands. On average, each year 160,000 Christians are martyred for their faith,[15] according to Dr. David Barrett, who I believe is the best church statistician today. Yet Dr. Barrett is also quick to point out that the reason for the astounding rise in martyrdom in our time is the growth of Christianity in our time. He says on average—from the days of the Roman Colosseum to the present-day killing fields in Sudan—one out of every two hundred Christians can expect to be martyred for his faith. During peacetime, during wartime. The bottom line is: at the present time, Christianity is bursting at the seams around the world. That's why we hear more and more about the persecuted church.

Therefore, it would seem very much as if we are witnessing in our day the fulfillment of Christ's statement in the Synoptic Gospels (Matthew, Mark, and Luke) that "the gospel is to be preached into all the world and then shall the end come." And the momentum for the spread of the Gospel seems to continue.

The Rise of False Messiahs

Jesus warned us that false christs would rise up. In our day, many false cults have arisen. Is that also an indication that these are the last days? On the other hand, there has always been a struggle with false doctrine. Paul even warned the early church of wolves in their own midst. Nevertheless, doesn't it seem to be worse in our day?

Paul Lee Tan writes, "There have been over 1,100 religious leaders in different parts of the world in the last fifty years who have claimed to be Christ and the savior of the world. Most of these false Christs have risen in Africa, in India or in the Orient and have spread into the West."[16]

Here are some insights from D. James Kennedy on the rise of the cults in our day:

> Is it hard for you to believe that 15 million people [in the U.S.] are on the fringes of Christianity, and yet have believed lies and know not Christ? Well, let me list for you just a few of the cults in existence today: The Jehovah Witnesses, the Christian Scientists, the Church of the Latter Day Saints (Mormonism), the Theosophical Society, the Church of the New Jerusalem, the Unity School of Christianity, the Unitarian church, the Alamo Christian Foundation, the Unification Church (Moonies), and the Way.[17]

And, of course, this list is by no means exhaustive.

We've seen mass suicides in the Jonestown massacre and in the Heaven's Gate cult. There was also David Koresh and the Branch Davidians. While it may be a matter of controversy whether or not they started the fire from within their compound that consumed them, it is a given that Koresh was a false christ. Interestingly, that cult went off the deep end years before because of an unbalanced emphasis on what? The end times. (We're back to Calvin's comment, "The study of prophecy either finds a man crazy, or it leaves him so.")

Although there are differences between competing cults, they all have at least one thing in common. They deny the eternal deity of Jesus Christ. They stumble on Him. Thus, in a very real sense, they reflect the *spirit* of "antichrist," which John talked about: "Who is the liar? It is the man who denies that Jesus is the Christ. Such a man is the antichrist—he denies the Father and the Son" (1 John 2:22). Thus all cults are in cahoots with the Antichrist (including the one to come, assuming there is a literal one to come).

The late eminent scholar Dr. Walter Martin, author of *The Kingdom of the Cults*, observed that in addition to denying the divinity of Christ, all cults disavow salvation by grace, justification by faith, and the Trinity. He further noted that virtually all cults have the following characteristics in common. They have a central figure who takes control of people's minds, and they have a central figure whose word or interpretation of the Bible is considered to be more important than the Bible. Tragically, 70 to 80 percent of all cult members came out of *professing* church backgrounds—former Baptists, Lutherans, Presbyterians, and so on.[18]

In our day, cults and interest in the occult seem to proliferate. With the New Age and disillusionment with the materialistic worldview, there is a new acceptance of supernatural phenomena. Palm readers have set up shop on main street. Interest in the occult seems to be growing all the time. Tim LaHaye adds, "There have always been cults and demon activity, but nothing in modern history is like today, and it is increasing."[19]

Spiritual Deception

In addition to the rise of cults, there has been a great deal of spiritual deception. At the time of World War II, Christianity was still very strong both in North America and much of Europe. Today the picture is quite different. We have seen a disillusionment of materialism, both in society in general and in the highest academic circles. From the universities to Saturday morning cartoons, we see a new interest in spirituality. There are more angels and other spiritual beings, like fairies and elves, in the stores than ever before. Stories of people meeting spiritual beings and having encounters with them are commonplace. The occult has made incredible inroads through some heavy strands of rock music and through vampire cults and the like. This whole new spiritual milieu can well open up the stage for the religion of the Antichrist.

Wars and Rumors of Wars

We've certainly had wars and rumors of wars in our day. Hal Lindsey asks, "War and more war. Has there ever been a time when the potential for self-destruction was as great as it is today?"[20]

At any given time, there are wars and rumors of wars throughout the globe. A war is defined as being an armed conflict, involving at least one government, and killing at least one thousand people a year. The Lentz Peace Research Institute of St. Louis reported that during the 1980s, there were more wars than there had been in the 1970s. They reported that during that decade, forty-two wars raged at various hot spots around our globe, killing more than five million people (either from direct killing or indirect fallout, such as famines). That comes down to about 120,000 people (62 percent of them civilians.) killed on average per each war. In the 1990s, we know that many have died in just the Gulf War (not Americans) and in Rwanda alone. Conflicts continue in Kosovo, Bosnia, Sudan, and so on.

Gustave Valbert calculated war statistics from previous centuries. He found that from 1496 B.C. to A.D. 1861, there were 3,130 years of war out of 3,358, and only 227 years of peace.[21] That means during 93 percent of recorded history there has been war, and only 7 percent of the time has there been peace. And then came the bloody twentieth century. The eminent British historian Paul Johnson points out that the twentieth century state has "proved itself the great killer of all time."[22]

Add to this the threat of nuclear war. When President John F. Kennedy addressed the United Nations on September 25, 1961, he said, "Today, every inhabitant of this planet must contemplate the day when it may no longer be habitable. Every man, woman, and child lives under a nuclear sword of Damocles, hanging by the slenderest of threads, capable of being cut at any moment by accident, miscalculation, or madness. The weapons of war must be abolished before they abolish us."[23] Tim LaHaye adds, "For the first time in human history man has the potential of destroying himself from the face of the earth."[24] Wars and rumors of wars indicate to futurists that we're closer to the end.

Famines, Earthquakes, and Signs in the Heavens

Jesus said, "There will be famines and earthquakes in various places" (Matt. 24:7). This has always been true, has it not? The situation, however, appears to be getting worse.

The famines experienced in the twentieth century have been the worst in recorded history. It's estimated that 27 million people starved to death in the wake of World War I and the revolutions that followed it.[25]

The communists bear a large responsibility for famines in the twentieth century.[26] For example, consider the 3.5 to 8 million (no one knows the exact number) Ukrainians whom Stalin starved to death during the 1930s to force them to conform to communism.

There is also famine in North Korea. Many are currently at a point of stunted growth and death. There again communism bears much of the blame for this starvation.

Even now many people in Sudan are experiencing widespread hunger. While nature may play a role in this tragedy, the militant Islamic regime in charge of that country bears much of the responsibility for that famine. The Arabs in northern Sudan have attempted to force their militant strand of Islam on the rest of the country, including the millions of Christians and animists in the south. As a result, some two million people (in the Christian regions) are currently at risk of starvation.

Meanwhile, it seems as if we're constantly hearing about earthquakes, and it would appear they are increasing in frequency and intensity. J. R. Church writes, "The twentieth century is proving to be the century for more earthquakes than ever before. . . . Out of the 13 most devastating earthquakes, ten have occurred in this century."[27]

Yet keep in mind that earthquakes have been a common phenomenon on our planet, presumably since the Fall. Count F. Montessus de Ballore, a Frenchman, studied earthquakes from 1885 to 1922. In his research, he found that there had been 171,434 earthquakes from antiquity to his time.[28]

Today's Technology

While many of the signs (wars, famines, and earthquakes) we've just looked at have occurred often in previous centuries—including the first century of the Christian era—there are some aspects of our age that make our period different from previous times. One of these is our burgeoning scientific and technological advancements. What we have witnessed in the twentieth century is absolutely astonishing! Life today is vastly different from life lived in the past. Consider the fact that the people living in the nineteenth century had more in common with people living two thousand years ago than they have with us. We experience those benefits everyday. The potential bad side is that our modern technology could pave the way for complete dominance over life.

We hear about microchips now being implanted in dogs to keep track of them. Could they one day be implanted in the hand or the forehead of a person? The Beast in Revelation "forced everyone, small and great, rich and poor, free and slave, to receive a mark on his right hand or on his forehead, so that no one could buy or sell unless he had the mark, which is the name of the beast or the number of his name" (Rev. 13:16-17). Many futurists caution that our advanced technology, which provides us with many wonderful things, could also be used to ultimately usher in the end.

One World Government

When President Bush announced to the world his push for a "new world order," many Christians sat up and took notice, especially premillennial dispensationalists. Was this the beginning of the end?

More and more people are thinking as global citizens. Our worldwide communications have accelerated. Large international organizations are common today, such as the U.N. or the International Monetary Fund. In some cases, their policies even have priority over the internal affairs of individual nations. Both a united Europe and a world government could be a logical next step.

Globally, we are much more interdependent both politically and economically than ever before. A crisis in one part of the world can quickly spark a worldwide, internationally charged situation.

Futurists believe the Beast of Revelation 13—that is, the Antichrist—will one day have worldwide control. John wrote, "He was given power to make war against the saints and to conquer them. And he was given authority over every tribe, people, language and nation" (Rev. 13:7). Thus, while the world moves toward becoming a "global village," the stage is being set for the rise of the Antichrist. Premillennialist Grant Jeffrey writes, "Despite the rise and fall of countless empires throughout history, there has never been a world government during thousands of years of human history."[29] Yet in the last days, argues Jeffrey and other premillennialists, it will be different. "For the first time in history, one man the future Antichrist, will have power 'over all kindreds, and tongues, and nations.'"[30]

Rebellion in the Last Days

Another potential sign that we are living in the last days is the increase of wickedness. Note what Paul wrote to Timothy:

> But mark this: There will be terrible times in the last days. People will be lovers of themselves, lovers of money, boastful, proud, abusive, disobedient to their parents, ungrateful, unholy, without love, unforgiving, slanderous, without self-control, brutal, not lovers of the good, treacherous, rash, conceited, lovers of pleasure rather than lovers of God—having a form of godliness but denying its power. Have nothing to do with them.
>
> They are the kind who worm their way into homes and gain control over weak-willed women, who are loaded down with sins and are swayed by all kinds of evil desires, always learning but never able to acknowledge the truth. Just as Jannes and Jambres opposed Moses, so also these men oppose the truth—men of depraved minds, who, as far as the faith is concerned, are rejected. But they will not get very far because, as in the case of those men, their folly will be clear to everyone (2 Tim. 3:1-9).

We see the evidence of a culture in rebellion against God every day

Maybe there have always been people like that, but as we approach what premillennialists believe to be the end, we will see more and more evil. We don't have to add any commentary to this passage. We see the evidence of a culture in rebellion against God every day. We see it in living color, in prime time, from coast to coast. It sounds as though the Apostle Paul was reading today's newspaper, watching the hottest new TV shows, or glancing at glossy magazines when he penned those words.

Premillennialist William T. James points out, "God's prophetic Word tells us plainly that the generation alive at the time of the coming of the Son of Man (Jesus Christ) will be indulging in precisely the same debasing activities as were the people alive just before the flood struck during Noah's day (read Genesis 6 and 7)."[31]

Putting It All Together

Put all these factors together, declare the futurists, beginning with the assumption that prophecy is to be taken literally, and voilà: Ours is the generation that will probably see Christ's return! No date can be given, but these are the last days. The signs pointing to it are numerous—all the details of the last two chapters notwithstanding.

Consider what William T. James, editor of *Foreshocks of the Antichrist*, has to say:

> Electrifying events bombard today's world with shock after shock that would have paralyzed previous generations with astonishment and fear. Yet we go about our daily lives tuning out all but the most shattering reports. The planet quakes both literally and figuratively while we rush toward what looks like an intensely stormy future. . . . The *European Union* awaits the *prince that shall come*, who will take the new Roman Empire of prophecy to world domination. . . . We find ourselves in truly momentous times. This generation regularly witnesses occurrences remarkably similar to those prophesied for the end of this earth age. If that is so, we stand on the launching pad poised to take part in a stupendous event: *the rapture*—that lightning-quick moment when Jesus Christ shouts to those saved during this church age, "COME UP HERE!" (Revelation 4:1).[32]

"Staggering Odds"

Grant Jeffrey did some calculations of the odds of many end-times prophecies being fulfilled at one particular time, and he found the odds staggering. The types of prophecies he's talking about include (in his own words and with his own numbering):

1. The Rebirth of Israel[33]
2. The Miraculous Restoration of the Hebrew Language[34]
3. Ancient Biblical Predictions about the Present Arab-Israeli Conflict[35]
4. The Return of the Ethiopian Jews to Israel in 1991[36]

5. The Astonishing Fertility of Israel[37]
6. Israel's Plans to Rebuild the Temple[38]
7. The Oil of Anointing[39]
8. Vessels for the Future Temple Worship[40]
9. The Revival of the Roman Empire[41] [He and other dispensationalists see the European Union fulfilling that role.]
10. The Rebuilding of Babylon[42] [under Saddam Hussein]
11. One World Government[43]
12. Preparations for the Mark of the Beast[44]
13. Worldwide Television Communications[45]
14. Knowledge and Travel Shall Increase in the Last Days[46]
15. Armies Preparing for the Battle of Armageddon[47]
16. God's Warning to Those Who Destroy the Earth[48]
17. A Military Highway across Asia and the Drying Up of the Euphrates River[49]

Jeffrey sees one sign after another being fulfilled in our days. What are the odds that all these events could happen in just *one* particular generation? He commences with the premise that a generation is forty years. So there have been fifty generations from the life of Jesus to our generation. "Therefore, the odds are 1 chance in 50 that any one of these specific prophecies will occur by coincidence in our lifetime."[50] He calculates that for any one generation to have five such prophecies fulfilled, the odds are 1 in 312.5 million.[51] For ten such prophecies, the odds are 1 in 97,500 trillion.[52] Therefore, he concludes, ". . . the staggering odds against these predictions occurring in our generation by coincidence strongly suggests that Jesus Christ will return to earth *in our lifetime*."[53] Because of such overwhelming evidence, premillennialist William T. James writes, "Foreshocks of the coming Antichrist are everywhere."[54]

The Tribulation

Understandably, the dispensationalists hold that the Tribulation is coming soon. Yet the question emerges: Will Christians go through it? We will deal with that in a later chapter. Nevertheless, I want to touch on one point because it relates to the Olivet Discourse. Matthew 24, Mark 13, and Luke 21 are the most important passages on the end times to Bible scholars; even scholars who disagree with one another would affirm that. Premillennialist Robert Van Kampen writes, "Thus, it is

Christ Himself who is responsible for giving His saints the most specific and significant prophecy concerning the end times—including an overview of these events in the Olivet Discourse, the time frame in which these events will occur in the book of Daniel, and the details concerning these events in the book of Revelation."[55]

This is an illuminating point. It helps further clarify the premillennial dispensational view on biblical prophecy. One passage provides the overview of coming events, another, the time frame, and yet another, the details. Thus we see again and again that virtually any topic on the end times, including whether the Tribulation is a past or future event, ultimately boils down to the principles of interpretation of prophecies in the Bible.

"We're Living in the Last Days!"

Many today point to what has just been related and state, "See! This is it! We're living in the last days!" Others, however, caution us because these things have happened before. In previous generations Christians have misread the signs and so misled their followers. Joel Green notes, "From the signs of the end given by Jesus, we are unable to construct an exact time-line leading up to the end, nor can we calculate the time of the end itself. All we can say is that we live in the end times, just as every Christian generation has."[56]

Conclusion

Regardless of one's understanding of the end times, it would seem Jesus' *unambiguous* intention was that we all should watch and wait for Him, that we should be ready, and that we should live our lives in such a way that we would not be embarrassed at His appearing.

With uncertain times ahead of us, with all the global threats to peace and prosperity, with the rise of fierce anti-Christian persecution worldwide, and with evil often winning the day in our era, it's important for us to know about the future. What will the millennium be like? What does it mean for our future? Did the prophet Daniel really foretell things that are coming true in our lifetime? And what about the Antichrist? Let's examine these key issues one after another and discover how they will impact our future.

Part Four

Issue by Issue

14

The Millennium

The lion may lay with the lamb, but the lamb won't get much sleep.

—Woody Allen

Imagine our world where the effects of sin have been reversed. Imagine a world where nature is no longer at war with itself. Imagine a world where death no longer holds the terrible threat it now retains. Imagine a world where there is no hostility. Yet, in contrast with John Lennon's secular vision, imagine a world blessed with a pure and undefiled religion and a world where the Christian ideal of "love thy neighbor" is finally put into widespread practice. Imagine a world under control of one person—and that person is none other than Jesus Christ Himself. In short, imagine the Millennium—at least that of historic and dispensational premillennialists and, to a lesser degree, that of the postmillennialists.

The Bible talks about a thousand-year period during which Christ reigns on earth. Is this a literal time period yet to come? Is it a literal period in effect now—conditional upon our obedience to the commands of Christ? Is this a figurative—that is, a symbolic—time we are now in? In this chapter, we will contrast different views on the Millennium.

What Is the Millennium?

One passage in Revelation is our only *direct* source on the Millennium. Revelation 20 tells us about the thousand years. It reads:

> And I saw an angel coming down out of heaven, having the key to the Abyss and holding in his hand a great chain. He seized the dragon, that ancient serpent, who is the devil, or Satan, and bound him for a thousand years. He threw him into the Abyss, and locked and sealed it over him, to keep him from deceiving the nations any more until the thousand years were ended. After that, he must be set free for a short time.

> I saw thrones on which were seated those who had been given authority to judge. And I saw the souls of those who had been beheaded because of their testimony for Jesus and because of the word of God. They had not worshiped the beast or his image and had not received his mark on their foreheads or their hands. They came to life and reigned with Christ a thousand years. (The rest of the dead did not come to life until the thousand years were ended.) This is the first resurrection. Blessed and holy are those who have part in the first resurrection. The second death has no power over them, but they will be priests of God and of Christ and will reign with him for a thousand years (Rev. 20:1-6).

Jay Adams sums it all up quite succinctly: "Negatively, the 1,000 years represents the binding of Satan. Positively, they represent the reign of the martyrs with Christ over his kingdom."[1]

What facts can be gleaned here?

- An angel from heaven imprisons Satan and binds him for a thousand years.
- Thus the Devil can't deceive the nations any more until the thousand years are up.
- At the end of that period, he is let loose for a short time.
- Meanwhile, the souls of martyrs live and reign with Christ during that time.
- This is "the first resurrection."
- The second death has no power over the saints ruling with Christ.

What about the other elements concerning the Millennium described at the start of this chapter? The answer to this question will be explored in depth.

Whole Theological Constructs

Theologian Philip Hughes points out that although this is the only passage dealing with the issue, whole theological constructs have been built around it. Hughes states:

> Yet despite the problems it presents, and although this is

> the only place in Scripture where this period of a thousand years is mentioned, it has frequently been treated as a key to the understanding of other prophetic passages, particularly in the Old Testament, or as a foundation on which elaborate eschatological superstructures have been built.[2]

Postmillennialist Loraine Boettner adds:

> Sound exegesis requires that the obscure passages of Scripture be read in the light of the clearer ones, and not *vice versa*. . . . Even the literal interpretation of the Premillenarians is not consistently literal, for it makes the chains in verse 1 and consequently also the binding in verse 2 figurative, often conceives of the thousand years as a long but undefined period, and changes the souls of verse 4 into resurrection saints.[3]

Premillennial dispensationalist Jack Van Impe strongly disagrees. He maintains that those who hold such positions are in opposition to the plain teaching of Scripture. In his book *Revelation Revealed*, he writes:

> Those who oppose the teaching of a literal one-thousand year reign of Christ upon earth are in direct opposition to the Word of God! Their claim that the doctrine is dangerously built on a single chapter of the Bible proves that they are not good students of God's Holy Word, for many passages both teach and reflect this truth. Let's investigate.
>
> First of all, if Israel has no future, dozens of Old Testament prophecies immediately go down the drain.[4]

Van Impe goes on to list a litany of messianic prophecies in the Old Testament. They include:

- The wolf shall lie with the lamb (Isa. 11:6).
- None shall be afraid (Micah 4:4).
- A king shall reign in righteousness (Isa. 32:1).
- "And in the days of these kings shall the God of heaven set up a king-

dom, which shall never be destroyed . . . and it shall stand for ever" (Dan. 2:44, KJV).[5]

- The Lord shall come to His temple (Mal. 3:1).

And so on.[6]

Therefore, concludes Dr. Van Impe, "Only the spiritually blind can deny the fact of a literal Millennium. Only the willfully ignorant can claim that the teaching is based on just one chapter of the Bible."[7]

Amillennialist Jay Adams takes issue with that idea. In Van Impe's quote, the "they" he refers to are an emerging brand of theologians who began as premillennialists and moved to a nonmillenarian perspective. Adams counts himself as one such theologian:

> In fact, apart from the twentieth chapter of Revelation, they wonder how anyone could come to the premillennial viewpoint at all. They freely admit that this one chapter is the sole basis for their belief. They have begun to demand that certain assumptions be proved. They ask, for instance, where biblical warrant may be found for identifying scores of Old Testament prophecies with the 1000-year period mentioned (but not described) in Revelation 20. They no longer can agree to the exploded "postponement theory," and having rejected that pillar of the dispensational system for the first time, they are able to see that Daniel's seventieth week (Daniel 9) is not parenthetically separated from the other sixty-nine by the church age, but was fulfilled in the time of Christ. They have carefully restudied Matthew 24 and the parallel passages in the other Gospels (especially in Luke 21) and now are convinced that much of what they once referred to as a "great tribulation" immediately prior to the second coming, rightly pertains to the destruction of Jerusalem in 70 A.D. With this, the entire matter of a future tribulation and Antichrist is brought into question. The futurist view of the Apocalypse, which asserts that the bulk of the book concerns a seven-year tribulation period at the close of this age, is so closely related to this latter point that it likewise must be submitted to thoughtful re-examination.[8]

It seems we're back to Ben Franklin: Yes, it is. No, it's not.

Here's a one-sentence summary from postmil Loraine Boettner on the idea of a nonliteral millennium: "Postmillennialists set forth a spiritual Kingdom in the hearts of men."[9] That's essentially what the Millennium means to him. It means that just like that mustard seed of faith, Christianity has begun to spread around the world. Thus the Millennium began at the time the church began. Historically, many have thought that to be the case. That explains what happened at the turn of the last Millennium. Note that in A.D. 999, thousands crammed into St. Peter's in Rome, awaiting the end of the world—since one thousand years had passed from the time Jesus had come to earth.

Three Different Views on the Millennium

As have already been discussed, there are basically three different views on the Millennium:

- (1) Premillennialism
  - (A) Dispensationalists
  - (B) Historic premillennialists
- (2) Amillennialists
- (3) Postmillennialists

Distinction Between Two Types of Premillennialists

An important distinction should again be made between the two major schools of premillennialists. There are those who believe the literal Millennium will be ushered in after the Tribulation. They do not believe in the secret Rapture of the church (which again is a relatively new view). Historic premillennialists, otherwise known as chiliasts, would include Irenaeus, Justin Martyr, and Tertullian. Historic premillennialists of modern times would include Donald Grey Barnhouse, J. Barton Payne, and George Eldon Ladd.[10] Another term for historic premillennialism is posttribulational premillennialism. John Calvin had a low view of this early form of premillennialism: "Not long after [the days of Paul] arose the chiliasts, who limited the reign of Christ to a thousand years. Their fiction is too puerile [childish] to deserve refutation."[11]

Dispensationalist Paul Lee Tan says, "In general, dispensational premillennialists are the most consistent in the literal interpretation of prophecy; covenant [historic] premillennialists less so; postmillennialists much less so; and amillennialists the least so."[12]

The more popular form of premillennialism is the dispensational variety. It is championed by such well-known writers as Hal Lindsey, John Walvoord, C. I. Scofield, Gleason Archer, Charles C. Ryrie, Dwight Pentecost, and Norman Geisler.[13] This elaborate view holds that the church is secretly raptured, then comes the Tribulation, and so on. Dispensationalism is the same as pretribulational premillennialism.

Amillennialism Versus Postmillennialism

There is not uniformity in how postmillennialism and amillennialism are defined or differentiated, although it would be safe to say neither holds to a literal thousand-year Millennium. These two schools of thought sometimes get lumped together, though different writers will use the terms differently from other writers. This only adds to the confusion that exists in the realm of end-times writings. For example, was St. Augustine an amillennialist or a postmillennialist? R. C. Sproul assigns him to the postmil camp.[14] Yet premillennialists Ice and Demy put him in the amil camp. They say he "abandoned premillennialism in favor of amillennialism."[15] Meanwhile, *The New International Dictionary of the Christian Church* defines postmillennialism as "an optimistic type of theology which predicts a 'golden age,' a Christianized millennium of predominantly human achievement before the Second Advent and the subsequent eternal realm."[16] The term was popularized by the controversial British theologian and "erudite clergyman," Daniel Whitby (1638–1726).[17]

The best way to summarize the postmillennial view in a word would be: optimism. It is the view that as the Gospel goes forth into all the world, Christianity will ultimately prevail, not in creating a perfect world, but a vastly improved one. Gary North holds to this view; he is the publisher of many books of a Christian Reconstructionist nature. First, he defines that term: "We who call ourselves Christian Reconstructionists proclaim a future worldwide revival and the steady, voluntary submission of people to God's law."[18] That statement sums up a major strand in postmillennial thinking—we win in the end (on earth, as well as in heaven). He clarifies this view even further: "We believe in revival. We believe in evangelism and foreign missions. So do all Christians. But we Reconstructionists have this unique outlook:

we believe that these gospel efforts will be successful in history."[19]

Postmillennialists, in the words of Loraine Boettner, who hold that position, believe "the Kingdom of God is now being extended in the world through the preaching of the Gospel . . ."[20]

Meanwhile, postmillennialists, writes *The New International Dictionary of the Christian Church*, see "the return of Christ as taking place after the millennium, which may be a literal 'golden age' on earth, or which may be symbolic of the first triumph of the Gospel, in this age."[21] In other words, some postmillennialists envision a literal Millennium yet to come—I say yet to come because there's been no literal Millennium as yet.

The other group of postmillennialists could easily be lumped in with amillennialists. About the latter group, *The New International Dictionary of the Christian Church* says, "They see the Revelation teaching as standing for the present age, the whole period between the ministry of Jesus on earth and His second coming."[22] It's safe to say in the nonmillenarian camp the differing positions are not always labeled correctly (usually by nonmillenarians, I might add).

Here are some of the theologians R. C. Sproul puts in the postmillennial camp: Eusebius, Athanasius, Augustine, John Calvin, Jonathan Edwards, J. Gresham Machen, and J. Marcellus Kik.[23] Meanwhile, Sproul puts the following in the amillennial camp: Jay Adams, G. C. Berkouwer, Louis Berkhof, Anthony Hoekema, and Abraham Kuyper.[24]

Amillennialism: No Millennium Per Se

When you read various books on the end times, what one writer has in mind when he pens the word "amillennialist" may be quite different from what another writer has in mind with the same word.

What exactly is amillennialism? It depends on who you ask. It certainly does not hold to a literal Millennium. As to this present age being the Millennium, I believe most would answer in the affirmative. Again, it depends on whom you ask. Postmillennialist Loraine Boettner says, "Amillennialism, too, differs from Postmillennialism in that it holds that the world is not to be Christianized before the end comes, that the world will in fact continue much as it now is, with a parallel and continuous development of both good and evil, of the Kingdom of God and the kingdom of Satan."[25] Again, the parable of the wheat and tares is the main model for the amillennialist.

On the other hand, Richard Kyle, author of *The Last Days Are Here Again*, states:

> For much of Christian history, amillennialism has been the predominate view. Amillennialists do not interpret Revelation 20 literally—in their opinion, it symbolizes certain present realities. Thus they do not believe that Christ will establish a literal earthly rule before the judgment. Rather, the glorious new heaven and earth will immediately follow the present dispensation of the kingdom of God.[26]

It's safe to say this about amillennialism versus postmillennialism:

- Neither holds to a literal Millennium—with the rare exception of some insignificant postmillennialists in the past.
- Both seem to say that if there is a Millennium, it is the current Church Age.
- The postmillennialists have a greater hope for the future because the spread of the Gospel will bring about positive change in our world.

The Millennium of the Premillennialists

Thomas Ice and Timothy Demy provide a description of the Millennium as premillennialists: "Revelation 20:1-7 says that Christ will reign for 1,000 years after His return to Jerusalem. The millennium is the capstone of history. It will be a time when Jesus Christ will be the focus of all creation, and He will reign and rule visibly over all the world in power and great glory."[27]

As we learned in the chapter on assumptions, the heart of the controversy on virtually all these end-times matters is how the Scriptures are to be interpreted. Dispensationalist Paul Lee Tan makes this very point when he says, "These eschatological systems are the result of varying hermeneutical approaches and procedures."[28]

The premillennialists essentially take the twentieth chapter of Revelation on the Millennium and square it with at least a dozen verses from other biblical passages to come up with a golden age that *God* will effect, not man. A form of postmillennialism (I believe all but dead now) used to teach that there was a golden age coming—a utopia—brought about by human progress—that is, the efforts of humankind. The realities of two world wars, the rise of fascism, communism, and just about every -ism to come down the pike fairly well undercuts such fanciful notions.

The dispensationalists argue that Revelation 20 is certainly not the only portion of the Scripture that talks about the Millennium. After quoting several Old Testament messianic passages (such as references to the conquering king), Donald Grey Barnhouse (historical premillennialist) says:

> We have quoted enough to show that the belief of Christians in a literal, earthly kingdom is not built on six verses in the book of Revelation, but that it is a theme that runs through the entire Word of God. Having established the fact of such a kingdom, we shall go on to show the urgent necessity for it, and the nature of this kingdom when the Lord will fulfill His Word."[29]

Meanwhile, the Millennium of the premillennialists is a literal millennium because the Bible is to be taken literally (remember Horatio Bonar's maxim: Literal if possible). Premillennialists obviously eschew spiritualizing the Bible. Consider these statements from premillennialists:

- "Spiritualizers find it hard to explain—and not one has even successfully attempted it—if the Scriptures do not mean what they say, why they do not say what they mean."

  —Charles Feinberg[30]

- ". . . it is necessary to understand that prophecy is usually literal and given in plain statements of Scripture. To be sure, symbolic and apocalyptic presentations of prophecy appear in many passages, but even here the Bible itself interprets these symbols as prophetic predictions. It simply is not true that prophecy is a hopeless puzzle that no one can understand."

  —John F. Walvoord[31]

- "The only dependable approach to prophecy, however, is the *literal method of interpretation*. This method assumes that Bible prophecy, written in regular human language, should be interpreted according to laws governing written communication. It is a trustworthy and God-honoring method of interpretation which takes the Bible at its word."

—Paul Lee Tan[32]

In other words, the Millennium is literal.

In addition, Hal Lindsey argues in his classic book, *The Late Great Planet Earth,* that since prophecy was literally fulfilled in Christ's first coming, then so also it will be literally fulfilled in His next coming. He notes:

> The real issue between the amillennial and the premillennial viewpoints is whether prophecy should be interpreted literally or allegorically. As it has been demonstrated many times in this book, all prophecy about past events has been fulfilled literally, particularly the predictions regarding the first coming of Christ. The words of prophecy were demonstrated as being literal, that is, having the normal meaning understood by people of the time in which it was written. The words were not intended to be explained away by men who cannot believe what is clearly predicted."[33]

Lindsey holds that Christians today know better than Christians in previous centuries because many are commited to the study of prophecy. "Today, Christians who have diligently studied prophecy, trusting the Spirit of God for illumination, have a greater insight into its meaning than ever before. The prophetic word definitely has been "unsealed" in our generation as God predicted it would be."[34]

What does our generation know about the Millennium, according to this school of thought? Here are some points on the Millennium from Jack Van Impe:

- The Devil is cast into the bottomless pit, which is not the same as the lake of fire, his ultimate fate. "Satan is incarcerated for ten centuries in order that peace, prosperity, happiness, and holiness may exist on earth during Christ's Millennial reign."[35]
- Sitting on the thrones of judgment during the Millennium are those who participated in the first resurrection. This includes "the Old

Testament saints, Church Age saints, and Tribulation saints."[36]

- ". . . procreation still takes place during this era of time because those who survived the Tribulation hour enter the Millennium with human bodies. The believers upon the thrones possess resurrected bodies and do not bear children, but the others do. Consequently, the children born during this one-thousand-year period are born with the old Adamic, or sin nature which has been an inherent part of man ever since the fall of man ever since the fall of Adam and Eve. Many of them, of course, accept Christ as their personal Savior, but many do not! . . . Satan's release, then, is to determine whether or not Christ is real to these children of the Millennium, or whether they have been submissive simply because He ruled with a 'rod of iron.'"[37]

Therefore, while things will be mostly idyllic during the Millennium, lurking beneath the surface, problems might be brewing.

An Anticlimactic Ending?

Postmillennialist Loraine Boettner argues that the Millennium of the premillennialist is strange in terms of its anticlimactic ending. When Satan is loosed after the one thousand years, he stirs up the enemies of God to rebellion. Boettner writes:

> What a Millennium the Premillennialist has!—a Millennium preceded by seven years of unparalleled confusion and suffering and persecution during the "Great Tribulation" and under the reign of Antichrist, and ending with a universal revolt and war against which the saints and even Christ Himself seem to be helpless and from which they are rescued only by fire from heaven![38]

Dr. Oswald Allis, a nonmillenarian, adds, "It is not pleasing to think of the Messianic King, the Prince of Peace, sitting enthroned as it were on a smouldering volcano."[39]

Yet the premillennialist might easily counter, take the matter up with the Lord. After all, it's the Bible that says Satan will be loosed after the one thousand years.

Meanwhile, nonmillenarians have problems with the whole framework of taking the Millennium literally. Former dispensationalist Jay Adams, who's now an amillennialist, believes the entire schema impedes proper biblical understanding. He writes in his book *The Time Is at Hand*: "Here is the crucial point—until futurist ideas of the Apocalypse are abandoned, it is impossible to come to a correct understanding of the millennium prophecy. . . . It is one of the major theses of this volume that a *realized* rather than a *futuristic* interpretation of Revelation is correct."[40]

The Monumental Work of St. Augustine

The City of God *managed to shape the thinking on the end times for more than a millennium*

As was previously discussed, throughout the centuries of the Christian era, no one has probably had a greater influence on thinking about the end times than the Bishop of Hippo, St. Augustine (354–430). A first-rate genius, Augustine's writings and arguments were to influence church doctrine for centuries to come. To this day, both Catholic and Protestant scholars highly respect Augustine. Indeed, Presbyterian theologian B. B. Warfield once stated, "every tendency of thought in the church was eager to claim for itself the support of his name."[41]

When the barbarians sacked Rome in 410 and Christianity was being blamed for its demise, Augustine wrote an apology, *The City of God*, to "restore confidence in the Christian church, which Augustine said would take the place of the earthly city of Rome."[42] This monumental book managed to shape the thinking on the end times for more than a millennium, and it's still influential. As was stated earlier, the church essentially became nonmillenarian under St. Augustine's tutelage, and such thinking remained dominant until the twentieth century. Augustine began his work in the year 413, and *The Scofield Reference Bible* is dated at 1909, which didn't become mainstream until a few decades later. That means Augustine's view basically shaped Christianity on this issue for 1,500 years. How's that for a legacy?

Augustine interpreted Scripture with Scripture. He began by differentiating the "two resurrections," which John talked about in Revelation 20. The first resurrection is essentially that of the new birth, being born again. The second resurrection is that which takes place on the last day—that is, Judgment Day. Recall the saying: "Born once, die twice. Born twice, die once." If you're born only once (and thus never born again), then you will experience death in this life and death in the life to come. If, however, you're born again, you're born twice, and you won't experience the "second death."

Jesus said, "I tell you the truth, whoever hears my word and believes him who sent me has eternal life and will not be condemned; he has crossed over from death to life. I tell you the truth, a time is coming and *has now come* when the dead will hear the voice of the Son of God and those who hear will live" (John 5:24-25, emphasis mine). Augustine argued this is the first resurrection—one has crossed from spiritual death to spiritual life. In the same passage, Jesus went on to talk about the second resurrection: "Do not be amazed at this, for a time is coming when all who are in the graves will hear his voice and come out—those who have done good will rise to live, and those who have done evil will rise to be condemned" (vv. 28-29). The condemnation of the unbelievers is the "second death."

From these verses, Augustine believed those who are born again are those who are experiencing the Millennium. They have been snatched out of the claws of the Evil One who has been bound. Augustine quoted Jesus to support his view: "No man can enter into a strong man's house, and spoil his goods, except he will first bind the strong man" (Mark 3:27, KJV). Then Augustine interpreted this verse to mean that Jesus has now bound the Devil so that he will no longer deceive the nations. Thus, we are free to go out and proclaim the Gospel and snatch people away from the Devil.

Augustine wrote:

> It was then for the binding of this strong one that the apostle saw in the Apocalypse "an angel coming down from heaven, having the key of the abyss, and a chain in his hand. And he laid hold," [John] says, "on the dragon, that old serpent, which is called the devil and Satan, and bound him a thousand years"—that is, bridled and restrained his power so that he could not seduce and gain possession of those who were to be freed.[43]

Augustine also said it's likely that the thousand years is not literal, but rather symbolic of "perfection to mark the fulness of time. For a thousand is the cube of ten."[44] He continued:

> Now the devil was thus bound not only when the Church began to be more and more widely extended among the nations beyond Judea, but *is now and shall be bound till the end of the world,* when he is to be loosed. Because even now men are, and doubtless to the end of the world shall be, converted to the faith from the unbelief in which he held them.[45]

Before we leave Augustine, I want to quote a premillennial dispensational source paying tribute to him. They don't agree with his interpretation on the Millennium, but they acknowledge his influence. Thomas Ice and Timothy Demy from their *Fast Facts on Bible Prophecy* state:

> Amillennialism came to dominate the church when the great church father and theologian Augustine (354–430) abandoned premillennialism in favor of amillennialism. It is no exaggeration to say that among the church's leadership (including the majority of Protestant reformers during the fifteenth and sixteenth centuries) amillennialism has been the most widely held view for much of the church's history.[46]

This is quite a statement in light of the fact that Dr. Ice is the director of the Pre-Trib Research Center in Washington, D.C.

Is This *the Time of the Millennium?*

While premillennialists hold that it is not, many nonmillenarians say that it is. Many past prestigious theologians did not believe in a literal Millennium, or if they did, they believed it was roughly equivalent to the Church Age. Consider just a smattering of these opinions from many who were Presbyterian or Reformed:

- Charles Hodge (1797–1878), Princeton professor, was a "leading American theologian of the nineteenth century" according to *The New International Dictionary of the Christian Church.*[47] He said:

> The Scriptural doctrine therefore, is consistent with the admitted fact that separate nations, and the human race as a whole, have made great advances in all branches of knowledge and in all the arts of life. Nor is it inconsistent with the belief that the world under the influence of Christianity is constantly improving, and will ultimately attain, under the reign of Christ, millennial perfection and glory.[48]

- A. A. Hodge (1823–1886) was Charles' son. Like his father he taught systematic theology at Princeton. He said:

> The Scriptures, both of the Old and New Testament, clearly reveal that the gospel is to exercise an influence over all branches of the human family, immeasurably more extensive and more thoroughly transforming than any it has ever realized in time past. This end is to be gradually attained through the spiritual presence of Christ in the ordinary dispensation of Providence, and ministrations of his church.[49]

- B. B. Warfield (1851–1921) succeeded A. A. Hodge's professorship at Princeton. Harold Lindsell says of him: "Perhaps no theologian of that age is as widely read and has had his books kept in print so long as Warfield."[50] Warfield said:

> Surely, we shall not wish to measure the saving work of God by what has already been accomplished in these unripe days in which our lot is cast. The sands of time have not yet run out. And before us stretch, not merely the reaches of the ages, but the infinitely resourceful reaches of the promises of God. Are not the saints to inherit the earth? Is not the recreated earth theirs? Are not the kingdoms of the world to become the kingdom of God? Is not the knowledge of the glory of God to cover the earth as the waters cover the sea? Shall not the day dawn when no man need say to his neighbour, "Know the Lord," for all shall know Him from the least

> to the greatest. O raise your eyes, raise your eyes, I beseech you, to the far horizon: let them rest nowhere short of the extreme limit of the divine purpose of grace. And tell me what you see there. Is it not the supreme, the glorious, issue of that love of God which loved, not one here and there only in the world, but the world in its organic completeness; and gave His Son, not to judge the world, but that the world through Him should be saved.[51]

Warfield added that at this time the King of kings is conquering the world through the spread of the Gospel: "According to the New Testament, this time in which we live is precisely the time in which our Lord is conquering the world for Himself; and it is the completion of this conquest which, as it marks the completion of His redemptive work, so it sets the time for His return to earth to consummate His kingdom and establish it in its eternal form."[52]

- J. G. Vos states:

> Prophecy shows that a time is coming when the kingdom of Christ shall triumph over all opposition and prevail in all the world. . . . Arts, sciences, literature, and property shall be consecrated to the advancement of the kingdom of Christ. The social institutions of men shall be regulated by gospel principles, and the nations as such shall consecrate their strength to the Lord.[53]

- The Puritans by and large held to nonmillenarian views. During the days of Cromwell in seventeenth-century Britain, some Puritan leaders, including John Owen, drew up the Savoy Confession in which they stated:

> As the Lord is in care and love towards his Church, hath in his infinite wise providence exercised it with great variety in all ages, for the good of them that love him, and his own glory; so, according to his promise, we expect that in the latter days, Anti-christ being destroyed, the Jews called, and the adversaries of the

> kingdom of his dear Son broken, the churches of Christ being enlarged and edified through a free and plentiful communication of light and grace, shall enjoy in this world a more quiet, peaceable, and glorious condition than they have enjoyed."[54]

- The Larger Catechism of the Westminster Confession adds:

> In the second petition [which is, Thy kingdom come] . . . we pray that the kingdom of sin and Satan may be destroyed, the gospel propagated throughout the world, the Jews called, the fullness of the Gentiles brought in; the Church furnished all gospel officers and ordinances, purged from corruption, countenanced and maintained by the civil magistrate: etc.[55]

J. Marcellus Kik elaborates on this confession:

> Thus these standards reveal that it was believed that Christ would dispose all things to the good of the church, that Christ would overcome the enemies of the church, that the church should pray that the kingdom of Satan be destroyed, the gospel propagated throughout the world, the Jews called, and the fullness of the Gentiles brought in. Surely the Westminster Standards would not encourage hope and prayer for things contrary to the Word of God.[56]

Postmillennialists: You Ain't Seen Nothing Yet!

Take the long view of history, argue the postmillennialists. It's taken centuries to get this far advanced. Maybe it'll take centuries more before we get it right. Boettner writes:

> The nineteen centuries that have elapsed since the Christian era began may well indicate that several more centuries, perhaps even millenniums, may be required, particularly if devastating wars yet remain to be fought,

> as is of course perfectly possible.
>
> Skeptics sometimes point to present day evils and tell us that we are living in a post-Christian age. But, no, there has never yet been a truly Christian age, nor has so much as one nation ever been consistently Christian. The age in which we are living is still pre-Christian.[57]

To which he adds, "Let Christians everywhere take seriously the command to evangelize the world and the work will be accomplished in a comparatively short time."[58]

The postmillennialists hold that once Christians obey Christ's mandates, we'll see some real changes in this world. Thus to the postmillennialists, we ain't seen nothing yet.

To premillennial dispensationalist M. R. DeHaan, however, the realities of history have discredited the postmillennial position:

> The Postmillennialist who had been preaching a better world getting better and better by the preaching of a so-called gospel and education and reform has abandoned his dream and taken refuge in the rickety and still more untenable theory of Amillennialism. This results from his failure to understand the mystery of the body of Christ. It was never God's program to convert the world in this dispensation. On the contrary, the Bible teaches clearly that this age will end in apostasy and wickedness, war and destruction."[59]

Yet Boettner points out:

> Premillennialists sometimes try to refute this general view by citing the question asked in Luke 18:8, "When the Son of man cometh, shall he find faith on the earth?" And they infer that the answer must be "No." But in order to give a negative answer to this question, it is necessary to ignore the many statements in Scripture which describe the latter day glory of the Church.[60]

Boettner is referring primarily to the messianic kingdom promises of the Old Testament, such as "All nations will be blessed through him, and they will call him blessed" (Ps. 72:17). Dispensationalists, of course, see such promises as to be fulfilled only at Christ's return.

Have There Been Improvements over the Centuries?

Yes, there have been many improvements over the centuries. For example, the average lifespan in the American colonies in 1750 was thirty-two. Today in the United States it's past seventy years.[61]

Boettner adds:

> What marvels must lie ahead when nations the world over are Christian—when the Millennium becomes a reality!
>
> Thus Postmillennialism holds that Christianity is to become the controlling and transforming influence not only in the moral and spiritual life of some individuals, but also in the entire social, economic and cultural life of the nations. There is no reason why this change should not take place over the entire earth, with pagan religions and false philosophies giving place to the true, and the earth being restored in considerable measure to that high purpose of righteousness and holiness for which it was created.[62]

He further states:

> That a great spiritual advance has been made should be clear to all. Consider, for instance, the awful moral and spiritual conditions that existed on earth before the coming of Christ—the world at large groping helplessly in pagan darkness, with slavery, polygamy, the oppressed conditions of women and children, the almost complete lack of political freedom, and the ignorance, poverty, and extremely primitive medical care that was the lot of nearly all except those who belonged to the ruling classes. Today the world at large is on a far higher plane.[63]

He also points out that more money is available for the service of the kingdom than ever before[64] and that 98 percent of the people in the world have the Bible in whole or in part available to them in their "native tongue."[65]

Postmillennialist Dr. James Snowden notes that we must compare where we are with where we've been: "The true way of judging the world is to compare its present with its past condition and note in which direction it is moving. Is it going backward, or forward, is it getting worse or better? It may be wrapped in gloomy twilight, but is it the twilight of the evening, or of the morning?"[66]

Consider all the positive aspects of our culture brought about by Christianity

Boettner observes, "Today we are living in an era that is relatively golden as compared with the first century of the Christian era. This progress is to go on until on this earth we shall see a practical fulfillment of the prayer, 'Thy kingdom come, thy will be done in earth as it is in heaven.'"[67] He would have us consider all the positive aspects of our culture brought about by Christianity.

In our highly anti-Christian age, where Christian bashing is a popular indoor sport, we forget that because of the spread of the Gospel, many positive things have come to our world. Many. For example:

- Hospitals as we know them began in the Christian era. In many countries, even to this very day, Christians establish hospitals in remote areas to express the love of Jesus Christ.
- Christ essentially initiated charity. Prior to Him, the ancient world was quite hostile. He initiated the "Good Samaritan" ethic. Even secular people engaged in charity today are imitating the example of Jesus Christ, whether they recognize it or not.
- Education has made great advances around the world because of the Gospel. Education for the masses, especially, became an ideal after the Reformation because the reformers felt that the only way their movement could hold sway was if people could read the Bible for themselves. Thus they had to know how to read.[68]
- The value of human life has improved dramatically wherever the Judeo-Christian view of humanity is present. Antilife pagan practices have often disappeared because of the Gospel. For example, it was the cultural norm in India for a widow to throw herself on her husband's funeral pyre. She either did it voluntarily or it was done to her.

William Carey and other missionaries lobbied the British government to halt this practice; only after much work on their part did the empire finally interfere with this centuries-old custom. Other examples include cannibalism and human sacrifice in other parts of the world. These practices have by and large disappeared because of the worldwide spread of the Gospel.

- Civil liberties ultimately have their foundation in Christianity. I remember reading about a dinner party discussion at the end of the nineteenth century during which someone was attacking the missionary enterprise. James Russell Lowell, the great Christian statesman, retorted:

> I challenge any skeptic to find a ten square mile spot on this planet where they can live their lives in peace and safety and decency, where womanhood is honored, where infancy and old age are revered, where they can educate their children, where the Gospel of Jesus Christ has not gone first to prepare the way. If they find such a place, then I would encourage them to emigrate thither and there proclaim their unbelief.[69]

No one can find such a spot because it doesn't exist.

I can go on and on, detailing ways in which the Gospel has changed—and continues to change—our world for the good.[70] Boettner points out:

> Looked at from the standpoint of present day events it may not be possible to say which way the tides are moving. But over the centuries there is progress, great progess if we look back five hundred, or a thousand, or two thousand years. Certainly many of those who tell us that the world is getting worse would change their minds very quickly if they suddenly found themselves back in colonial days, or in the Dark Ages, or in the pre-Christian era.[71]

Dr. W. G. T. Shedd, another postmillennial theologian, says:

> The circle of God's election is a great circle of the heav-

> ens and not that of a treadmill. The kingdom of Satan is insignificant in contrast with the kingdom of Christ. In the immense range of God's dominion, good is the rule, and evil is the exception. Sin is a speck upon the azure of eternity; a spot upon the sun. Hell is only a corner of the universe.[72]

Contrasting Visions

Thus we clearly see two very different visions of the Millennium. The one literal, the other not. One sees the messianic prophecies fulfilled literally through the kingdom Christ ushers in and centered in Jerusalem. The other sees these prophecies fulfilled throughout the Christian era and even now as the Gospel goes forth into all the world.

Loraine Boettner states the Millennium will not necessarily be a period of holy perfection:

> There seems to be a general impression that when we speak of a Millennium we mean a time when the world will be sinless or practically so. We do believe that a time is coming when the people of the world in general will be Christians, a time when Satan will no longer be able to "deceive the nations" (Rev. 20:3). But we do not believe that the Kingdom in this world, even in its millennial fullness and power, will be a perfect or sinless state. Nor do we believe that every person will be a Christian. Yet it is not uncommon to find pre- and amillennial writers inferring or declaring that such are the tenets of Postmillennialism, and using such terms as "ideal perfection," "a perfect world," "convert every individual," and "sinless perfection," to describe the postmillennial position. No representative Postmillennialist teaches those things. Certainly such was not the teachings of Hodge, Dabney, Shedd, Strong, Snowden, or Warfield. Nor is it the teaching of Scripture. Sinless perfection belongs only to the heavenly life."[73]

Premillennialists, on the other hand, question the idea that the Devil has been bound and is bound in our day. We clearly examined that view in an earlier chapter. From every indication, "The devil is alive and well and living on planet earth," to quote Hal Lindsey.

Conclusion

Because Christians have been arguing about the Millennium for centuries, I don't imagine we're going to resolve all these conflicts this side of paradise. Yet wait a minute: forget the details for a moment. What's the overall point of the Millennium? Let's put it this way: Who wins in the end? God does and the Lord Jesus Christ.

When we realize that whether you hold to the premil view that Christ *will* conquer one day or the amil or postmil view that He *is currently* in the process of conquering the earth, the truth remains: Christ's Kingdom will prevail for all eternity.

15

Daniel's Seventieth Week

Prophecy does not work out its own fulfillment, but stands as a witness until after the event has taken place.[1]

—R. B. Girdlestone

One of the most interesting and disagreed-upon passages regarding Bible prophecy pertains to Daniel's Seventieth Week. The prophet Daniel likely completed the book which bears his name by about 530 B.C.[2] He was a Jewish exile living in Nebuchadnezzar's Babylon. He saw many things about the future, perhaps more than anyone else in all the Scriptures (with the exception of John who penned Revelation). What Daniel wrote still comforts and encourages God's people to this day.

It also provides much fodder for debate over the end times.

The Book of Daniel is believed to be one of the most important portions of the Bible on the issue of the end times. Or is it? Is that in itself an interpretation? Some preterists hold that statement is based on an assumption they don't share. (They see this book as containing prophecies that were in the future for Daniel, but from our perspective they were fulfilled long ago.) Futurists, on the other hand, see them as in the *future*.

Premillennialist John Walvoord says, "Few passages in the Old Testament are more important to prophetic understanding than Daniel 9:24-27."[3] That particular passage deals with Daniel's "seventy weeks," a source of much discussion and debate among students of eschatology.

Before we hear different interpretations about the seventy weeks, let's put it in context. Astoundingly, Daniel saw the rise of kingdoms before anyone even knew about them.

The Overall Context of the Seventy-Weeks Prophecy

First of all, long before Daniel's vision on the seventy weeks, King Nebuchadnezzar had a dream, and none of his magicians or "wise men" could help him unlock the mystery of that dream. Yet Daniel, a Jewish exile with an honored reputation, was called upon to do the impossible: To tell the king what he had dreamed and then interpret it (see Dan. 2).

Daniel told the king what he had dreamed, and the king excitedly confirmed that was correct. Daniel saw a statue in the king's dream composed of four parts—each part symbolic of a kingdom. First there was:

- The head of gold. Interpreters believe this to be the contemporary rule of the Babylonians (612–539 B.C.).
- The chest and arms of silver. This is interpreted to be the reign of the Medes and Persians (539–331 B.C.).
- The belly and thighs of bronze. This is held to be the rule of the Greeks (331–63 B.C.).
- The legs of iron and the feet part iron and part clay. This is generally thought to be the Roman Empire (63 B.C.–A.D. 476). Moreover, some premillennial dispensationalists interpret the toes as representing a revived Roman Empire yet to arise sometime in the future.

The Bible foretold these events with pinpoint accuracy. This is why some liberal Bible scholars try to date Daniel much later than when he actually wrote it, not because there's any historical, archeological, or textual evidence, but only because their antisupernatural bias forces them to argue that it *had* to be written after these events. Liberal scholars begin with their assumption that miracles and the supernatural are impossible; then they read their unbelief into the Bible. Walvoord writes, ". . . these prophecies are so accurate and so detailed that liberal interpreters reject the possibility that this was written by Daniel in the sixth century B.C."[4] Nevertheless, archeology has proved them wrong.[5]

Now, let's examine the passage itself.

Thus Saith the Lord, Through Daniel

In the ninth chapter of Daniel, he talked about the "seventy 'sevens.'" It is from this passage that some contend the Great Tribulation will be seven years. Here's Daniel 9:20-27:

> [20] While I was speaking and praying, confessing my sin and the sin of my people Israel and making my request to the Lord my God for his holy hill—[21] while I was still in prayer, Gabriel, the man I had seen in the earlier vision, came to me in swift flight about the time of the evening sacrifice. [22] He instructed me and said to me,

> "Daniel, I have now come to give you insight and understanding. [23] As soon as you began to pray, an answer was given, which I have come to tell you, for you are highly esteemed. Therefore, consider the message and understand the vision:
>
> [24] "Seventy 'sevens' are decreed for your people and your holy city to finish transgression, to put an end to sin, to atone for wickedness, to bring in everlasting righteousness, to seal up vision and prophecy and to anoint the most holy.
>
> [25] "Know and understand this: From the issuing of the decree to restore and rebuild Jerusalem until the Anointed One, the ruler, comes, there will be seven 'sevens,' and sixty-two 'sevens.' It will be rebuilt with streets and a trench, but in times of trouble. [26] After the sixty-two 'sevens,' the Anointed One will be cut off and will have nothing. The people of the ruler who will come will destroy the city and the sanctuary. The end will come like a flood: War will continue until the end, and desolations have been decreed. [27] He will confirm a covenant with many for one 'seven.' In the middle of the 'seven' he will put an end to sacrifice and offering. And on a wing of the temple he will set up an abomination that causes desolation, until the end that is decreed is poured out on him."

Three Main Positions on Daniel's Seventy Weeks

Many different groups interpret these eight verses quite differently. Here is one way to divide the views on Daniel's seventy weeks:

(1) Preterist Position A. Daniel's prophecy was entirely fulfilled by the second century B.C. Antiochus Epiphanes and the high priest of Israel are the key players in this drama.

(2) Preterist Position B. Daniel's prophecy was entirely fulfilled by the first century A.D. Jesus is the main character. When He was cut off (crucified), the die was cast for the end of Jerusalem, even though that was to come forty years later.

(3) Futurist Position. The first sixty-nine weeks of Daniel 9 were ful-

filled through Christ's first coming. The last week will not come until immediately after the Rapture, which will then inaugurate the Great Tribulation (it will last precisely seven years, according to Dan. 9). Even if Antiochus Epiphanes was a foreshadow of things to come, there is a future "abomination that causes desolation" to come. Therefore, a future temple will be built.

The following charts will help distinguish these three main positions.

There's another view that I won't address in detail, and that is the multiple fulfillment view. This position holds that all three views are essentially true. These events were fulfilled in the past, and they'll be fulfilled again in the future. I am not addressing this view in detail because virtually everything that will be said about the other views could also apply to the multiple fulfillment position.

A Few Preliminary Observations

Before exploring the three views further, here are a few basic observations on Daniel 9:

(1) There will be a total of seventy sevens. Virtually all commentators

DANIEL'S SEVENTY WEEKS

PRETERIST POSITION A

7 year-weeks= 49 years	The 62 year-weeks= 368 years		Last year-week #70= 7 years	
587 B.C.	538 B.C.	170	167	164/63
Destruction of Jerusalem and the going forth of the prophetic word.	Return to Jerusalem and reinstatement of the high priestly office, the anointing of the high priest, Jeshua.	High Priest Onias III dies (last high priest).	167 B.C. The end of sacrifices. The altar of Zeus set up in the wing of the temple. Intense persecution.	Antiochus dies (the destroyer).

PRETERIST POSITION B (sometimes called "the traditional view")

7+62=69 year-weeks

458 B.C.	A.D. 26 – A.D. 30	A.D. 70—Destruction of Jerusalem
"From the going forth of the command to restore and build Jerusalem"—Artaxerxes's decree to Ezra in 458 B.C.	"Until the anointed one, the ruler comes"—Jesus is baptized. After 62 weeks the anointed one will be cut off—Jesus' death in A.D. 30.	The Prince (Jesus) shall come in judgment against Jerusalem. The Jewish sacrificial system is abolished (for all time). (The gap between the Messiah's death and the destruction of Jerusalem is explained by the notion that the die was cast in A.D. 30, not 70.)

DISPENSATIONAL VIEW

7+62=69 year-weeks =483 years[6]	The Prophetic Parenthesis=the Time of the Church	Seventieth year-week 7 years, The Tribulation	
445 B.C.	A.D. 33	Rapture	Millennium
"From the going forth of the command to restore and build Jerusalem"—Nehemiah's building the walls of Jerusalem—Nehemiah 2:1-8.	"Until the anointed one, the ruler comes"—Jesus appears. After 62 weeks the anointed one will be cut off—Jesus' death and destruction of Jerusalem.	"One week to secure the covenant." In the middle of the week, end of sacrifices. Intense persecution during Tribulation.	Coming of Christ for judgment.

say that each "seven" or "week" symbolizes a seven-year period. That being the case, that would mean there will be a 490-year period from the time of the decree through its fulfillment. The first grouping of sevens will be seven (forty-nine years); the next grouping will be sixty-two sevens (434 years) and one seven (seven years). It is essentially that last seven that this controversy is all about.

(2) Nevertheless, *when* did the decree go out? Bible scholars answer that differently as well. In his book *Major Bible Prophecies*, Dr. John Walvoord lists four decrees mentioned in the Bible related to the rebuilding of Jerusalem. Each of these is a candidate for the decree of Daniel 9:

1. The decree of Cyrus in 583 B.C. in relation to rebuilding the temple.
2. The decree of Darius a little later to confirm Cyrus' decree.
3. The decree of Artaxerxes, which authorized Ezra to rebuild the temple.
4. The decree of Artaxerxes in 445 or 444 B.C., which authorized Nehemiah to rebuild Jerusalem and its walls.

Walvoord, a leading dispensationalist, argues if this last one were the case, then "it would provide fulfillment for the 483 years by A.D. 33."[7]

According to historic premillennialist J. Barton Payne, author of *Encyclopedia of Biblical Prophecy*, Artaxerxes' decree through Ezra is the proper starting point. Therefore, Jesus' "baptism will occur in A.D. 26, 483 years after Ezra will have received the decree by which he would begin to rebuild Jerusalem."[8]

Meanwhile, dispensational writers usually begin with the decree of Nehemiah in 444 B.C., notes Payne, thus bringing the date to the triumphal entry of Christ into Jerusalem.

E. B. Pusey and other theologians hold another view. They maintain that the correct starting point is the decree Artaxerxes issued to Ezra in 458 B.C.[9] Artaxerxes' decree concerns not only the temple but also the reconstruction of the city. When one calculates the prophecy from this date, we end up with the sixty-nine weeks ending in 26 A.D. with the Messiah being "cut off" in 30 A.D.

(3) It's safe to say preterists and futurists disagree over this passage and the Olivet Discourse perhaps more than any other passage of the Bible. (Virtually everyone fights over Revelation.) A reminder: because well-meaning Bible scholars interpret them differently, we need humility and to avoid being dogmatic when we approach the Scriptures.

A Close Look at Verse 24

When we read only Daniel 9:24 and not the rest of the passage, it is amazing how accurately it would seem to be that Jesus Christ fulfilled it. Daniel said, "Seventy weeks are determined for your people and for your holy city, *to finish the transgression, to make an end of sins, to make reconciliation for iniquity, to bring in everlasting righteousness, to seal up vision and prophecy, and to anoint the* Most *Holy*" (Dan. 9:24, NKJV, emphasis mine). The traditional view (held by those of Preterist Position B and some futurists) holds that the starting point was Artaxerxes' decree to Ezra (458 B.C.) and was fulfilled when Jesus died for our sins.

Antiochus Epiphanes

Besides the four potential decree dates just explored whereby Jesus becomes the anointed one of this prophecy, there is yet another interpretation by Christian theologians. It is the one listed as Preterist Position A. This view maintains that the decree in question is the word that went out in 587 from the prophet Jeremiah about the return and the rebuilding of Jerusalem. This view brings the conclusion of the seventy weeks to the Maccabean time (in the mid-second century B.C.).[10]

Let's back up for a history lesson. There are necessary historical details that are important for people of all views to understand.

Israel was not been a free nation from the time the Babylonians took the nation into captivity in 586 B.C. until 1948. After the Babylonian captivity, the Medes and Persians overran it. Then came the meteoric rise of Alexander the Great and his sudden demise. He, too, controlled Palestine. After him, the Egyptian Ptolemies and the Syrian Seleucids fought over the tiny country as well; eventually the Syrians won. All of this Daniel predicted with great accuracy, even the fact that upon the death of Alexander the Great, his kingdom would be immediately divided into *four* kingdoms.[11]

An exceedingly evil Syrian ruler arose in the second century before Christ. Antiochus IV Epiphanes ruled Syria from 175 to 164/163 B.C. (The exact date of his death is disputed.) Antiochus hated the Jews and despised their religion. He desecrated the temple from 171 to 165 B.C., provoking the Maccabean revolt, which was ultimately successful. (It is from this revolt that Hanukkah was born.)

Oskar Skarsaune, who holds Preterist Position A, describes the following scenario of the seventy weeks: The starting point is the year 587 B.C. This is the year the prophetic word went out from Jeremiah to rebuild the city after it would lie in ruins for seventy years (Jer. 25:11; 29:10-14). Thus the seventy weeks of Daniel 9 commenced when the seventy years of Jeremiah began. Daniel received the revelation of the seventy weeks while he read the Book of Jeremiah and sought to understand the meaning of the seventy years. This is the context of the seventy weeks: "I, Daniel, understood from the Scriptures, according to the word of the Lord given to Jeremiah the prophet, that the desolation of Jerusalem would last seventy years. So I turned to the Lord God and pleaded with him in prayer and petition, in fasting, and in sackcloth and ashes" (Dan. 9:2-3). God answered Daniel's prayer and revealed to him the prophecy about the seventy weeks. Those who hold Preterist Position A remind us that the context of this passage is the key to understanding it.

Continuing with Skarsaune's Preterist A interpretation: Leaving Jeremiah's time, we move forward by seven-year weeks (forty-nine years) from 587 to 538 B.C., the year King Cyrus gave the Jews permission to return from Babylon to Jerusalem to start rebuilding the temple (Ezra 1). After that (516 B.C.), the office of the high priest was reinstated. The first postexile high priest was Jeshua (Ezra 3). He is believed to be a picture of the Christ to come and is described as such in Zechariah 3:1-10 and 4:14.

This view also contends that Jeshua was the anointed one to come because of his high priestly office, which had been defunct for many years. Jeshua was "anointed the most holy" (Dan. 9:24) at the dedication of the new temple (Ezra's was smaller than Solomon's), completed and dedicated in 516 B.C. This concludes the seventy years of Jeremiah (587–516).

According to this view, thus far, the first seven weeks of Daniel (forty-nine years) have been fulfilled. Next, for sixty-two weeks (434 years) the high priestly office continues intact until the murder of the high priest Onias III in 170 B.C., which was just before Antiochus IV Epiphanes conquered Jerusalem. Preterist Position A believes that the last week (the last seven years) began at that time, lasting from 170 to 164/163 B.C.

Antiochus posed a serious threat to the Jews. First, he abolished the sacrifices. Second, he placed a statue of a pagan god (Zeus) in the temple. This act was highly offensive to the monotheistic Jews. Next, he killed thousands of Israelites. All of this lasted 2,300 days.[12] Daniel had been told: "It [the abomination that causes desolation] will take 2,300 evenings and mornings; then the sanctuary will be reconsecrated" (Dan. 8:14).

The Jewish persecution under Antiochus reached its climax after 3 1/2 years, and it was at that time, in the year 167 B.C., that the altar of Zeus was set up in the wing of the temple in Jerusalem, and the daily sacrifices ended. This was the abomination that causes desolation. At the end of

Daniel's Seventieth Week, the destroyer dies. Antiochus Epiphanes fulfilled this prediction when he died in the year 164/163. Thus, according to this view, the whole seventy weeks took place from 587 to 163 B.C. with the detailed last week from 170-163 B.C.

One other point about Preterist Position A. Preterists believe the confusion and difficulty of interpreting this passage comes about when we insist that Jesus was the anointed one of Daniel 9:25. They certainly believe Jesus of Nazareth is *the* Anointed One (the Messiah), but they don't believe He is the anointed one of Daniel 9:25. They argue that the "anointed one" was a term often applied to the high priest. Furthermore, they provide an argument from silence: Although the New Testament cites numerous Old Testament passages, that Jesus fulfilled, the New Testament does not cite Daniel 9:25 as a messianic prophecy.

Nevertheless, was Antiochus Epiphanes a picture of things to come (as would be held by Preterist Position B and the Futurists)? Was he a foreshadow of what was to take place in the first century? For example, we read earlier the opinion that the Roman army was an abomination to the Jews—and that its presence in the temple in A.D. 70 was the reoccurrence of "the abomination that causes desolation."[13] Was Antiochus Epiphanes, as futurists would hold, a foreshadow of what is *yet* to come?

49 [7 x 7] + 434 [62 x 7] +7 [1 x7] = 490

When Daniel talked about the seventy weeks, he broke it down into groupings of seven, sixty-two, and one. Postmillennialist J. Marcellus Kik, who holds Preterist Position B, contends that the total length of time prophesied brings us through Christ's death and the Jews' self-destructive choice of death over life by rejecting their Messiah and killing His disciples. Kik writes, "The first period of 49 years was to accomplish the rebuilding of the city. . . . The 483 years (7 plus 62 weeks) takes us up to the ministry of Christ. During the last week of years the Messiah was to be cut off. We know that after three and a half years of his ministry the Anointed One suffered a violent death."[14]

Dispensationalist founder C. I. Scofield, a futurist, has the following to say about the seventy weeks. Note that his major divergence with Kik would be over the *last* of the 490 weeks:

> These are "weeks" or, more accurately, sevens of years;

> seventy weeks of seven years each. Within these "weeks" the national chastisement must be ended and the nation re-established in everlasting righteousness (v. 24). The seventy weeks are divided into seven = 49 years; sixty-two = 434 years; one = 7 years (vs. 25-27). In the seven weeks = 49 years, Jerusalem was to be rebuilt in "troublous times." This was fulfilled, as Ezra and Nehemiah record. Sixty-two weeks = 434 years, thereafter Messiah was to come (v. 25). This was fulfilled in the birth and manifestation of Christ. Verse 26 is obviously an indeterminate period. The date of the crucifixion is not fixed. It is only said to be "after" the threescore and two weeks. It is the first event in verse 26. The second event is the destruction of the city, fulfilled A.D. 70. Then, "unto the end," a period not fixed, but which has already lasted nearly 2000 years. To Daniel was revealed only that wars and desolations should continue (cf. Mt. 24:6-14). The N.T. reveals that which was hidden from the O.T. prophets (Mt. 13:11-17; Eph. 3:1-10), that during this period should be accomplished the mysteries of the kingdom of Heaven (Mt. 13:1-50), and the out calling of the Church (Mt. 16:18; Rom. 11:25). When the Church-age will end, and the seventieth week begin, is nowhere revealed.[15]

Thus dispensationalists view the gap between the sixty-ninth and the seventieth week persisting to this very day.

Kik, however, argues:

> The prophecy records that this cutting off of Christ was *after* the sixty ninth week. There are those who maintain that the last week of this prophecy has as yet not been fulfilled in history. This amounts to a denial of the plain import of the prophecy that the death of the Anointed One was to be after the sixty ninth week and during the seventieth week. H. A. Ironside writes: "between the sixty ninth and the seventieth weeks we have a Great Parenthesis which has now lasted over nineteen hun-

> dred years. The seventieth week has been postponed by God Himself who changes the time and the seasons because of the transgressions of the people." Notice that it is Dr. Ironside who declares that the week has been postponed. God does not state it, nor does his Written Word.[16]

Consider this sobering thought, says Kik, "If the seventieth week were postponed we would still be in our sins!"[17]

Kik also notes counterarguments:

> The only valid objection against this general interpretation is that the destruction of Jerusalem did not occur within the seventieth week—within the period of seven years. The seventy weeks extended to about 33 A.D. The destruction of Jerusalem, of course, came in 70 A.D. A close examination of the passage in Daniel does not disclose any definite statement that the people of the prince were to cause this destruction within the seven years. Within the seven years the destruction of the city *was determined* by its rejection of Christ and his apostles. Because of this rejection the people of the prince that shall come shall destroy the city and the sanctuary.[18]

In Kik's opinion, "Jerusalem became a 'carcass' during the seventieth week."[19] He adds, "Daniel prophesied that the events he enumerated were to occur in the continuous period of 490 years. . . . The Scriptures and history have revealed that the prophecy of Daniel has been wonderfully fulfilled. The Scriptures do not tell us that the seventieth week has been postponed. If it were postponed, I repeat, we would still be in our sins and without hope."[20] Why? Because the Messiah would not have been cut off; Jesus would not have died for our sins.

A Future Abomination that Causes Desolation?

Why do we always hear that the Great Tribulation will last seven years? Because of this passage. The futurist view of dispensationalists is that as Daniel was looking into the future, he saw the immediate future of the next few centuries. Then he saw something else that was yet to happen, and still has not happened. To give an analogy to explain this view, think of a person on one mountaintop looking across to what looks like only one other mountaintop. In reality, he is seeing two—one relatively close and the other far away—but from his view, both appear to be one. In the same way, argues the futurist, Daniel was seeing things that would unfold in his near future and then something else that would unfold much later. Dispensationalist Ed Hindson comments, "Daniel's prophecy looks all the way down the corridor of time until the end. He tells us there is one great 'abomination of desolation' still to come."[21]

Why do we always hear that the Great Tribulation will last seven years?

The evil man in this passage who desecrates the temple is the Antichrist (even if Antiochus Epiphanes was a prototype of what's to come). In fact, this is one of four key passages to tell us about him—the others are 1 John 2:22, 2 Thessalonians 2:3-4, 8-10, and Revelation 13. If this interpretation is correct, the implication is that the temple will have to be rebuilt.

The Jigsaw Puzzle Method of Prophetic Interpretation?

As we've seen throughout this book, the heart of the end-times controversy is the mode of interpreting the Bible prophecy. A clear example is how writers interpret the seventy weeks of Daniel 9. The Norwegian theologian Oskar Skarsaune, a nonmillenarian, calls the dispensational view the "jigsaw puzzle approach." Daniel 9 provides the frame of the puzzle, and then bits and pieces from the Old and New Testament are placed into this frame to create a picture of the future. Gary DeMar adds that the dispensationalists hold that the most important piece of information in prophecy is the seventy weeks prophecy.[22]

For example, prewrath premillennialist Robert Van Kampen makes the following statements, demonstrating how Daniel 9 provides the framework of the dispensational understanding of the great tribulation to come:

> Those who hold to the premillennial return of Christ also agree that just prior to the thousand-year reign of Christ there will be a **seven-year period** of trouble on earth, beginning mildly and increasing in intensity as

> this period progresses. . . . The **seven-year** tribulation period will begin when this man who becomes Antichrist makes a **seven-year** treaty with Israel, who will, once again, be living in her own homeland when the treaty is signed (Dan. 9:27). **Three-and-a-half years** later, those who refuse to worship Antichrist or refuse to take his mark (666) will become the targets of his severe persecution, a persecution unlike any the elect of God has ever known. Antichrist's unprecedented persecution of the elect of God (Matt. 24:21) and the nation of Israel (Dan. 12:1), which initiates the final half of the **seven-year** tribulation period, is referred to as a time of *great tribulation*, the term Christ specifically gives to this time of intense persecution in His Olivet Discourse to His disciples (Matt. 24:21).[23]

In other words, Daniel 9 provides the prophetic *framework* for the whole picture and the belief that the Great Tribulation will last seven years.

Here's another representative sample that demonstrates that the seven years in the seven-year tribulation comes from Daniel's seventy weeks. In his book *Revelation Revealed*, dispensationalist Jack Van Impe writes:

> There is no doubt about the literalness of this **seven-year period**. Daniel's first sixty-nine weeks (see Daniel 9:24-26) totaled 483 years. . . . The formula is so clear that a child can grasp it. . . . One does not have to be a mathematical wizard or a calculus genius to discover that the Tribulation is a full **seven years** in duration. Take it literally![24]

The futurist view of dispensationalists is that the first sixty-nine weeks gives the time until Christ's crucifixion. Next, there follows an in-between time of undetermined length (in which we now live) called the time of the Gentiles or the church time. Then comes the last week. As a result, there is an enormous gap between verse 26 and 27 in Daniel 9—a gap that thus far has lasted nearly two millennia. This last week will be the fulfillment of Christ's return, the Great Tribulation, the rise of Antichrist, and the various judgments. With this view providing the mechanism, the hunt is on throughout the Bible for verses and passages to put into this prophetic jigsaw puzzle.

Why the Gap?

Preterists (both A and B types) ask, "So why the gap between the sixty-ninth and the seventieth weeks?" Gary DeMar points out, *"Nothing in the text of Daniel 9:24-29 implies a 'gap.'"*[25] He adds, ". . . dispensationalists need a gap between the feet and the toes of Nebuchadnezzar's statue. . . ."[26] Note the reproduction of a chart by dispensationalist Clarence Larkin from one of the Bible prophecy conferences of many years ago. The toes are extended quite long to account for the present church age.

Ed Hindson writes:

> Premillennialists see a gap of time, the Church Age, separating the legs and the toes, with the stone falling at the *second* coming of Christ, during the final stage of Gentile history.
>
> In Nebuchadnezzar's vision, the stone fell on the ten toes and obliterated the statue to dust, the wind blew the dust away, and the stone filled the whole earth. Premillennialists argue that this has not yet happened. They believe this is a prophetic picture of Christ's return to set up His kingdom on earth at the beginning of the millennium (His 1,000-year reign).[27]

The dispensational view is predicated on the belief that prophetic time is not counted when Israel is out of the land.[28] Loraine Boettner thinks it would be strange for God to have not made that long, long gap clear to us. He provides analogies from everyday life:

> If in our present day social affairs of business contracts we attempted to insert hidden parentheses of days or months or years we would get into trouble immediately. Suppose that a traveling companion asks me how far it is from New York to Denver, and I inform him that it is 70 miles. We travel that distance, and beyond, but haven't reached Denver. So he says to me, "You said it was 70 miles from New York to Denver. But we have already traveled more than that and we still haven't come to

> Denver." Then I explained to him, "Oh, but there is a parenthesis in there of 2,000 miles that I didn't tell you about. You see, the speedometer is set so that it registers only the first 69 miles, which is country through which I enjoy traveling, then it doesn't register again until we enter the last mile going into Denver.". . . Now if we attempted such chicanery what would be the result? Such trifling would, of course, be condemned as puerile and dishonest. In all of our dealings we assume that the 70th mile follows immediately after the 69th mile, and the 70th week follows immediately after the 69th week. Nowhere in Scripture is a specified number of time-units, making up a described period of time, set forth as meaning anything but continuous and consecutive time. Likewise, the 70 weeks in Daniel's prophecy are 70 links in a chain, each holding to the others, a definite measure of the remaining time allotted to the nation of Israel before the coming of the Messiah.[29]

Scientific Hermeneutics

Duke Divinity School professor George Marsden, author of *Fundamentalism and American Culture*, thinks the dispensational school of thought (that believes in the gap) arose out of the desire to essentially apply the scientific method to the interpretation of the prophetic verses of Scripture. Dr. Marsden writes:

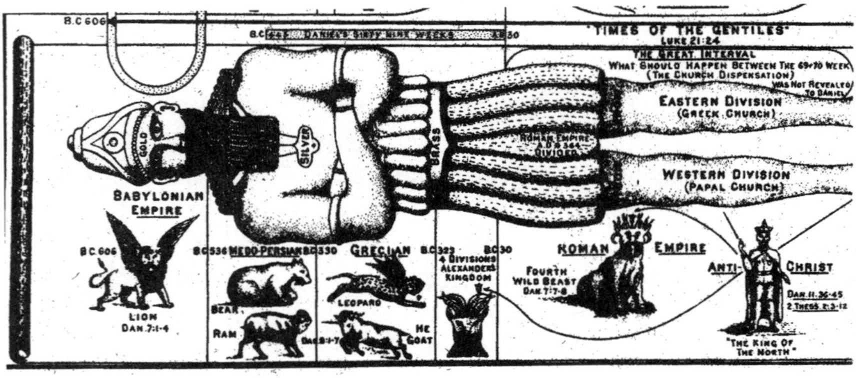

> Dispensationalist leaders regarded these methods of dividing and classifying as the only scientific ones. Scofield, for example, contrasted his work to previous "unscientific systems." . . . Induction had to start with the hard facts, and dispensationalists insisted that the only proper way to interpret Scripture was in "the literal sense," unless the text or the context absolutely demanded otherwise. . . . The belief that the facts and laws they were dealing with were matters of plain common sense was basic to the dynamics of the movement.[30]

He adds an observation similar to that of the Norwegian scholar Oskar Skarsaune, cited earlier: "In this view Scripture was an encyclopedic puzzle. It was a dictionary of facts that had been progressively revealed in various historical circumstances and literary genres and still needed to be sorted out and arranged."[31]

The first problem with this interpretation, says the nonmillenarian, is the random use of Bible passages and disregard for context. Therefore, the details are quite different among various dispensational writers themselves.

The second problem, argue the nonmillenarians, is the direct application of Old Testament prophecies to our time without going through the New Testament to discover how these passages were interpreted in the New Testament. They contend that to jump like a leapfrog over the New Testament, where the major prophecies of the Old Testament are discussed, interpreted, and developed, can lead to erroneous conclusions.

On the other hand, the dispensationalists hotly dispute the idea that they ignore the New Testament's citation of the Old Testament. They

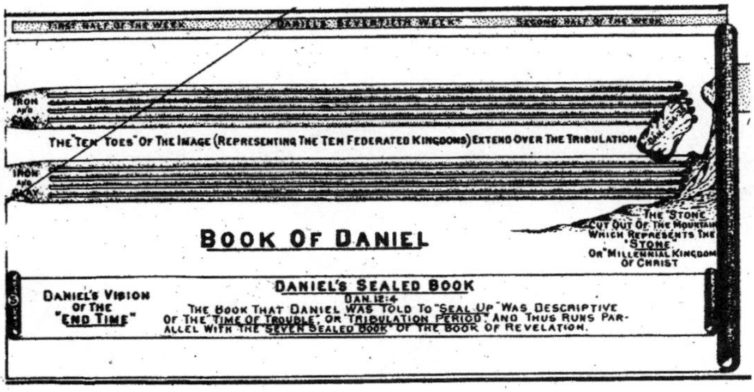

Reproduction of premillennialist Clarence Larkin's chart on the Book of Daniel.

point out that the only way we can know about future fulfillment of the end-times prophecies is by looking at the way Jesus fulfilled predictions about His first coming. Obviously, this requires looking at both the Old and New Testaments. As we read in an earlier chapter, here are the arguments of two dispensationalists:

- Charles Feinberg: "The only way to know how God will fulfill prophecy in the future is to ascertain how He has done it in the past."[32]
- Sir Robert Anderson of Scotland Yard: "There is not a single prophecy, of which the fulfillment is recorded in Scripture, that was not realized with absolute accuracy, and in every detail; and it is wholly unjustifiable to assume that a new system of fulfillment was inaugurated after the second canon closed."[33]

Furthermore, dispensationalists believe that as Daniel was looking into the future, he was seeing events both in the near future and in the far future.

Do you see how we're back to the question of assumptions? Again, interpretation of prophetic passages is the heart of the controversy on the end times.

Conclusion

Once more we see God's people divided over the minutia of details on end-times prophecies (if this indeed is an end-times prophecy). Therefore, we are reminded once more to search the Scriptures even more diligently "to see if these things be so." The Westminster Confession says, "All things in Scripture are not alike plain in themselves, nor alike clear unto all." This is certainly true about the seventy weeks of Daniel.

16

The Rapture

The Rapture: The Hope of the Church [1]

—Grant Jeffrey

It's been called:

- The blessed hope
- The Great Snatch
- The translation of the saints
- The ultimate trip
- Project Disappearance[2]

What is *it*? Why, it's the Rapture, of course. Let's consider this important Christian doctrine and some of its developments in the last two centuries. Above all, the passage that teaches it—1 Thessalonians 4—does indeed give "blessed hope" in the light of humanity's worst enemy—death.

Splitting the Second Coming?

The dispensationalists hold that there are two parts to the second coming of Christ—first, the Rapture, and then "the revelation."

Dispensationalist M. R. DeHaan of the Radio School of the Bible defines the Rapture aspect as "the secret sudden coming of Christ for His own."[3] Even if this doctrine was not formally verbalized until 1830, dispensationalists believe it is implicit in the teaching of the Scriptures because of their foundational view that God has one program for the church and another for Israel. DeHaan asserts that "the Rapture has to do with the Church only, whereas the Revelation has to do with Israel and the nations."[4]

In short, Christ first comes in the Rapture for His church; then He comes in judgment seven years later at the end of the Great Tribulation. Dave MacPherson sums it up this way: "The Second Coming of Christ is in two stages. First He comes *for* the saints and then later He comes back *with* the saints."[5] Christ establishes His earthly throne in Jerusalem and reigns for one thousand years. His presence ushers in the Millennium.

Postmillennialists and amillennialists, on the other hand, neither accept this scenario nor do they necessarily use the term "Rapture." Historically, the term of choice was the "resurrection." The key difference between the dispensationalists and the nonmillenarians is the *timing* of this event. Incidentally, we must point out that dispensationalists themselves have differing views on the timing.

To some, the Rapture takes place before the Tribulation.

To others, it takes place in the middle of the Tribulation.

And still to others, it takes place at the end of the Tribulation.

To the nonmillenarians, it takes place at the end of the world on the last day—the Day of Judgment. It takes place when God raises the dead, both good and bad, and judges everybody.

While the critics argue that dispensationalism *splits* the Second Coming into two parts—the Rapture and "the revelation"—I think it's only fair to point out that preterists divide the Second Coming into at least two parts as well—His coming in judgment in A.D. 70 and His final advent. Meanwhile, there are some nonmillenarian theologians who argue that there are several comings of Christ, that is:

1. At His resurrection.
2. At Pentecost.
3. In judgment in A.D. 70.
4. In the death of believers.
5. His final once-and-for-all return, which ends the world.

What Saith the Lord?

Before we plow too deeply into the controversy over the Rapture, let's answer the question: "What saith the Lord?" Verses from 1 Thessalonians 4 describe what is popularly called "the Rapture" (and historically, "the resurrection"). Paul wrote, speaking for the Lord:

> Brothers, we do not want you to be ignorant about those who sleep, or to grieve like the rest of men, who have no hope. We believe that Jesus died and rose again and so we believe that God will bring with Jesus those who have fallen asleep in him. According to the Lord's own word, we tell you that we who are still alive, who are left till the coming of the Lord, will certainly not precede

> those who have fallen asleep. For the Lord himself will come down from heaven, with a loud command, with the voice of the archangel and with the trumpet call of God, and the dead in Christ will rise first. After that, we who are still alive and are left will be caught up together with them in the clouds to meet the Lord in the air. And so we will be with the Lord forever. Therefore encourage each other with these words (1 Thess. 4:13-18).

The context of this passage from Paul's letter is that the Christians in Thessalonica were expecting the imminent return of Christ. Yet some of them had died. The survivors were concerned that those who had passed away were going to miss out on the Lord's return. Therefore, Paul was writing them to comfort them. They are words of great encouragement, for death has been the biggest enemy of humanity since the Fall, but no longer does death have such power over Christians.

The Rapture, the Resurrection, or Both?

As was stated earlier, historically the passage that teaches "the Rapture" has been one of two key passages on the resurrection (not just of Christ, but of believers); the other passage is 1 Corinthians 15. This is what St. Augustine wrote in the fifth century on 1 Thessalonians 4:

> For "the hour is coming, and now is, when the dead shall hear the voice of the Son of God; and they that hear shall live," i.e., shall not come into damnation, which is called the second death; into which death, after the second or bodily resurrection, they shall be hurled who do not rise in the first or spiritual resurrection. For "the hour is coming" (but here He does not say, "and now is," because it shall come in the end of the world in the last and greatest judgment of God) "when all that are in the graves shall hear His voice and shall come forth." He does not say, as in the first resurrection, "And they that hear shall live." For all shall not live, at least with such life as ought alone to be called life because it alone is blessed. For some kind of life they must have in order to

> hear, and come forth from the graves in their rising bodies. And why all shall not live He teaches in the words that follow: "They that have done good, to the resurrection of life"—these are they who shall live; "but they that have done evil, to the resurrection of judgement"—these are they that shall not live, for they shall die in the second death. They have done evil because their life has been evil; and their life has been evil because it has not been renewed in the first or spiritual resurrection which now is, or because they have not persevered to the end in their renewed life.[6]

Now jumping forward to the sixteenth century, read what the Reformer John Calvin had to say about the same passage:

> [Paul] again says that the *dead who are in Christ*, that is, who are included in Christ's body, will *rise first*, that we may know that the hope of life is laid up in heaven for them no less than for the living. He says nothing as to the reprobate, because this did not tend to the consolation of the pious, of which he is now treating. He says that those that survive will be carried up together with them. As to these, he makes no mention of death: hence it appears as if he meant to say that they would be exempted from death. Here Augustine gives himself much distress, both in the twentieth book of *The City of God* and in his Answer to Dulcitius, because Paul seems to contradict himself, inasmuch as he says elsewhere, that *seed cannot spring up again unless it die*. (1 Cor. xv.36.) The solution, however, is easy, inasmuch as a sudden change will be like death. Ordinary death, it is true, is the separation of the soul from the body; but this does not hinder that the Lord may in a moment destroy this corruptible nature, so as to create it anew by his power, for thus is accomplished what Paul himself teaches must take place—*that mortality shall be swallowed up of life*. (2 Cor. v. 4.)[7]

Calvin continued into verse 17 (1 Thess. 4) by stating:

> Now, to assign to Christ a thousand years, so that he would afterwards cease to reign, were too horrible to be made mention of. Those, however, fall into this absurdity who limit the life of believers to a thousand years, for they must live with Christ as long as Christ himself will exist. We must observe also what he says—*we shall be*, for he means that we profitably entertain a hope of eternal life, only when we hope that it has been expressly appointed for us.[8]

A Major Shift in the Nineteenth Century

Now, let's fast-forward again to the nineteenth century because up to that time the church was generally in accord with regard to the end times. Christ would return, and the world would apocalypse—that is, come to an end.

As was already noted, a new view arose around 1830, which introduced the now-popular view of the secret Rapture. Someone once quipped, "The *secret* pre-trib rapture is so secret that the church never heard of it for 1800 years."[9]

Dave MacPherson has written several books on the controversy about the Rapture. The books themselves are revolutionary. He discovered that all roads lead back to Port Glasgow, Scotland, to a teenaged girl named Margaret Macdonald. McPherson writes:

> Margaret Macdonald's revolutionary revelation of a two-stage Second Coming came to her as she studied various Scripture passages in the spring of 1830 in Port Glasgow, Scotland. One of her unique thoughts was that the first stage (the Rapture) would take place before the revealing of the Antichrist—an idea that had never been heard of in Church history before she expressed it! Not long after her revelation, she wrote down her account of everything and sent handwritten copies of it to a number of Christian leaders. *The Morning Watch*, a leading British publication, quickly copied some of her distinc-

> tive notions. Her revelation was first published in Robert Norton's *Memoirs of James & George Macdonald, of Port Glasgow* (1861), pp. 15-18.[10]

Pretrib, Midtrib, Posttrib

Whenever you hear the terms "pretribulation," "midtribulation," and "posttribulation," they refer to the timing of the Rapture. Is the Rapture before the tribulation (*pre*tribulation)? Does it take place during the Tribulation (*mid*tribulation)? Or does it come after the Tribulation (*post*tribulation).

The question for the dispensationalist is: Which comes first, the Rapture or the Tribulation? Dispensationalist Robert Van Kampen calls on us to rethink the timing of the Rapture. He personally shifted from being pretrib to a variation of midtrib, which he labels "prewrath." He writes:

> Plainly stated, the core truth is this: *the persecution by Antichrist during the great tribulation will be the wrath of Satan* (Rev. 12:12), *not the wrath of God. When the sign of the sun, moon, and stars is given in the heavens, the wrath of Satan against the elect of God will be terminated, the faithful to God will be raptured, and then the wrath of God will begin against the wicked who remain, ending with the battle of Armageddon*. Thus, the Rapture of God's saints has to occur sometime during the second half of the tribulation period, during Antichrist's persecution of God's elect. Plain and simple! No more, no less. Once you get that right, everything else falls together perfectly![11]

Van Kampen is quite concerned about the timing because it could mean that this generation of Christians could go through the terrible time of Tribulation, even though many of them have thought they would be spared such an horrific event. He adds:

> Yet those who hold to the pretribulaton Rapture position insist that "the elect" who will undergo this horrible time of persecution will not be the church, but the

> nation of Israel. However . . . Israel is not saved until after the seven-year tribulation period is complete. Referring to this time of Gentile domination of Jerusalem, Christ had earlier, while still in the temple, taught His disciples that "Jerusalem will be trampled under foot by the Gentiles until the times of the Gentiles be fulfilled" (Luke 2:24). Paul specifically tells the church in Rome that Israel will not be saved "until the fulness of the Gentiles has come in" (Rom. 11:25-26), paralleling Daniel's prophecy that "everlasting righteousness" will be brought in to the nation of Israel only after the seven-year tribulation period (seventieth week) is complete (Dan. 9:24). Thus, the elect of God—*you*—who for the sake of Christ's name will undergo persecution at the hands of Antichrist at the midpoint of the tribulation period (Matt. 24:9) cannot be the newly saved nation of Israel because she will not be saved until after the tribulation period is complete, until after "the fulness of the Gentiles has come in"![12]

Van Kampen certainly does not take this matter lightly. The implications could be quite consequential, especially to our families. He writes:

> Because the stakes are so high, your view of end times may determine whether you, your children, or your grandchildren survive the onslaught of Antichrist or die at his hands if someday you have to face this "great tribulation [persecution], such as has not occurred since the beginning of the world until now, nor ever shall" (Matt. 24:21)![13]

Although he may be classified as a premillennialist, Robert Van Kampen holds to the position that the day of the Rapture is the same as "the Day of the Lord"—the day of final judgment: "The true children of God will be given relief from their affliction *when* the day of the Lord's wrath comes, 'when the Lord Jesus shall be revealed from heaven with His mighty angels in flaming fire.' Not one moment earlier, not seven years earlier, but on the same day, at that precise moment!"[14]

One man, weaned on the dispensationalist school of thought, became convinced that the *pre*tribulational Rapture is essentially wishful thinking. His name is Oswald J. Smith, and he wrote a pamphlet, *Tribulation or Rapture—Which?*, wherein he states:

> Now, after years of study and prayer, I am absolutely convinced that there will be no rapture *before* the Tribulation, but that the Church will undoubtedly be called upon to face the Antichrist, and that Christ will come at the close and not at the beginning of that awful period. I believed the other theory simply because I was taught it by W. E. Blackstone in his book "Jesus is Coming", the Scofield Reference Bible and Prophetic Conferences and Bible Schools; but when I began to search the Scriptures for myself I discovered that there is not a single verse in the Bible that upholds the pre-tribulation theory, but that the uniform teaching of the Word of God is of a post-tribulation rapture.[15]

> ***Paul wrote these words that now divide Christians to encourage us***

On the other hand, the preterists say, "What are you worried about? All of this already happened in A.D. 70. The Tribulation is over." Either way, we can and should expect persecution because, as 2 Timothy 3:12 informs us, those who desire to live godly lives in Christ Jesus can expect such trouble.

We should also point out that the historical premillennialists do not hold to the secret Rapture view of the dispensationalists. D. Martyn Lloyd-Jones of that school holds: "It is important to realize that you can be a futurist without believing in the preliminary rapture of the saints."[16]

Encouraging Words

Why did Paul write these words that now divide the Christian community two millennia later? He wrote them to encourage us. Look away from the controversy for a minute. Look at the big picture. There is freedom from the anguish of death. There is hope for life everlasting. This is no small point. We know in the long run that life has meaning. It could be said that death is humanity's chief foe. It certainly holds many in fear—although, according to *The Book of Lists*, more people are afraid of going to the dentist and of public speaking than they are of death.[17]

Sometimes we become so wrapped up in the details of Christ's coming that we lose sight of the big picture. You would almost think that the gulf between premils and the postmils, between the pretribs and the preterists, between the dispensationalists and the amils is so wide and huge that it is larger than the gulf between a Christian view of death and any other view of death. That's simply absurd! Jesus rose from the dead; He is the "firstfruits" of the resurrection. Remember, long before the term "Rapture" became widely used, the common term to describe what Paul teaches in 1 Thessalonians 4 is the "resurrection." Many people to this day prefer to use that term to describe the phenomenon.

We are similar to reverse Victorians. In that era, talk about sex was hushed, while talk about death was open. In our time, talk about sex is open (too open, in my opinion), while talk about death is largely hushed. Noted thanatologist Elisabeth Kubler-Ross points out the irony of our view toward death: "The more we are making advancements in science, the more we seem to fear and deny the reality of death. How is this possible?"[18] Yet the Christian need not fear death.

A Fascinating Contrast

Because Jesus rose from the dead and because Jesus is coming back, we have the assurance that death is not the major menace many fear it to be. The difference between a Christian view of death and a pagan one is miles apart. Thus we must be careful to not fall into a trap of dividing ourselves over the Rapture so much that we miss the main point of the passage—we who know Christ have hope in death.

To get a glimpse of that wide gulf between pagan and believer regarding death, consider the thoughts on the grim reaper from many skeptics. Author Herbert Lee Williams compiled the following quotes:

- Ernest Hemingway: "There is no remedy for anything in life . . . death is a sovereign remedy for all misfortunes."
- The Earl of Beaconsfield: "Youth is a mistake, manhood a struggle, old age a regret."
- Voltaire: "Son, choose your (Christian) mother's way, not mine; she has chosen the better part."

- Eugene O'Neill: "Life's only meaning is death."
- H. L. Mencken: "What the meaning of life may be, I do not know; I incline to believe it has none."
- Matthew Prior: "He alone is blessed who ne'er was born."
- Robert Ingersoll: "If there be a God, let him have mercy on my soul."
- Friedrich Nietzsche: "If man has a why for his life he can bear with almost any how."[19]
- W. E. Lecky: Death is "the melancholy anticlimax to life."[20]

And on and on it goes.

Think about it logically. Suppose, like the modern secularist, we maintained that life is just the product of time plus chance plus matter. Ultimately life would be meaningless to us, and death the inevitable end. This, however, is not true for the Christian, and it was Paul's goal in this wonderful passage to assuage the fears of Christians whose loved ones had already died.

Now let's consider the words of dying Christians. What a contrast!

- D. L. Moody: "Earth is receding, heaven is opening, God is calling me!"
- John Wesley: "Best of all, God is with us!"
- Martin Luther: "Into thy hands I commend my spirit; God of truth thou hast redeemed me!"
- John Knox: "Come Lord Jesus, I commit body, soul and spirit into Thy hands. I have tasted of the heavenly joys where presently I shall be!" After uttering a deep sigh, he said, "Now it is come!"[21]

Because we're so familiar with the New Testament's teaching on the resurrection, it's easy to take it for granted. We should be ever mindful of death because ultimately this earth is not our home. Martin Luther once said, "Even in the best of health we should have death always before our eyes [so that] we will not expect to remain on this earth forever, but will have one foot in the air, so to speak."[24] Pascal reminds us that only Christ is the source of this knowledge: "Apart from Jesus Christ we know not what our life is, nor our death, nor God, nor ourselves."[24]

Conclusion

We have seen how well-meaning Christians differ on a lot of the details regarding the Rapture. Yet, isn't that just bickering over the details? In the big picture, we can positively affirm:

(1) One day, we're leaving here.

(2) Jesus is taking us up to be with Him.

(3) Death is not the end of it all.

This passage on the Rapture/resurrection should not *divide* us. It should *comfort* us! We've become so bogged down with the mechanics that we've too often lost the big picture.

In closing, I'm reminded of a story Robert Ervin Hough tells. A farmer was visited by a preacher who asked him how it was going. "Oh, fine," said the farmer, "but I was stung by a bee." Although it still annoyed him, he quickly added, "Well, there is one thing that brings me a good deal of satisfaction anyway; that bee will never sting another man!" "Why," asked the other man, "did you kill it?" "No, but do you not know that a bee has only one sting, and when it stings a man, it leaves the sting in him?" To this, Hough concludes, "Death [for the Christian] has but one sting, and that one was lodged in the body of Christ on the cross."[25] Amen.

17

The Rebirth of Israel

God has a program for the world, the Church, the nations and for His people Israel.[1]

—M. R. DeHaan

Most dispensationalists of today believe the single most important event in recent times is the rebirth of Israel as a nation in 1948 and Israel's complete recovery of Jerusalem in 1967. Read virtually any book on the end times, and the dispensationalists "key" on this historic event.

- In *The Late Great Planet Earth*, Hal Lindsey says, "We have seen how current events are fitting together simultaneously into the precise pattern of predicted events. Israel has returned to Palestine and revived the nation. Jerusalem is under Israeli control. . . . It's happening. God is putting it all together. God may have His meaning for the 'now generation' which will have a greater effect on mankind than anything since Genesis 1."[2]
- In *Is the Antichrist Alive and Well?* Ed Hindson asserts, "The tiny nation of Israel is the geographical focal point of Bible prophecy."[3]
- Thomas Ice and Timothy Demy write, "Modern Israel is prophetically significant and is fulfilling Bible prophecy . . . there will be *two* end-time regatherings—one before the tribulation and one after the tribulation."[4]

These sample quotes are just the tip of the iceberg.

Nevertheless, not all Bible-believing Christians necessarily agree with their statements. The purpose of this chapter will be to look at Israel and its relationship with the church.

As a preliminary observation, consider the Old Testament prophesies that the Jews will be gathered in their homeland, and Israel will be restored physically and spiritually. "This is what the Sovereign Lord says: 'I will take the Israelites out of the nations where they have gone. I will gather them from all around and bring them back into their own land. I will make them one nation in the land, on the mountains of Israel. . . . I will save them from all their sinful backsliding, and I will cleanse them. They will be my people, and I will be their God'" (Ezek. 37:20-22, 23).

The question is, When did this take place—centuries before Christ as preterists hold or in 1948 when the Jews reestablished their nation?

Meanwhile, Paul cautioned Gentile Christians in Rome not to be arrogant or to believe that they are better because they received what the Jews rejected (see Rom. 11). It all happened so that the Gentiles would be gathered into the kingdom. He told them "not [to] be conceited: Israel has experienced a hardening in part until *the full number of the Gentiles* has come in. And so all Israel will be saved" (Rom. 11:25-26, emphasis mine). What does it mean when Paul said all Israel will be saved? D. Martyn Lloyd-Jones gives his view:

> Thus the conclusion of this interpretation of the words "all Israel shall be saved" is that they mean the total of all believing Jews in all ages and generations, all whom God has foreseen shall infallibly be fulness of the Jews. There are some, and I am among them, who believe that Paul does teach in this chapter that before the end there will be large numbers of conversions among the Jews. It will be astonishing and it will rejoice the hearts of believers then alive. It will be like life from the dead.[5]

Is the Church the New Israel?

Has God abandoned His covenant with the Jews? If you read church history, you would think the vast majority of theologians through the centuries thought He had. In his book *Armageddon: Appointment with Destiny*, Grant Jeffrey observes:

> Historically, over the last two thousand years, many in the Church have "written off" Israel and ignored the eternal covenant promises that God made to His Chosen People, the Jews. Many scholars have mistakenly taught that God rejected and abandoned Israel forever when the majority of Israel rejected Jesus Christ as their Messiah.[6]

A huge area of controversy between different Christian schools of thought relates to Israel. For example, as we've already seen, the dispensationalists hold that God has one plan for the Jews and another for the church. When Jesus presented the Gospel and God's kingdom to the Jews, they rejected Him and it. So God went into Plan B and created the mystery of the church. Thus the promises of the Old Testament prophets about the worldwide expansion of God's reign were all put on hold until Israel is regathered and until they recognize that Jesus is their Messiah.

On the other hand, the nondispensationalists contend that this teaching is wrong. The church was not Plan B. God knew in advance what was going to happen. The church, which initially was made up of virtually all Jews, was His agency to spread the faith to the whole world. Joel B. Green writes:

> In the Old Testament, Israel was known as the people of God: in Hebrew, *qahal*; in Greek, *ekklesia*. It is of no little consequence that the early church took over for themselves the Old Testament designation for Israel—the *ekklesia* of God. In this same vein, Paul seems to equate true Israel with Christians, whether Jews or Gentiles (see Rom. 2:25, 28-29; Gal. 3:7; Phil. 3:3).[7]

Are the church and Israel the same? Is the church "spiritual Israel"? Are we "the new Israel"? What does the Bible say? Paul stated, "A man is not a Jew if he is only one outwardly, nor is circumcision merely outward and physical. No, a man is a Jew if he is one inwardly; and circumcision is circumcision of the heart, by the Spirit" (Rom. 2:28-29).

Paul added in the same letter, "For not all who are descended from Israel are Israel. Nor because they are his descendants are they all Abraham's children. . . . It is not the natural children who are God's children, but it is the children of the promise who are regarded as Abraham's offspring" (Rom. 9:6-8).

Nonmillenarian Philip Edgcumbe Hughes points out, "It is the contention of dispensationalists that the Old Testament did not foresee or foretell the coming of this present age of the Christian church."[8] Hughes feels so strongly about this that he even pens these words: "We fear that the dispensationalist method of interpretation does violence to the unity of Scripture and to the sovereign continuity of God's purposes, and cavalierly leaves out of account a major portion of the apostolic teaching—that, chiefly, of the Acts and the Epistles—as unrelated to the perspective of the Old Testament authors."[9]

Obviously, premillennialists disagree. Leading dispensationalist C. I. Scofield gives us this commentary: "The apparent failure of the Old Testament promises concerning the Davidic kingdom was explained by the promise that the kingdom would be set up at the return of Christ (Acts 2:25-31; 15:14-16)."[10] So God's promise for the Jew is different than for the Christian.

Scofield goes on to add:

> A distinction must be observed between "the last days" when the prediction relates to Israel, and the "last days" when the prediction relates to the church. . . . Also distinguish the expression the "last days" (plural) from "the last day" (singular); the latter expression referring to the resurrections and last judgment. . . . The "last days" as related to the church began with the advent of Christ (Heb. 1:2), but have especial reference to the time of declension and apostasy at the end of this age (2 Tim. 3:1; 4:4). The "last days" as related to Israel are the days of Israel's exaltation and blessing, and are synonymous with the kingdom-age. . . . They are "last" not with reference to this dispensation, but with reference to the whole of Israel's history.[11]

If that's the case, then Hughes poses these questions:

> Is this church period a parenthesis, a stop-gap, made necessary by the contingency of the rejection by the Jews of the kingdom at Christ's first coming? . . . Was God's position one of doubt and uncertainty, so that he had to wait and see what the answer of the Jews would be? And when it turned out to be a negative answer was he forced to resort to an emergency measure until such time as he could put his original plan into effect?[12]

Implied in his questions is the answer: No. Hughes goes on to make these observations:

- "Certainly, the apostles do not appear to have regarded the era of the church as a parenthesis outside the scope of the prophetic vision. On the Day of Pentecost, for example, Peter assured his large Jewish audience that the sending forth of the Holy Spirit is 'what was spoken by the prophet Joel.'"[13]

- "If there is a difference between the 'kingdom' and the 'church,' the apostles and evangelists of the New Testament seem to have been unaware of it."[14]

Accordingly, nondispensationalists hold that God's promises for the expansion of His program into all the world have been going on for the last two millennia through the agency of the church. The stone that has become a mountain is filling the whole earth, and one day every knee shall bow and acknowledge that Jesus is Lord.

One other observation here. Some nonmillenarians believe God will do something special for Israel at the end of time that will compel them to accept Jesus as their Messiah. They base this view on Romans 11, in which the Apostle Paul said, "all Israel will be saved." This view then holds that from the time of the rejection of Christ by the Jews until the very end of time, the church of Jesus Christ are the chosen people, not the Jews. Yet at the end, God will do something special for the Jews as well.

Is Modern-day Israel a Fulfillment of Prophecy?

Is the modern-day state of Israel the long-awaited fulfillment of prophecy that many writers today assert that it is? It has been stated so often that to even ask that question sounds like heresy! Certainly, we can all marvel at the seemingly miraculous way they have survived attacks from all sides when considerable odds have been against them. Yet again, is the birth of Israel as a nation in 1948 the fulfillment of prophecy?

Listen to this statement from premillennialist Grant Jeffrey's *Armageddon: Appointment with Destiny*:

> On May 15, 1948, after almost nineteen hundred years of devastation and persecution, Israel became a nation—in the precise year foretold by the prophet Ezekiel over twenty-five hundred years earlier. Therefore, based on Christ's promise in Matthew 24:32-34, our generation is the first group of Christians in history with a sound foundation for believing that, within our natural life span (forty to seventy years), we will witness the amazing

> events concerning the Second Coming of Christ. . . . We are the first generation in history that can, in light of the firm scriptural authority of Matthew 24:32-34, respond in confidence to Christ's command, "And when these things begin to come to pass, then look up, and lift up your heads; for your redemption draweth nigh" (Luke 21:28).[15]

In other words, the clock started ticking in 1948. This generation will not pass away until all these things happen. We've already seen different opinions on this statement (including those who believe it was fulfilled in A.D. 70; that is, within the generation of those who actually heard those words). The most significant part of Jeffrey's quote is the important role Israel plays in the fulfillment of Bible prophecy.

Van Kampen puts it this way: "In 1948, Israel became a nation. In 1967, Israel regained control of Jerusalem. These two events are critical; they had to occur before the events outlined in the Olivet Discourse could commence. Summer is not yet come, but the branch—God's ancient people, the Jews, so to speak—is definitely tender and the leaves are beginning to bud."[16]

Now listen to the other side of the dispute. John Wilmot states, "Today a resettled people has assumed the title ['Israel'] and applies it also to their country. . . . The only entitlement to the name of 'Israel' is from spiritual relationship to Jesus Christ."[17]

Similarly, postmillennialist Loraine Boettner argues:

> The assumption of modern Premillennialism, and particularly of Dispensationalism, that at the Coming of Christ a Jewish kingdom will be re-established in Palestine proceeds on a false principle, which is that God still has a special purpose to be served by the Jewish people as a nation. But the fact of the matter is that there is no further need for such a kingdom.[18]

Boettner goes on to cite Jesus' statement of judgment to the Jewish leaders (in light of their rejection of Him, their own Messiah): "Therefore I tell you that the kingdom of God will be taken away from you and given to a people who will produce its fruit" (Matt. 21:43).

Interestingly, this view is even echoed by nondispensational premillennialists. For instance, D. Martyn Lloyd-Jones, writes, "It is a simple fact that our Lord never spoke about the restoration of the Jews to the Holy Land. Never. There is no reference to it in all His teaching."[19]

Paul wrote that the Jews have received a temporary hardening. Yet at the end of time, their eyes will be opened. They will recognize Jesus Christ as their own Messiah and "all Israel will be saved" (Rom. 11:26). What does Paul's statement mean? Are we seeing the fulfillment in our day because proportionately more Jews are coming to faith in Jesus as their Messiah than ever before? That's an interesting thought, but keep in mind that many people from *every* group are coming to faith at this present time.

Students of history marvel at the amazing ways the Jews have managed to defend themselves in modern-day Israel. Against all odds, against incredible numbers of armed Arabs attacking them, over and over, this tiny, fledgling nation has managed to win the many wars brought against her since her rebirth in 1948. Many writers feel this alone is evidence that God is on the side of modern-day Israel. After giving his readers a brief history lesson on how the modern state of Israel has survived attack after attack, Ed Hindson writes:

> Each of these conflicts was unsuccessful in eliminating the tiny nation of Israel. It should be obvious by now that she is back in her land by a miracle of God. The prophet Amos promised: "I will bring back my exiled people Israel; they will rebuild the ruined cities and live in them. . . . I will plant Israel in their own land, never again to be uprooted from the land I have given them" (Amos 9:14,15). God is clearly fulfilling His promise.[20]

Can One Be Pro-Israel Even If Not Thinking the Modern-day State Doesn't Directly Fulfill Biblical Prophecy?

Is it possible to be pro-Israel and yet believe that the modern nation of Israel no more fulfills biblical prophecy than the bombing of Kosovo? Some writers think so. There are many who admire Israel, if for nothing else than for the wonderful job they have done and do to promote Holy Land tours. Israel, especially Jerusalem, contains sites that are holy to three different religions. In the past, while in Islamic or Christian hands, there has not been as much ready access to these holy sites for the pilgrims of rival faiths. Modern Israeli Jews, however, have allowed a certain level of freedom to devotees from around the world.

Many believe (and I'm one of them) that Israel is currently the best friend the United States has in the Middle East. To believe that, must one subscribe to the theory that modern-day Israel is the fulfillment of prophecy unfolding before us in our times? Not necessarily. Nor does it mean Israel can do no wrong. There should be justice for the thousands of Palestinian refugees. Even Shimon Perez says there should be a Palestinian state.

Meanwhile, the Arab enemies of Israel are also enemies of the Gospel. There is a global war against Christians in our time—often at the hands of Muslim extremists. Those who hate Israel are often those who kill Christians in their own country. Suffice it to say that Israel is a key ally of the United States and indeed deserves our support.

The entire world owes a great debt to the Jewish people, thanks to Jesus Christ

Moreover, I believe it's important to treat Jews with respect and dignity. Do you realize every Jew is actually a blood relative of the Savior? The whole world is in debt to the Jewish people. The whole world! God has blessed our planet because of the Jews through the agency of the church of Jesus Christ. As Benjamin Disraeli, a Jewish prime minister of England in the nineteenth century, said:

> The pupil of Moses may ask himself whether all the princes of the House of David have done so much for Jews as that Prince who was crucified. . . .
>
> Had it not been for [Jesus], the Jews would have been comparatively unknown, or known only as a high Oriental Caste which had lost its country. Has not He made their history the most famous history in the world?
>
> The wildest dreams of their Rabbis have been far exceeded. Has not Jesus conquered Europe and changed its name to Christendom? All countries that refuse the cross wilt, and the time will come when the countless myriads of America and Australia will find music in the Songs of Zion, and solace in the parables of Galilee.[21]

Indeed, the entire world owes a great debt to the Jewish people, thanks to Jesus Christ. Yet the world has been rather ungrateful, even those who profess to be followers of Jesus.

"I Will Bless Them That Bless Thee and Curse Them That Curse Thee"

God said to Abraham, "I will bless those who bless you, and whoever curses you I will curse" (Gen. 12:3). Many believe to bless the Jews brings a blessing and to curse them brings a curse. Grant Jeffrey writes, for example, that England was blessed as a nation from the time of Cromwell (mid-seventeenth century) through the mid-twentieth century. Certainly, in the last century, under Queen Victoria, the sun never set on the British Empire. Cromwell gave rights to the Jews, rights that had been denied them in previous monarchies of England. Jeffrey notes, "The British Empire's prosperity and world power can be traced to the reign of Lord Cromwell. The Jews returned and prospered in England and all her colonies."[22]

Meanwhile, nearly three hundred years later, in the early part of this century, England reneged on its pro-Israel Balfour Declaration of 1917. Israel, he points out, received only 17.5 percent of the land promised her in the Balfour Declaration.[23] Worse than that, the Jewish people did not have a homeland to which they could flee from Hitler's persecution during the Nazi terror. As a result, Jeffrey declares:

> It is not improbable that the decline of Britain from its exalted status as the preeminent superpower that "ruled the seas" to its diminished position as a second-level power is connected to her abandonment of the Jews and their national homeland. In this same period, 1917–1948, England lost her vast empire, one-quarter of the globe, and even lost the southern part of Ireland.[24]

Is God Finished with the Jews?

Some dispensationalists dispute the view the church has held for centuries—that is, that God is essentially finished with the Jews or that the church is the New Israel (which Paul declared in his letters to the

Romans and Galatians). They add that this view has led to anti-Semitism. There is no question that the Christian era has been marred and is forever stained with blood by wicked chapters of anti-Semitism. Hal Lindsey points out:

> Most theologians from Augustine onward had declared the promises and blessings of Israel null and void and transferred them to the Church—without the curses, of course. Most anti-Semitism within the professing Christian church from that time onward was fueled by the belief that God was finished with the Jew as a special people and nation. Therefore, making life "difficult" for the Jew became almost a mark of religious dedication.[25]

Tragically, anti-Semitism *is* an ugly part of church history.[26]

The irony of professing Christians, who have persecuted Jews through the ages as "Christ-killers," is that the generation responsible for His death was judged most severely. Forty years after the Jews cried out to Pilate, "Let his blood be on us and on our children!" (Matt. 27:25), they received in full the judgment for their responsibility of having the Son of God crucified. That's it. No more.

Gary DeMar says that curse ("Let His blood be upon us") was fulfilled in that one generation and *only* that one: "The curse was fulfilled in A.D. 70 upon the generation that uttered the oath. To continue to futurize events that are certainly fulfilled prophecy can only do more harm. Many modern-day evangelicals and fundamentalists unwittingly contribute to widespread anti-Semitism."[27]

Why does he say that? Ideas have consequences. He quotes Grace Halsell's book, *Prophecy and Politics: Militant Evangelists on the Road to Nuclear War*, wherein she states:

> Convinced that a nuclear Armageddon is an inevitable event within the divine scheme of things, many evangelical dispensationalists have committed themselves to a course for Israel that, by their own admission, will lead directly to a holocaust indescribably more savage and widespread than that any vision of carnage that could have generated in Adolf Hitler's criminal mind."[28]

Commenting on this, Gary DeMar says, "It is time that we take the Bible seriously and jettison a system of interpretation that accepts massive slaughter around the world as inevitable."[29]

Dwight Wilson adds, "For the premillenarian, the massacre of Jewry expedited his blessed hope. Certainly he did not rejoice over the Nazi holocaust; he just fatalistically observed it as a 'sign of the times.'"[30] He says, unfairly it would seem to me, that they did not fight anti-Jewish persecution "because persecution was prophetically expected."[31]

Meanwhile, there is no "Christian" justification for anti-Semitism. None. Thankfully, anti-Semitism seems to have become quite unpopular in our day, especially in Christian circles. The nation of Israel has virtually no greater non-Jewish friend than that of the Christian community in North America.

Nevertheless, nonmillenarians argue just because there has been anti-Semitism in the Christian era doesn't necessarily mean that the church is not the spiritual Israel. Nor does it necessarily mean that modern-day Israel is the fulfillment of ancient biblical prophecy. It's certainly the U.S.'s favorite ally in the Middle East, and it plays a critical role in the fight for world peace, but it's not necessarily the fulfillment of the restoration promises of the Old Testament, such as Ezekiel 37 ("dem bones, dem bones"), which preterists tend to believe were fulfilled B.C. c. 516, in the days of Ezra and Nehemiah.

Nonmillenarian Gary DeMar writes, ". . . the entire New Testament is silent on the subject of Israel's restored nationhood."[32] But wait a minute! Listen to what Jesus said, "Jerusalem will be trampled on by the Gentiles *until the times of the Gentiles are fulfilled*" (Luke 21:24, emphasis mine). This statement seems to imply a time limit of some sort on how long the Gentiles are allowed to run roughshod over Jerusalem.

DeMar further says this about the 1948 rebirth of Israel as a nation and Hal Lindsey (but he might as well have said it about all premillennialists today): "Without this keystone [modern Israel], the predictive elements in Lindsey's prophetic blueprint are nothing more than that scattered bricks on an unorganized building site."[33]

It's been nearly nineteen centuries since the Jews had their own homeland. Persecuted and hounded from one "Christian" nation to another, they suffered heavily under the church-states of Christendom. Within roughly a century after the rebirth of millenarianism, Israel as a nation is reborn. Is there a link there? Dispensationalism, says Hal Lindsey, helped pave the way for that rebirth because its prophetic scenario for the future saw the need for Israel to be reborn. Ideas have consequences. He mentions Lord Balfour of the Balfour Declaration, which moved Britain to help the Jews reestablish a homeland in Palestine:

> Lord Balfour had become an avid believer in the literal interpretation of Bible prophecy, through the influence of John Darby's extensive ministry. As a result, he believed that God could not lie to the Jewish people when He promised to return them to their own land and reestablish the State of Israel.[34]

Ideas have consequences.

I've never understood anti-Semitism among professing "Christians." Don't we worship a Jew? In reality, those who are born again often aren't anti-Semitic; it is only those outwardly Christian who don't know the Lord who discriminate against the Jews.

Now, as commendable as it is to completely condemn anti-Semitism,[35] none of these considerations alters whether or not the New Testament teaches that the church is the new Israel. Even if one believes that it is, it does not necessarily mean one believes God is through with Israel. Nonmillenarians who believe the church is the new Israel are divided over whether or not God has future plans for the Jewish nation. For example, Hughes writes, "We have seen that the fulness of the Gentiles will be attained when the evangelization of all peoples in every corner of the world has been completed. It is by evangelization, too, that the fulness of Israel will be achieved."[36]

Hughes continues, "God's choice of the Israelites was no *carte blanche*, however, permitting them to live carelessly without fear of retribution. Privilege always means responsibility. . . . It was for purposes of blessing that the children of Israel were chosen by God—not blessing limited to themselves, however, but blessing intended for all nations of the earth." Then he adds, "The Gospel was always intended to be universal in scope, and that this was stated with explicit clarity in the promise given to Abraham that in his seed all the nations of the earth would be blessed."[37]

Premillennialists like to point out that nonmillenarians are inconsistent. They want the curses applied to Israel but the blessings applied to the church.

Conclusion

It is interesting to note that whether we're talking about the dispensationalist view of Israel or the nonmillenarian view, there is the underlying belief that Israel will one day have to deal with Jesus. He is an inescapable imperative for all of us, Jew or Gentile. As the Book of Hebrews puts it, He is the One to whom we must give account (Heb. 4:13).

18

The Antichrist

***Whoever refuses to confess that Jesus Christ is come in the flesh is Antichrist.*[1]**

—St. Polycarp

Late one night in Berlin in the 1930s shortly after the Nazis' rise to power, historian Herman Rauschning had tea and pastries in Hitler's apartment with some of the Nazi leaders. In addition to der Fuhrer, Joseph Goebbels and Julius Streicher were also there. The discussion eventually turned to religion, and Hitler vehemently pronounced his anti-Semitic and anti-Christian views. One can picture him virtually foaming at the mouth as he exclaimed:

> It is not merely a question of Christianity and Judaism. We are fighting against the most ancient curse that humanity has brought upon itself. We are fighting against the perversion of our soundest instincts. Ah, the God of the deserts, that crazed, stupid, vengeful Asiatic despot with his powers to make laws! . . . That poison with which both Jews and Christians have spoiled and soiled the free, wonderful instincts of man and lowered them to the level of doglike fright. . . . I am the Lord thy God! Who? That Asiatic tyrant? No! The day will come when I shall hold up against these [the ten] commandments the tables of a new law. And history will recognize our movement as the great battle for humanity's liberation, a liberation from the curse of Mount Sinai. . . .[2]

Thus spoke one of history's leading candidates for the Antichrist. Is it any wonder that many Christians in his day thought he might be *it*—the Antichrist, the man of lawlessness, the Beast? Hitler certainly reflected the spirit of the Antichrist.

Who is the Antichrist? Is there a literal beast yet to come or was he Nero, as some theologians maintain? In this chapter we will see what the Bible, history, and various writers have to say about the Antichrist.

Here again opinions differ on whether the Antichrist is a real person or whether the term is symbolic. However, it would seem that the vast majority of church leaders through the ages believe he is a real person. Whether it was Nero or someone yet to come or perhaps even a series of men is open to debate.

Through the ages, people have nominated a number of "candidates" for the title of Antichrist. Here's just a partial list.

- Nero
- The pope (to many Reformers)
- Martin Luther (to many Catholics then)
- Napoleon
- Robert Owen, nineteenth-century socialist
- Kaiser Wilhelm II
- Benito Mussolini
- Adolph Hitler
- Josef Stalin
- Pope Pius XII
- Pope John XXIII
- Moshe Dayan
- Pope John Paul II
- Anwar Sadat
- Jimmy Carter
- Pat Robertson
- Sun Myung Moon
- Henry Kissinger
- Nikita Krushchev
- John F. Kennedy[3]
- King Juan Carlos of Spain
- Mikhail Gorbachev
- Saddam Hussein
- Bill Clinton—with Hillary as the False Prophet[4]

A few of these names, such as Nero, Hitler, or Stalin, do not seem so far-fetched as candidates for the Antichrist. Nevertheless, the above suggestions are highly speculative, akin to date-setting. I recall a rumor that was circulating in 1984 that even Ronald Wilson Reagan might be the Antichrist—notwithstanding all his positive references to God or the Bible. And what was the "evidence" that the President might be the Beast?

Ronald is six letters.

Wilson is six letters.

Reagan is six letters.

In other words: He is 666!

How ridiculous can all this mindless speculation get! No wonder some people dismiss prophecy altogether. Sadly they throw the baby out with the bathwater. Interestingly President Reagan left the White House in 1989 and moved back to Bel Air, California, where he changed the number on the address of his new home to 668 Saint Cloud. It had been 666. He wanted to avoid the mark of the beast.[5]

So Is There a Literal *Antichrist?*

It would seem that many, if not most, scholars through the ages do believe in a real person yet to come. St. Augustine made these points about the Antichrist when commenting on 2 Thessalonians and Paul's reference to the "man of lawlessness." To provide the context of Augustine's quote he commences with the Bible verse from 2 Thessalonians 2:7:

> "For the mystery of iniquity doth already work: only he who now holdeth, let him hold until he be taken out of the way: and then shall the wicked be revealed.". . . I frankly confess I do not know what he means. I will nevertheless mention such conjectures as I have heard or read.
>
> Some think that the Apostle Paul referred to the Roman empire, and that he was unwilling to use language more explicit, lest he should incur the calumnious charge of wishing ill to the empire which it was hoped would be eternal; so that in saying, "For the mystery of iniquity doth already work," he alluded to Nero, whose deeds already seemed to be as the deeds of Antichrist. And hence some suppose that he shall rise again and be Antichrist. Others, again, suppose that he is not even dead, but that he was concealed that he might be supposed to have been killed, and that he now lives in concealment in the vigor of that same age which he had reached when he was believed to have perished, and will live until he is revealed in his own time and restored to his kingdom. But I wonder that men can be so audacious in their conjectures.[6]

While Augustine dismisses the idea that the Antichrist will just be a risen-from-the-dead Nero, he does not dismiss the notion of a real person yet to come that will be the Antichrist.

The Antichrist and False Messiahs

The Antichrist is believed to be the main character in the last act of the drama of the ages. Before the curtain goes down, he must appear. From the time of Pentecost until the last day (the Day of the Lord), the church has been struggling against evil. Yet many believe one particular man, the Antichrist, will play a pivotal role in the battle between good (that is, God and Christ) and evil (that is, the Dragon and the Beast) in the last days.

Before the curtain goes down, the Antichrist must appear

The word "Antichrist" appears only in the letters of the Apostle John. Several other biblical writers, Job, Daniel, Paul and again John in Revelation, talk about an evil man, "the Man of Lawlessness" and "the Beast." Many interpreters (but certainly not all) assume that these are all different descriptions of one person. The reason for believing it is the same man is that the descriptions of him in the different passages are quite similar. Antichrist is a spirit, an idea, and a concrete person.

From the first-century claims to messiahship by Simon Magus to the modern-day false prophets, there have been many who have professed to be the Christ, the Messiah. Jesus warned, "Watch out that no one deceives you. For many will come in my name, claiming, 'I am the Christ,' and will deceive many" (Matt. 24:4-5). Even those in the preterist school would agree that His warning against false christs and spiritual deception applies to all time—even if they think that in the immediate context in which He said these words He was warning about imposters to arise around the time of Israel's destruction in A.D. 70.

In one way all spiritual imposters are antichrists because, as John said in his first letter, there are many antichrists: "Dear children, this is the last hour; and as you have heard that the antichrist is coming, even now many antichrists have come" (1 John 2:18). What do they all have in common? "It is the man who denies that Jesus is the Christ. Such a man is the antichrist—he denies the Father and the Son" (v. 22).

John also provided the test of any spirit and any spiritual power: "Every spirit that acknowledges that Jesus Christ has come in the flesh is from God, but every spirit that does not acknowledge Jesus is not from God. This is the spirit of the antichrist, which you have heard is coming and even now is already in the world" (1 John 4:2-3). In other words, any person or religious group that does not believe that Jesus is God and that He is the promised Messiah displays the spirit of the Antichrist. Yet with all that said, there seems to be *one* particular Antichrist who will come on the scene during the last days.

Antichrist, the World Ruler

Revelation talks about "the Beast" and says of him that "he was given authority over every tribe, people, language and nation" (Rev. 13:7). The idea of a world ruler is nothing new. From Alexander the Great through the Roman Empire to the British Empire, world kingdoms have come and gone. None of the empires the world has seen has had total power—it wasn't possible. Yet today, there are technologies in force that make it quite possible.

The Book of Daniel talks about a terrifying and frightening beast that is blasphemous and boastful. "It crushed and devoured its victims and trampled underfoot whatever was left. It was different from all the former beasts, and it had ten horns" (Dan. 7:7). What did Daniel mean by the ten horns? He later elaborated, "The ten horns are ten kings who will come from this kingdom. After them another king will arise, different from the earlier ones; he will subdue three kings. He will speak against the Most High and oppress his saints and try to change the set times and the laws. The saints will be handed over to him for a time, times and half a time" (vv. 24-25). Yet Daniel had said a day of reckoning would come for the Beast: "As I watched, this horn was waging war against the saints and defeating them, until the Ancient of Days came and pronounced judgment in favor of the saints of the Most High" (vv. 21-22).

Some point out that if Daniel's prophecies were referring only to the kings and kingdoms of antiquity, they would not have been repeated in the Book of Revelation since this book was written after the fall of Jerusalem in A.D. 70. Yet there is some evidence for the view that this book was written before that time.

Let's take a moment to look at the preterist view on the subject. Then the rest of the chapter will be devoted to the futurists' considerations.

Was Nero the Antichrist?

First of all, let's keep in mind the primary purpose of the Book of

Revelation. John wrote this book in part to encourage his fellow Christians, who were undergoing life-threatening persecution. Talking about the Beast of Revelation 13 and the False Prophet, Joel B. Green, author of *How to Read Prophecy*, writes:

> How would John's first readers have understood these images? Already in New Testament times, the emperor of Rome was increasingly seen not only as an agent of the gods, but as a god himself. For many, the emperor was the deity who guaranteed sustenance and fulfillment in life. Thus he was to be worshiped *as a god*. This state of affairs constituted no small problem for Christians, who gave their highest allegiance to their Lord and who looked to him, not to the Roman emperor, for daily provision. As this imperial religion developed further, the state would harass Christians more and more, pressing them to renounce Christ in favor of emperor worship. In such a context, the beast from the sea would have symbolized the deified emperor. His counterpart from the earth would have represented those persons—priests, philosophers, and the like—who promoted the imperial religion.[7]

THE ANTICHRIST

Daniel's Foreview

Fourth Wild Beast
Dan. 7:7, 8, 19, 20, 23-25.

The Little Horn Of The He-Goat
Dan. 8:8-12, 23-25.

Green adds, "This is a political antichrist, the Roman emperor demanding divine adoration. In claiming for himself the title *Lord* the emperor became for Christians a rival Christ, an antichrist."[8]

This thought is repeated among many nonmillenarians (of which Green may or may not be a member): Nero was likely the beast of Revelation 13, the Antichrist. R. C. Sproul affirms that in his book, *The Last Days According to Jesus*. There is clear evidence that they think that John was writing in a hidden way so that his readers might read between the lines and deduce that Nero was the Beast. For example, Caesar Nero is in the Greek: *Neron Kesar*. In the Hebrew it is: *nrwn qsr*. Hebrew letters have numerical value; when Nero's name is added up in Hebrew, guess what it equals? Gary DeMar says, "When we take the letters of Nero's name and spell them in Hebrew, we get the following numeric values: n = 50, r = 200, w = 6, n = 50, q = 100, s = 60, r = 200 = 666."[9]

Nevertheless, amillennialist G. C. Berkouwer cautions against any dogmatic assertion for the meaning of 666: "Through the course of the centuries this number 666 has been shrouded in mystery. One cannot reassure himself with the thought that the number will remain mysterious for a longer or shorter time, to be revealed later."[10]

Nero was the first Roman emperor to initiate the persecution of Christians. He was a very sick man. Sometimes Christians were tied up,

The Wilful King
Dan. 11:36-39.

Paul's Foreview
2 Thess. 2:3-12

John's Foreview

Beast Out Of The Sea
Rev. 13:1-7

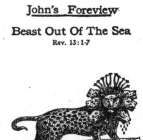

covered with pitch, stuck up on poles in his gardens, and then lit up for his amusement. Literally! It is said that even though his guests were generally pagans, they were so revulsed at this that they felt sorry for the Christians. Then, of course, there were the Christians who were thrown to the lions. Of those evil days, historian John Foxe, author of *Foxe's Book of Martyrs*, reports:

> Whatsoever the cruelness of man's invention could devise for the punishment of man's body, was practiced against the Christians—plates of iron laid unto them burning hot, deep dungeons, racks, strangling in prisons, the teeth of wild beasts, gridirons, gibbets and gallows, tossing upon the horns of bulls. . . .[11]

And it was Nero who started the official persecution of Christians.

His Family Life

Obviously Nero was a psychopath. What kind of person was he in his personal and family life? Here is what Dr. James Kennedy and I wrote about Nero in *What If Jesus Had Never Been Born?*:

> He had received the finest of pagan philosophical educations, and yet he degenerated into one of the worst conceivable men. He visited brothels, frequently in disguise. He practiced, as one historian says, "lewdness on boys . . . striking, wounding, murdering." He took a mistress. He wanted to have an affair with her and his wife objected. What do you do in a case like that? Well, it should be obvious to any and all: you simply kill your wife!—which is what he did. But his mother objected. So he killed his mother. But he wasn't completely without feeling. In fact, when he looked down on her corpse at her funeral he said, "I did not know I had so beautiful a mother."
>
> And so he married his mistress. Then one day she made the sad mistake of nagging him because he came home late from the races. She was in the latter stages of

> pregnancy. Nero kicked her in the stomach, killing both her and the child. Keep in mind, this was the ruler of the world at that time![12]

A beast indeed. Even if there is a future Antichrist to rise, Nero serves as his *prototype*. It is fortunate that he was a first-century despot without modern technology available to him.

Meanwhile, clearly not all nonmillenarians necessarily think that Nero was the Antichrist. Even St. Augustine, whom we could call "the father of amillenarianism," believed there was an Antichrist *yet* to come.[13]

We will now consider some potential points about the Antichrist and the spirit of Antichrist. I say "potential" points because they will be mostly futuristic considerations. If the preterists are right and Nero was the Antichrist, then these points are essentially irrelevant. Nevertheless, henceforth we will describe the Antichrist and what the Bible says about him—with the implicit understanding that this is a futuristic interpretation.

Some Potential Considerations on the Coming Antichrist

Paul explained to the Thessalonians that the day of the Lord's coming cannot come before the man of lawlessness comes:

> Don't let anyone deceive you in any way, for that day will not come until the rebellion occurs and the man of lawlessness is revealed, the man doomed to destruction. He opposes and exalts himself over everything that is called God or is worshiped, so that he sets himself up in God's temple, proclaiming himself to be God (2 Thess. 2:3-4).

Paul said the lawless one is now held back, but when the restraint is gone:

> The lawless one will be revealed, whom the Lord Jesus will overthrow with the breath of his mouth and destroy by the splendor of his coming. The coming of the lawless one will be in accordance with the work of Satan displayed in all kinds of counterfeit miracles, signs and wonders, and in every sort of evil that deceives those who are perishing (2 Thess. 2:8-10).

What is the restraint that Paul was talking about? What is the secret power of lawlessness? Arguably, it's the law itself. When the man of lawlessness comes, and the restraint (the law) is taken away, then society degenerates into complete anarchy, that is, lawlessness.

The German historian Herman Rauschning gives an interesting example from recent history that demonstrates "the secret power of lawlessness." He tells how ordinary, decent, and even kind people changed under the influence of the Nazis. Their faces became hard, and they lost concern for others. They became greedy and quick to take advantage of any weak person. They developed new habits, took mistresses, and started living above their means. They abused anybody in their path. It was as if they took on a new personality or as if they were possessed. How was it that a good family man could change to the point where he could torture an innocent person and even murder little children and then go home to his wife and kiss his children goodnight? Even after the war, these people viewed themselves without guilt, because they had just followed orders and therefore felt no personal responsibility for their actions. They had no conscience because they had erased their scruples, living by instinct rather then conscience. Certainly, Hitler and the Nazis reflected the spirit of the Antichrist.

The Beast

"Nothing on earth is his equal—a creature without fear. He looks down on all that are haughty; he is king over all that are proud" (Job 41:33-34). This description of a massive animal (a dinosaur?) from the ancient book of Job is strikingly similar to the description of the Beast from Revelation 13. The title of "the Beast" suggests that he is not quite human, or more than human, or less than human. John says: "And I saw a beast coming out of the sea. He had ten horns and seven heads . . . and on each head a blasphemous name" (Rev. 13:1).

The Beast will derive his power from Satan: "The dragon gave the beast his power and his throne and great authority" (Rev. 13:2). In Genesis we first meet Satan as a serpent, a snake, but in the Book of Revelation, he is a dragon—some sort of full-grown fierce and deadly reptile. As sin will be full-grown at that time when judgment is about to fall, so also will Satan be more and completely what he is—namely evil.

As the wild beast has an insatiable lust for blood and dominion, so too will the Antichrist. These were certainly characteristics of Adolf Hitler. When he was told of the torture of the Jews, he laughed, and he rejoiced upon hearing of the genocide taking place in the concentration camps. When some Nazi officers and other German leaders realized the extent of Hitler's evil, they attempted to assassinate him in 1944. They failed and were all tortured to death with piano strings. They were hung until they almost died. Then they were revived. Then they were hung again until near death. Then revived again. The process took three hours, and Hitler had it filmed for his own enjoyment. He was a human beast. People who enjoy the suffering of others are not only perverse but are also beastly. The Antichrist will be such a wild beast.

IMAGE OF THE BEAST

Spiritual World Leader

Revelation 13:2-4 says:

> The dragon gave the beast his power and his throne and great authority. One of the heads of the beast seemed to have had a fatal wound, but the fatal wound had been healed. The whole world was astonished and followed the beast. Men worshiped the dragon because he had given authority to the beast, and they also worshiped the beast and asked, "Who is like the beast? Who can make war against him?"

The power behind and within the Antichrist will come directly from the Devil himself. As Christ was one with the Father, so will the

Antichrist be one with the Devil in purpose and power.

In antiquity the state was usually almighty, and the ruler was often seen as divine. From the caesars of Rome to the emperor of Japan, sovereign rulers have been worshiped and feared by their subjects. The Antichrist will be worshiped after he has been mortally wounded and comes back to life. This also is a counterpart to Christ's death and resurrection. This miracle will firmly establish the Antichrist as divine and worthy of worship and praise.

It's easy to picture Satan coming to the Antichrist with the same proposition he presented to Jesus. "The devil took him to a very high mountain and showed him all the kingdoms of the world and their splendor. 'All this will I give you,' he said, 'if you will bow down and worship me'" (Matt. 4:8-9). If such a scenario takes place, the Antichrist will not resist as Christ did, but he will take the Devil up on his offer; he will bow down to the Devil and for a while all the kingdoms of the world will be his. Because the Antichrist will be totally sold out to the Devil, Paul called him "the man of sin" (2 Thess. 2:3, NKJV).

The False Prophet

Revelation seems to describe not just the Antichrist but also an unholy trinity comprised of Satan, the Beast, and the second beast—or the prophet of the Beast. This prophet of the Beast will glorify the Beast and do many miraculous signs:

> Because of the signs he was given power to do on behalf of the first beast, he deceived the inhabitants of the earth. He ordered them to set up an image in honor of the beast who was wounded by the sword and yet lived. [Here again, we see a counterfeit sign alluding to Christ's death and resurrection.] He was given power to give breath to the image of the first beast, so that it could speak and cause all who refused to worship the image to be killed. He also forced everyone, small and great, rich and poor, free and slave, to receive a mark on his right hand or on his forehead, so that no one could buy or sell unless he had the mark, which is the name of the beast or the number of his name.

> This calls for wisdom. If anyone has insight, let him calculate the number of the beast, for it is man's number. His number is 666 (Rev. 13:14-18).

This prophet's goal will be to glorify the Beast and to compel people to worship him. He will also be given great spiritual power. "He performed great and miraculous signs, even causing fire to come down from heaven to earth in full view of men" (Rev. 13:13). Do not be under the illusion that the Antichrist and his prophet will use their spiritual powers for healing and helping the weak and the sick (except possibly in rare circumstances, and only to deceive). These are Christian ideals and not those of the Antichrist. Instead, he will use his power for control and dominion just as the Devil is using his.

Worldwide Persecution

The Antichrist and his state will persecute the Christians and conquer and kill the saints. "He was given power to make war against the saints and to conquer them" (Rev. 13:7). Christian persecution is as old as the church. In fact, an average 0.5 percent of Christians (or one out of every 200) have always been martyred for their faith.[14] Although martyred Christians usually have furthered Christianity and increased the growth of the worldwide church, in the last days the Antichrist and his government will defeat the saints for a while. The persecution of that time will be without equal. Nevertheless, there will be a limit to the allotted time of the persecution.

Again, these views are primarily from a futuristic point of view.

A Thought from St. Augustine

As we noted in an earlier chapter, nonmillenarian St. Augustine believed that when Jesus came the first time He bound the Devil that he might no longer deceive the nations. Jesus asked, "How can anyone enter a strong man's house and carry off his possessions unless he first ties up the strong man?" (Matt. 12:29). Furthermore Paul said, "And having disarmed the powers and authorities, he made a public spectacle of them, triumphing over them by the cross" (Col. 2:15). As we watch the Gospel go from nation to nation, and as we observe people coming to faith all over the world, we see the light of the Gospel and the kingdom of God advancing, and the power of Satan diminishing as he must flee from the power of the cross.

Martin Luther called Satan God's "dog on a leash." He said the Devil can go no further than God allows. Yet at the end of the age God will lengthen the leash and let the dog run. Thus God will temporarily give Satan back the power he had before Christ came. That will be the time of the Antichrist and that would explain why his power will be so great.

Conclusion

Ultimately, evil will be done away with. The Antichrist will be no more for "the Lord Jesus will overthrow [him] with the breath of his mouth and destroy [him] by the splendor of his coming" (2 Thess. 2:8). Satan, who inspired the Antichrist, will also be cast into hell forever. At that time, the kingdom, glory, and power will *fully* belong to our Lord Jesus Christ.

While orthodox theologians of different stripes may argue whether the kingdom has or hasn't come to earth, is or isn't present on earth, to what degree it does or does not operate in the world today, they would all agree that one day His kingdom will have complete rule. Thus the future (however the details may work out) belongs to the Lord. Paul Little writes, "The coming of Christ will bring the rule of Antichrist to an end. It is the great event of which all Scripture looks forward. The Old Testament prophets spoke of it, though the first and second comings often merged in their thinking."[15]

Therefore, however the details of the Antichrist may work out (or *did* work out in the first century, if the preterists are correct), we know that Jesus has conquered the Devil. It's only a matter of time before the full effects of that defeat are worked out on planet earth.

We know who wins in the end.

Thus the future belongs to Christ, not the Antichrist.

19

And What About . . . ?

It is better to ask some of the questions than to know all of the answers.[1]

—James Thurber

The multitude of differing views we've examined naturally leads to many questions. The purpose of this chapter is to address those miscellaneous questions that naturally arise from such a diversity of opinions.

Is the Temple to Be Rebuilt?

Some have said that premillennial dispensationalism is the rebirth of Judaism in that it implies a renewal of the Jewish system, including a temple for the Jews, which of course they've not had for nearly two thousand years. There are some Orthodox Jews in Israel who would very much like to see the temple rebuilt and are working to that end. Nevertheless, they are still by far in the minority at this present time, but the movement is starting to go "mainstream."[2] Dispensationalists, thinking that what Jesus spoke about in the Olivet Discourse is *yet* to be fulfilled, believe the temple will be rebuilt.

Some premillennial dispensationalists believe at some time to come, two future temples will be built. (For clarity's sake, we will call these temples 4 and 5. Temple 1 refers to Solomon's temple, destroyed by Nebuchadnezzar in 586 B.C.; Temple 2 was the modest, downscaled version of Ezra; Temple 3 was Herod's temple, which was standing in Jesus' day.) Temple 4 is described as the "tribulation temple," and Temple 5 will be the fulfillment of the prophecies of the last few chapters of Ezekiel.

Randall Price, author of *Jerusalem in Prophecy*, believes Jesus spoke of two temples in the Olivet Discourse—one to be destroyed, that is, Temple 3, Herod's temple (Matt. 24:2); and the other to be desecrated, that is, Temple 4, the Tribulation temple (Matt. 24:15).[3] Price writes, "Two Temples have been built and destroyed in Israel's past. According to prophecy, two more will yet be built in the future."[4] (Seemingly Ezra's temple was so modest that writers often dismiss it; in fact, it was reported that when they completed it, they themselves wept because it was a mere shadow of Solomon's temple.)

At present, rebuilding the temple (Temple 4) would seem unlikely. When I was in Israel in 1997, our guide pointed out that one of the holiest places for all Muslims is the Dome of the Rock. You've probably seen the picture of this mosque many times. The Dome of the Rock is holy to Muslims for two reasons. First, this mosque houses "the Rock" of Mount Moriah. It is believed it was here that Abraham attempted to offer Isaac as a sacrifice. As descendants of Abraham (through Ishmael), this plot of ground is holy to them. Second, according to Islam, Muhammad ascended into heaven from the same place.

Bob Ware

Dome of the Rock

Our tour guide pointed out that if the faction of Jews (strictly Orthodox) who wants the temple rebuilt pushes too hard for it, this could cause World War III and bring an army of some two hundred million Muslims from all over the world down on Israel. Furthermore, he said that the vast majority of Israelis today are secular minded and would not care about the temple being rebuilt—certainly not at such a price.

Meanwhile, dispensationalists believe it will be rebuilt because prophecy demands it. In *The Late Great Planet Earth*, after briefly touching on the difficulties fraught with rebuilding the temple, Hal Lindsey minces no words: "Obstacle or no obstacle, it is certain that the Temple will be rebuilt. Prophecy demands it."[5] Preterists, however, disagree. They believe those prophecies related to the temple were already fulfilled in A.D. 70.

Nineteenth-century theologian David Brown, who wrote a critique of premillennialism (especially of the dispensational variety) reminds us that in the Book of Hebrews "the sacrifices mentioned by Ezekiel are those very ones which are done away by Christ."[6] Brown adds:

> Scripture affords no warrant for expecting the restoration of *Jewish peculiarities* during the millennium; that the literal way of interpreting those prophecies which are thought to express this, is not, cannot be, gone through with by either Christians or unbelieving Jews; that it brings out opposite and contradictory results, and so must be a false principle of interpretation.[7]

Meanwhile, Gary DeMar maintains that the premise that there has to be a new temple is wrong. In the context of the Olivet Discourse, Jesus was asked about the temple that stood at that time (Temple 3): "The temple that Jesus said would be destroyed is the same temple with the same stones that was pointed out to Jesus by His disciples. No future temple is in view. Jesus gives no indication that He has a future temple in mind. [Temple 4] But what if the Jews rebuild the temple? Such a temple will [have] nothing to do with the fulfillment of any part of this prophecy."[8] Then, in case anyone misses the point, he adds, "*Not one verse in the New Testament mentions the need for a rebuilt temple*. In fact, just the opposite is stated. The temple of God in the New Testament is quite obviously the church of Christ with Jesus as the 'cornerstone' (1 Peter 2:7)."[9]

Postmillennialist J. Marcellus Kik supports this view with what could be viewed as the coup de grace argument:

> The catastrophe of Jerusalem really signalized the beginning of a new and world-wide kingdom, marking the full separation of the Christian Church from legalistic Judaism. The whole system of worship, so closely associated with Jerusalem and the Temple, received, as it were, a death blow from God himself.[10]

Nevertheless, some premillennialists would essentially seek to revive biblical Jewish worship. Commenting on Temple 5, premillennial dispensationalist Paul Lee Tan explains, ". . . while animal sacrifices have been done away at the cross, there is no reason why some *reminders* of Christ's perfect and final sacrifices should not be allowed—both during the present church age and the millennial age."[11] Preterists would ask,

"By reviving the Old Testament sacrificial system?"

Critics of this idea note that much of the Book of Hebrews contrasts the old sacrificial system with Christ's once-and-for-all death. For instance, it says, "He [Jesus] sets aside the first [covenant] to establish the second. And by that will [the will of God], we have been made holy through the sacrifice of the body of Jesus Christ once for all" (Heb. 10:9-10). Historic premillennialist D. Martyn Lloyd-Jones addressed that whole idea: "In reply, those friends [dispensationalists] say that the Temple and its sacrifices will only be a kind of memorial of what our Lord has already done. But can you really believe such a thing?"[12]

Nonmillenarians contend this whole idea of a revised sacrificial system shows the fallacy of dispensationalism for taking prophecy literally. Keith Mathison, author of a critique of this view, *Dispensationalism: Rightly Dividing the People of God?*, says, "Jesus did not come as a literal lamb with four legs and wool, and neither will a future millennium come with literal bloody sacrifices [in a future temple]."[13]

Furthermore, a case can be made that in the New Testament, the word "temple" does not always refer to a literal building. Jesus said of His own body, "Destroy this temple, and I will raise it up again in three days" (John 2:19). Paul said that believers are the temple of the Holy Spirit (1 Cor. 6:19). John said in the Apocalypse that in the New Jerusalem he did not see a temple, for the Lord God Almighty and the Lamb are its temple (Rev. 21:22).

Will People Be Saved after the Rapture?

Will the church be complete at the return of Christ? That is to say, will there be more people who will come to faith in Jesus *after* the Rapture? Of course, pretribulational premillennialists believe there will be. During the Great Tribulation, many Israelites will turn to faith in Christ as never before in history. Paul Lee Tan writes, "The Spirit will be poured upon the nation Israel and many Gentiles will be saved (Rev. 7:9-17)."[14]

Will the church be complete at the return of Christ?

On the other hand, postmillennialist David Brown disagrees with that notion: "The Church will be absolutely complete at Christ's coming. If this can be established, the whole system falls to the ground."[15] He adds, "No plain reader of the Bible ever doubts that the

Church will be completed ere Christ comes"[16]

Brown cites 1 Corinthians 15:22-24: "In Christ all will be made alive. But each in his own turn: Christ, the firstfruits; then, when he comes, those who belong to him. Then the end will come."[17] Brown further states, "Christ the *first-fruits*; afterward they that are Christ's (the *full harvest* of them) at his coming. . . . Can anything be more decisive than this? What commentator explains it otherwise?"[18] In other words, the end occurs right after Jesus comes for His own.

Dispensationalists would rebut that view by arguing that one must differentiate two descriptions of the Lord's return (the Rapture and the revelation). M. R. DeHaan writes:

> There are two classes of Scripture passages which speak of the coming again of Christ. These are very easy to recognize and differentiate if we bear in mind a few simple principles. . . . The Rapture, or the secret coming, is seldom directly mentioned except in type in the Old Testament. Virtually all the references in the Old Testament deal with the glorious appearing at the close of the Tribulation and the commencement of the Millennium. In the New Testament, however, we find both aspects of the Lord's coming mentioned. The reason for this becomes immediately clear when we remember that the Rapture has to do with the Church only, whereas the Revelation has to do with Israel and the nations. In the Old Testament days there was no Church. That was a mystery not revealed until after the Day of Pentecost and then revealed by the Holy Spirit through Paul and the other apostles. The Old Testament saints and prophets knew nothing about the Church. She did not come into existence until after the rejection of the Lord at His first coming.[19]

How Many Judgments Are There?

Historically, the church has affirmed one judgment of believers and nonbelievers alike at the end of time. As the Apostles' Creed puts it, ". . . from thence [the right hand of God the Father, almighty] he [Jesus] shall come to judge the living and the dead."[20]

In the dispensational system, however, there are at least two, sometimes even more, judgments. The *Scofield Reference Bible* lists seven judgments.[21] W. E. Blackstone, who wrote *Jesus Is Coming* (first published in 1878), put the number of judgments at four. These are his own words and numbering:

1. The Judgment of the Saints for their works.
2. The Judgment of the living nations, who are upon the earth at the Revelation. Jesus is Judge of the *quick* (or living) and *dead.*
3. The Judgment of the dead at the Great White Throne.
4. The Judgment of angels, into fire "prepared for the devil and his angels." The ungodly go there first. Compare Revelation 19:20 with Revelation 20:7-10; 2 Peter 2:4; and Jude 6.[22]

Modern dispensationalists often whittle the number down to just two—the believers' judgment (the Bema seat) and the Great White Throne judgment.

Critic David Brown feels this is wrong. He writes:

> There is no department of divine truth more deeply and dangerously affected by the pre-millennial scheme than that which relates to the judgment. . . . For a large portion of the human race it provides no judgment at all. . . . This whole scheme of the judgment makes no provision whatever—nor does it pretend to make any—for judging the vast multitudes of believing men by whom the world is to be peopled during the millennium. They are not among those judged *before* the millennium, for they are not then born; and they are not among those judged *after* it, for none but the wicked are expected to be judged then. And so *they are not judged at all;* that is to say, this scheme *makes no provision* for their being judged."[23]

Brown feels quite strongly that there is to be a once and for all judgment: ". . . the simultaneous presentation of the whole human race, in a resurrection-state, before the great white throne—is unambiguously announced in Scripture."[24]

Dispensationalists Thomas Ice and Timothy Deny disagree:

> There are several times of judgment in the future, each with a specific purpose, end, and constituency. To speak of a single, all-encompassing judgment day is incorrect. There are different judgments for believers' works, Old Testament saints, tribulation saints, living Jews at the end of the tribulation, Satan and the fallen angels, and unredeemed people.[25]

Nonmillenarians, however, argue that the Bible speaks of only one judgment, which will take place at the end of time. To be judged will be the righteous and the unrighteous. Here's what amillennialist and former premillennialist Jay Adams has to say on the subject:

> Since premillennialists have [at least] two judgments, they must decide which is the *great* day of judgment. The premillennial scheme, of course, forces them into the unhappy position of deciding that the resurrection and judgment of the *wicked* is the great day, while the revelation of the Savior and the rapture of the church must be a lesser one! Jude referred to the great day, of course, because there was no other. From the biblical evidence, no doubt should be entertained about the length of the period of salvation. At the coming of Christ, Scripture expressly says, the door will be shut.[26]

Nevertheless, dispensationalists hold that when you map out all the different Bible verses on the end times and put them together, they end up teaching more than one judgment. Postmillennialist J. Marcellus Kik cites three passages (Matt. 16:27; 1 Cor. 4:5; and 2 Tim. 4:1) and then concludes: "All these passages confirm the teaching of Matthew 25:31-46 that the final judgment takes place at the second coming of Christ."[27]

One of them, 2 Timothy 4:1, seems to be obviously direct: "I charge thee therefore before God, and the Lord Jesus Christ, who shall judge the quick and the dead *at his appearing and his kingdom*" [KJV, emphasis mine].

In the sheep and goats passage, we hear about *all the nations* being judged. Kik writes, "It is rather difficult to picture all nations of the earth gathered together in the small land of Palestine."[28] To this, he adds:

> The premillennialist, however, maintains as a cardinal and fundamental tenet of his system of eschatology that the throne of glory is an earthly throne set up in the material city of Jerusalem. The temporal throne of David is to be reconstructed in Jerusalem. . . . As a matter of fact there is not one passage in the New Testament which gives definite information of a personal reign of Christ upon a temporal throne in the material city of Jerusalem! What seems to be hidden to the apostles has been revealed by uninspired men.[29]

Such a remark would certainly offend dispensationalist Paul Lee Tan, who holds that as Christians we will be accountable one day for how much we have taken the prophetic word of the Bible literally. He cites Revelation 1:3, KJV, which states: "Blessed is he that readeth, and they that hear the words of this prophecy, and keep those things which are written therein: for the time is at hand." Like other dispensationalists, Tan believes Christians will be held accountable for our good works (or lack thereof) at the Bema Seat of Christ (not to be confused with the Great White Throne judgment, which they believe is only for the non-believers). Tan holds that one of the criteria of judgment is how we've reacted to the prophetic word:

> It is obvious that there is only one order of future events, and therefore only one system of prophecy is correct. When before the Bema Seat of Christ, are we not expected to be able to say to the Lord, "Lord we took you at your word, we interpreted the future as you have literally revealed it"? Christ's words to Thomas may again be heard, "Blessed are they that have not seen, and yet have believed" (John 20:29).[30]

Before leaving the subject of the judgment(s), let's hear from the most respected theologian of the later part of the Middle Ages, St. Thomas Aquinas (1224–1274). What he has to say tends to confirm the point that the idea of separate judgments (as opposed to just one) is relatively new: "For all will be judged at once; each will know his own sin and the sins of all others: each then, will know at once the justice of the judgment in each case. . . . It is most probably that the whole judgment will be enacted and received mentally, not audibly."[31] He also states, "All human beings without exception will be present at the general judgment."[32]

Are These the Last Days?

At the beginning of the Book of Acts in the *Scofield Reference Bible*, we read: "The apparent failure of the Old Testament promises concerning the Davidic kingdom was explained by the promise that the kingdom would be set up at the return of Christ (Acts 2:25-31; 15:14-16)."[33]

Scofield adds:

> A distinction must be observed between "the last days" when the prediction relates to Israel, and the "last days" when the prediction relates to the church. . . . The "last days" as related to the church began with the advent of Christ (Heb. 1:2), but have especial reference to the time of declension and apostasy at the end of this age (2 Tim. 3:1; 4:4). The "last days" as related to Israel are the days of Israel's exaltation and blessing, and are synonymous with the kingdom-age.[34]

This entire matter goes back to the point we heard earlier in the chapter on Israel: that nation holds the key to God's prophetic clock. To many dispensationalists the clock stopped in A.D. 70 when Israel ceased being a nation and did not start ticking again until 1948 with the rebirth of Israel.

Nevertheless, David Brown argues that the kingdom was not postponed, despite the Jews' rejection of Jesus:

> We have seen that the kingdom of Christ is just the kingdom of grace in the hands of the Mediator—a kingdom already in existence—virtually ever since the fall, and formally since his ascension to the right hand of power; and that it will continue unchanged, both in character and form, till the final judgment, when, in its state of glory, it becomes "the everlasting kingdom of our Lord and Saviour Jesus Christ"—"the kingdom of Christ and of God."[35]

Philip Edgcumbe Hughes also disagrees with Scofield's notion that the era of the church is separate from what was prophesied in the Old Testament: "Certainly, the apostles do not appear to have regarded the era of the church as a parenthesis outside the scope of the prophetic vision. On the Day of Pentecost, for example, Peter assures his large Jewish audience that the sending forth of the Holy Spirit is 'what was spoken by the prophet Joel.'"[36]

Nonetheless, Scofield counters, "The Dispensation of the Kingdom . . . begins with the return of Christ to the earth, runs through the 'thousand years' of His earth-rule, and ends when He has delivered up the kingdom to the Father."[37]

Is Postmillennialism Really Dead?

Remember the classic story about a newspaper that erroneously printed the obituary of Mark Twain—before he had died? He was in London when he read the bad news, so he cabled the Associated Press on June 2, 1897, with this classic reply: "The report of my death was an exaggeration."[38] I think when it comes to the postmil position, there is ample evidence that it is viewed as dead by some—mortally wounded by World War I and finished off by World War II. For example, premillennialist Lewis Sperry Chafer writes:

> Of the three contentions—postmillennialism, amillennialism, and premillennialism, or as the latter was known in the early centuries from the Greek designation, chiliasm—postmillennialism is dead. Whether the present insane, corrupt condition of the world killed the theory by the contradiction of its own developing character, or these latter times so magnified its inconsistencies that it died, future historians must determine.[39]

Nevertheless, there's also ample evidence that it still exists today, for example, in conservative Presbyterian circles. Methinks the funeral has been perhaps announced prematurely.

Hal Lindsey echoes Chafer's sentiments that the postmillennialist position is dead. He writes:

> There used to be a group called "postmillennialists." They believed that the Christians would root out the evil in the world, abolish godless rulers, and convert the world through ever increasing evangelism until they brought about the Kingdom of God on earth through their own efforts. Then after 1000 years of the institutional church reigning on earth with peace, equality, and righteousness, Christ would return and time would end. These people rejected much of the Scripture as being literal and believed in the inherent goodness of man. World War I greatly disheartened this group and World War II virtually wiped out this viewpoint. No self-respecting scholar who looks at the world condition and the accelerating decline of Christian influence today is a "postmillennialist."[40]

"*Used* to be?" ask the postmils. Postmillennialists are no longer in the majority, but there are still plenty of postmillennialists alive today. To paraphrase Gary DeMar, the postmil position is not dead; it's just buried under millions of premillennial paperbacks.[41]

"Wait a minute!" cries the postmillennialist. Overall, things are getting better when you get a more complete overview. Besides, the postmillennialist would add, how we define what we mean by "the Millennium" makes a big difference (as we've discussed in previous chapters).

Conclusion

When we consider the various views on the Second Coming within the evangelical camp, we see such divisions we almost wonder whether anybody agrees on anything. Nevertheless, as we'll clearly see in the next chapter, we must remember that Bible-believing Christians have far more in common with one another than we have with nonbelievers, despite the minutia of details that may seem to draw us apart.

In this chapter, we've listened to various sides on several issues. One of those we've often heard from was David Brown, a postmillennialist who wrote a rebuttal to premillennialism in the nineteenth century. Although he obviously disagreed with the position, he still asserted in his book that he welcomed the fresh study on the Second Coming, which premillennialists brought to the church. If it makes us good Bereans, then the debate is welcome. We close out this chapter with Dr. Brown's words:

> Pre-millennialists have done the Church a real service, by calling attention to the place which the second advent holds in the Word of God and the scheme of divine truth. If the controversy which they have raised should issue in a fresh and impartial inquiry into this branch of it, I, for one, instead of regretting, shall rejoice in the agitation of it.[42]

Part Five

Practical Applications

20

Common Ground on the Return of Christ

For every one reference to the first coming of Christ as the baby of Bethlehem, there are eight references to His final, His second, coming.[1]

—D. Martyn Lloyd-Jones

Have you ever noticed how often the "experts" get it wrong? Seriously, if you track the predictions and prognostications of even our leading authorities, it's often a hit-and-miss proposition. For example, consider these "prophecies" made by various people:

- "There is not the slightest indication that [nuclear] energy will ever be obtainable. It would mean that the atom would have to be shattered at will."

  —Dr. Albert Einstein, 1932
- "This is the biggest fool thing we have ever done . . . the bomb will never go off, and I speak as an expert in explosives."

  —Admiral William Leahy, advising President Harry Truman on the U.S. Atomic Bomb Project, 1945
- "The thought of being president frightens me. I do not think I want the job."

  —Ronald Reagan, Governor of California, 1973
- "While theoretically and technically television may be feasible, commercially and financially I consider it an impossibility, a development of which we need waste little time dreaming."

  —Lee de Forest, American inventor of the audio tube, pioneer in development of radio and TV, 1926
- "*Gone with the Wind* is going to be the biggest flop in Hollywood history. I'm just glad Clark Gable will be the one falling on his face and not Gary Cooper."

  —Gary Cooper, 1938
- "I do not consider Hitler to be as bad as he is depicted. He is showing

an ability that is amazing, and he seems to be gaining his victories without much bloodshed."

—Mahatma Gandhi, May 1940

- "You ain't goin' nowhere . . . son. You ought to go back to drivin' a truck."

  —Jim Denny, manager of the Grand Old Opry, firing Elvis Presley after one performance, September 25, 1954[2]

The Prophecies of God

Human prophecies are usually less reliable than next month's weather forecast. In contrast, we have the Word of God, which is completely reliable. The Bible is our source of knowledge of the first and second comings of Jesus Christ. We know, therefore, with certainty that Jesus is coming back. We have His word on it, and you can't do better than that. Yet as we've seen repeatedly, well-meaning Christians with various views dispute *when* He's coming and *how* it will all work out.

Although it's a given that there are sincere Bible scholars who hold to different views on the matter of the Second Coming, it's important we keep it all in perspective. It's critical we not become too divided on all the little of details that we miss the big picture: *He's coming back.* Amen and Amen. Even so, come quickly, Lord Jesus.

Evangelicals All Agree That the Bible Is the Word of God

Those who look forward to Christ's return believe in the authority of the Bible, which we believe is the Word of God. What it says on all things, including Christ's Second Coming, we believe is true. Thus we have much more in common with one another—even if we are divided by various views on how to interpret prophecy and the differences that flow from that starting point than we do with liberal theologians who deny that He's coming back.

Just because someone has a different approach to certain passages—because he or she believes that's the way God intended us to interpret it—shouldn't call into question his or her loyalty to the Scriptures. To do that is just as ridiculous as questioning somebody's patriotism if he or she question whether the United States should engage in XYZ military operation.

Home on the Mountain Range

Think of it this way. Suppose bands of theologians, writers, and speakers are on a huge mountain range. Now that mountain range comprises various hills. People are often leaving one hill and joining another hill on the same range, to and fro. Some of the hills have far more people than other hills, even though there's plenty of room for all of them. Some of the mounds on this mountain range are well defined; others are not. Although these people are on different hills, they are all on the same range. This mountain range consists of those who believe in the second coming of Christ. Each large hill represents the major different views, that is, dispensational premillennialism, historical premillennialism, amillennialism, and postmillennialism. There are even some hills populated with those who have eclectic or hybrid views.

Perhaps in the valley at the foot of the range are some misguided people. They are misguided because although they believe in Christ, they somehow have missed the point that He is coming back or have not heard it. I'm sure that the thief on the cross, whom we know from our Lord's own lips was saved, had no clue of the Second Coming. Theoretically, there could also be some believing theologians on a very low slope, who are convinced that the Scriptures teach Christ came back in A.D. 70, and He won't be coming back again. These are "*full* preterists." They claim to believe in Christ, but they believe His Word teaches this hotly disputed doctrine. Despite the great divergence of opinions, those on this mountain range hold that the future belongs to Christ.

Now, way across the valley on a completely different mountain range are nonbelievers. Although this mountain range is in sight on a clear day, it is miles away. That mountain range also comprises various hills with bickering subjects trying to explain why their hill is the best. Behold, some of the people even have clerical collars, that is, they receive their pay from the church of Jesus Christ, but they do nothing but tickle people's ears and promote unbelief from their pulpits. All the people on this range decidedly do not believe in Christ's return. They are sure about one thing: The future belongs to man, not God. They scoff, "Where is this 'coming' he promised? Ever since our fathers died, everything goes on as it has since the beginning of creation'" (2 Peter 3:4).

Meanwhile, back on the first mountain range, many of the subjects are bickering among themselves about the various hills they occupy. Each camp can produce a myriad of Scripture verses to back up why its position is the best one. Some become so angry in their bickering that they lose sight of the fact that they're essentially on the same side and on the same mountain range. They virtually cannot differentiate between those on the nearby hills with those on the far-off mountains. It's my way or the highway.

If anybody thinks these theological disputes are new at all, listen to what a theologian from the second century had to say. These words are from Justin Martyr: "I and others, who are right-minded Christians on all points, are assured that there will be a resurrection of the dead and a thousand years in Jerusalem, which will then be built, adorned, and enlarged, as the prophets Ezekiel and Isaiah and others declare." Yet in the same passage he also adds, "many who belong to the pure and pious faith and are true Christians think otherwise."[3]

A person is not considered heretical on the basis of his or her millennial view

A twentieth-century postmillennialist writer, Keith Mathison, echoes Justin's point: "A person's doctrine of the millennium is not an indication of orthodoxy the way other doctrines such as the Trinity and the deity of Christ are. Someone who does not believe in the Trinity is a heretic. But a person is not considered heretical simply on the basis of his or her millennial view. There can be differences among genuine Christians."[4]

Listen to this poignant thought from premillennial dispensationalist writer E. Schuyler English, author of the 1954 book *Re-Thinking the Rapture*. Note that many of the theologians he cites are not well known today. One could easily substitute today's better-known writers and speakers who are at various places on the spectrum and his wonderful point still comes through. Here's what Dr. English says:

> How tragic it would be if such esteemed and beloved saints, all now with the Lord, as James M. Gray, A. C. Gaebelein, H. A. Ironside, and William L. Pettingill on the one hand; G. H. Pember, J. A. Seiss, D. M. Panton, and J. Hudson Taylor on another; and George Müller, S. P. Tregelles, Dan Crawford, and Henry W. Frost on still another, should have pointed the finger at those in other

> groups, crying, "Heretic!" and refusing to have fellowship one band with another! Yet the first four of these brethren were pre-tribulationists; the second four, partial-rapturists; and the last four post-tribulationalists. They are in the glory now, and in whatsoever way any of them, or all of them, erred, they are now instructed as to the truth, we can be sure. May we, therefore, be kept from bitterness in any remarks that we make, and bear in mind that controversy in itself is not wrong but is an instrument for the guardianship of the truth as opposed to error. Let us endeavor to guard, in it all, "the unity of the Spirit in the bond of peace."[5]

In other words, picture amillennialists R. C. Sproul or Gary DeMar pointing fingers at premillennialists Hal Lindsey or Jack Van Impe and yelling, "Heretic!" And vice versa. Meanwhile, miles and miles away on the nonbelievers' mountain range rest the true heretics.

It does no good to question someone's faith or loyalty to Scripture as the Word of God because they have a different view on the end times. Or sometimes, they'll get in little digs on the other side—some subtle, some not so subtle. One acerbic postmillennialist even went so far as to refer to Hal Lindsey's volumes as "novels" when the clear context of what he was describing were Lindsey's nonfiction books.[6]

I also find dogmatism on the other side, even when it is subtle. One premillennial writer said, "Those who believe this [elaborate premillennial scenario he just described] are called "Premillenarians" because they believe the Word of God concerning the coming again of Christ to set up His kingdom *before* the Millennium."[7] Does this imply that someone holding another position doesn't believe the Word of God? I'm reminded of the Joey Adams' joke about two ministers who argued about particulars of the faith. Just before they parted, one got in the last word, "Let us go our separate ways. You continue to worship the Lord in your way, and I will continue to worship Him in His."[8]

Meanwhile, there are those who hold to their positions so strongly that you would think there's no other tenable position held by Bible-believing Christians. One premil writer says, "There can be no doubt that the 'Abomination of Desolation' is Antichrist, the 'beast' of Revelation 12-13, who will have 'a mouth speaking arrogant words and blasphemies and authority to act for forty-two months' (Rev. 13:5), the one Paul refers to as the 'man of lawlessness,' who 'takes his seat in the temple of God, displaying himself as being God' (2 Thess. 2:3-4)."[9] No doubt? There are so many differing interpretations related to the end times. To me, "no doubt" is too strong a phrase, especially in light of the preterist position on A.D. 70, as we saw detailed in previous chapters.

Note this dogmatism: "There is no doubt that the Antichrist has already been born."[10] No doubt? Well, maybe he's right. Who knows? Maybe the Antichrist *has* been born and *is* alive and well on Planet Earth. Only one hitch—I'm quoting St. Martin of Tours who lived in the fourth century!

We often find "no doubts" from those on the other side as well. Preterist Gary DeMar says, "Fulfilled prophecy is being interpreted as if it is unfulfilled prophecy."[11] Postmillennialist Gary North says of the Great Tribulation: "What the Bible teaches is that it took place in A.D. 70, and Christians did not go through it."[12] Implied in those statements is a "no doubt."

Here's a statement I find difficult to accept. "Those who oppose the teaching of a literal one-thousand year reign of Christ upon earth are in direct opposition to the Word of God!"[13] Bible-believing Christians who disagree would say they don't oppose the Word of God, but rather the writer's particular interpretation of the Word.

Some posttribulationists don't appreciate what they perceive as the dogmatic stance of some pretribulationists. For example, Alexander Reese protests:

> All down the centuries the Church expected Christ's Coming after the arrival of Antichrist, according to the teaching of Christ and His Apostles. Only in 1830 did a school arise that treats with intolerance, and often with contempt, the attitude of those who had looked for Him in the manner just named. Not the slightest respect was paid to a view that had held the field for 1,800 years.[14]

Meanwhile, as we fight among ourselves on our hills separated by rather minor crevices, we forget we're all on the same mountain range. It's time to hoist a huge flag bearing Blaise Pascal's advice:

In essentials, unity.
In nonessentials, liberty.
And in all things, charity.

That's an excellent message and is probably as appropriate for this subject as any within Christian theology.

Thus there is great need to see that there is more that unites us, even with our various opinions, than separates us. All that said in no way minimizes our need to keep searching the Scriptures and studying for ourselves while at the same time living lives that are ready for His return at any moment.

Now let's explore the big picture of what we can agree on when it comes to the end times.

Overview of the Biblical Witness—Restoration

The central themes of the Bible are Creation, the Fall, and Restoration. The entire history of humankind is the history of how God fixes what was broken and destroyed by the Fall. The restoration process hinges upon the coming of the long-awaited Messiah. When Jesus came, it was as if the true King came into an enemy-occupied land and established the true and right kingdom or at least established the pivotal beachhead for what is to come. C. S. Lewis once put it masterfully in his book *Mere Christianity*. This is how he described the history of the world and the Incarnation:

> This universe is at war . . . it is a civil war, a rebellion . . . we are living in a part of the universe occupied by the rebel. Enemy-occupied territory—that is what this world is. Christianity is the story of how the rightful king has landed, you might say landed in disguise, and is calling us all to take part in a great campaign of sabotage. When you go to church you are really listening-in to the secret wireless [radio] from our friends: that is why the enemy is so anxious to prevent us from going. He does it by playing on our conceit and laziness and intellectual snobbery.[15]

God has always had His people on earth, but from the time His church was established, the kingdom has had a special foothold on earth. Even those who subscribe to the Scofieldian notion that the kingdom was completely postponed when the Jews rejected their rightful Messiah believe when Jesus returns, the restoration of this sin-sick world will be made complete. When Christ returns to planet earth, the war between good and evil will finally be over (with the exception of the end of the Millennium when Satan is loosed for a very short time).

Whether you believe that Millennium is the same as the messianic or Interadvent Age or that there is a literal Millennium on earth to come, we know that the kingdom of Christ is an eternal one. All of God's elect who have come to believe in Christ during the time of the Church Age have gone over from death to life. The second death (which means eternal punishment) cannot touch them.

One day all sin and evil will be judged and done away with, and all the ungodly will be doomed (2 Peter 3:7). All things will be made new. There will be a new heaven and a new earth (Isa. 65:17-19; 2 Peter 3:13; Rev. 21:1). Even Jerusalem will be new—whether that refers to that literal city in Palestine or not. John said, "I saw the Holy City, the new Jerusalem, coming down out of heaven from God, prepared as a bride beautifully dressed for her husband" (Rev. 21:2). All the individual believers will also be restored to what God created us to be. For in the instant of His coming, we will be clothed in immortality. Our salvation will go from sanctification to glorification in the blinking of an eye. We will be made perfect and sinless, and we will be forever with the Lord (1 Cor. 15:51-53). These are wonderful truths to try to comprehend. Why then bicker over details?

This is our redemption that we are waiting for, the fulfillment of all God's work. This is the time when "the kingdom of the world has become the kingdom of our Lord and of his Christ, and he shall reign for ever and ever" (Rev. 11:15).

The Centrality of the Cross

Writers at virtually every point of the spectrum agree on the centrality of the cross. That includes those who think that the temple will be rebuilt and that animals will be sacrificed on the altar once again as a commemoration of Christ's sacrifice—a view nondispensationalists *vehemently* reject. Nonetheless, those who claim to believe in such animal sacrifices to come will quickly assert that only the blood of Christ, shed at Calvary, can forgive people from their sins. "Salvation," asserts Hal Lindsey, "is always by grace through faith alone."[16] Amen.

Some nonmillenarians have complained about the success of Hal Lindsey's best-selling blockbuster *The Late Great Planet Earth.* (Thirty million copies have been sold to date).[17] They claim that their complaints are based on their disagreement with his eschatology, but I have pointed out to them that even if they disagree with his view of the end times, they should recognize the marvelous ways God has used that book to help bring people into His kingdom. I can think of two wonderful Christians, both of whom now eschew Lindsey's eschatology, yet who came from skeptical backgrounds to a faith in Christ because they read *The Late Great Planet Earth.* Today both are serving the Lord in significant ways.

We can all agree that salvation is by grace alone

Charles Spurgeon once said, "Never forget the three whats. What from? Believers are redeemed from hell and destruction. What by? By the precious blood of Christ. What to? To an inheritance incorruptible, undefiled, and that will not fade away."[18] So we can all agree on the centrality of the cross and that salvation is by grace alone.

Areas Where We Dispute the Timing but Not the Phenomenon

Much of the dispute between the differing camps on the end times gets down to the timing of the scenes to come.

We may dispute the timing on the Rapture. That issue is even disputed among premillennialists themselves. But that there will be an instantaneous translation of the saints one day is not up in the air. Will there be a second chance to repent should the Rapture occur before the great tribulation? I wouldn't advise anybody to stake his or her eternal destiny on it.

Is the great tribulation a past event or will it happen in the future? Or were the events of A.D. 70 a foretaste of what is to come? We shall see when it happens. Again, hindsight is always 20/20. Meanwhile, let's not have unnecessary tribulation in the church from wrestling too stridently over the issue.

Does God have two divine plans—one for Israel and one for the church?

While the theological debate may rage on that issue, keep in mind the big picture: Even premillennial dispensationalists view Jews in the end times accepting Jesus as their Messiah. Thus Jesus is the inescapable divine imperative. He is the one whom none of us can avoid dealing with. Not one person on earth. One day every knee shall bow to Him and acknowledge He is Lord to the glory of God the Father (Phil. 2:9-11).

Furthermore, I think we can all vehemently agree now at the turn of the century that any and all anti-Semitism is wrong. Yet I think we should also realize that the modern country of Israel is not infallible. When it attempts to make laws attempting to stop the spread of Christianity in the land of its birth, surely it is opposing the work of God in that respect. When it denies basic human rights and justice to law-abiding Palestinians, that too is wrong.

The Antichrist is also a controversial issue. Yet I think we can all agree that the spirit of the Antichrist is to be opposed whenever it rears its ugly head, inasmuch as it is up to us. It does seem that the spirit of the Antichrist is more active in our time than in previous generations. On television, for example, scoffers openly blaspheme Christ in living color from coast to coast.

Whether Nero was *the* Antichrist John had in mind or whether there's one *yet to be*, the overall point is that Christ will one day vanquish that Antichrist. Although he may wage war against believers and kill them, in the end he will not succeed, nor will any force that rears its ugly head against Jesus the Christ. Not that they haven't tried!

- Herod tried to eradicate Christianity while it was yet in its infancy.
- The first-century Jewish establishment tried to strangle the Christian faith, but its capital was destroyed and the temple laid waste.
- Ancient Rome tried to annihilate Christianity at least ten times, but the religion of the catacombs prevailed.
- During the Middle Ages, corruption from within and the Islamic invasion from without threatened to choke the faith to death.
- The wars of religious sectarianism that followed the Reformation devastated much of Europe, once again threatening Christianity. Nevertheless, Christ won out.
- The communists and fascists in the twentieth century shed the blood of more Christian martyrs than in all previous centuries combined. Yet at the end of the century, Christianity is on the rise, and those two movements on the wane.

And on and on it goes.[19]

Jesus Christ *is* the conquering king.

Therefore, although the spirit of the Antichrist often seems to prevail in this world, one day Christ will vanquish Satan and his minions, including the Antichrist and all other antichrists, once and for all. Who is the Antichrist? Who will he be? Is he alive today? What are the mechanisms by which he operates? Well-meaning Christians may well dispute the particulars. Yet make no mistake about the important point: Anyone who opposes Jesus Christ has chosen the wrong side.

What about the Millennium? Are we in it now in that it is the Church Age? Is it yet to be? Is there no such literal thing? This is a matter that we won't necessarily know until we get there. Meanwhile, we can all agree that between now and the time of Christ's once-and-for-all return or the Rapture (whichever comes first), let us not abandon our responsibility on two fronts: (1) evangelism and discipleship; and (2) social responsibility (to be salt in our decaying culture).

If the Lord should tarry and not return for even a century or more, what kind of world will we leave to posterity? As long as the United States is a democratic republic and we have the right to be heard, then out of love for our neighbors, we ought to promote what is good and right. Not that we would bring in the Millennium through our efforts, but nor should we think we somehow fulfill prophecy by letting America "go to hell in a handbasket."

Take the issue of future judgment. Historical premillennialists and nonmillenarians believe there is one final judgment at the end of time. Premillennial dispensationalists have a more elaborate picture. They even disagree among themselves as to how many judgments there are. Yet at the end of the day, Bible-believing Christians agree that each human being will face judgment. The saved will go to heaven forever; the unsaved to hell.

A Permanent Moratorium on Date Setting

We can also agree on no more date setting. All this does is bring discredit and dishonor to the Lord. This has happened over and over in history. Let's call for a moratorium on date setting—on what Gary DeMar calls "Last Days Madness." "The 1988 experience of the now discredited Edgar Whisenant," says Tim LaHaye, "and the 1994 date setting of Harold Camping, do nothing to build confidence in the soon coming of

Christ. Instead, they disillusion many."[20]

I think it's safe to say we need to watch and pray and to wait for Christ to return. We also need to be busy doing His work as long as we can so that He will find us as good and faithful servants when He appears.

Why Is It Taking So Long?

A good question often asked is why the Lord's return taking so long. Let's go to 2 Peter 3 for the answer. According to J. Barton Payne's *Encyclopedia of Biblical Prophecy*, Peter's second epistle is one of the books of the New Testament most concerned "proportionately" with the future. Payne writes, "Of its brief 61 verses, 25, or 41% are involved in prophecy. These refer to 11 separate forecasts, commencing in the latter part of chapter 1 and continuing on throughout the remainder of the epistle."[21]

This is what the apostle Peter had to say about "the Day of the Lord":

> First of all, you must understand that in the last days scoffers will come, scoffing and following their own evil desires. They will say, "Where is this 'coming' he promised? Ever since our fathers died, everything goes on as it has since the beginning of creation." But they deliberately forget that long ago by God's word the heavens existed and the earth was formed out of water and by water. By these waters also the world of that time was deluged and destroyed. By the same word the present heavens and earth are reserved for fire, being kept for the day of judgment and destruction of ungodly men.
>
> But do not forget this one thing, dear friends: With the Lord a day is like a thousand years, and a thousand years are like a day. The Lord is not slow in keeping his promise, as some understand slowness. He is patient with you, not wanting anyone to perish, but everyone to come to repentance.
>
> But the day of the Lord will come like a thief. The heavens will disappear with a roar; the elements will be destroyed by fire, and the earth and everything in it will be laid bare.
>
> Since everything will be destroyed in this way, what

> kind of people ought you to be? You ought to live holy and godly lives as you look forward to the day of God and speed its coming. That day will bring about the destruction of the heavens by fire, and the elements will melt in the heat. But in keeping with his promise we are looking forward to a new heaven and a new earth, the home of righteousness.
>
> So then, dear friends, since you are looking forward to this, make every effort to be found spotless, blameless and at peace with him. Bear in mind that our Lord's patience means salvation (2 Peter 3:3-15).

In other words, what the scoffer sees as slowness is in reality God's patience. Some of those very skeptics may end up later becoming Christians because of that patience.

A tragic aspect of this scoffing is that it is often found among the clergy in our day. Dr. James Montgomery Boice, author and pastor, says:

> I've been in ministerial gatherings when, for example, a friend of mine would stand up to argue a point. He'd quote the Bible and afterwards people would say to him, "Matt, why are you always quoting the Bible when you stand up to talk about something? Don't you know, nobody believes the Bible anymore?" I was in a gathering where I was one of the speakers, and I spoke about the fall of man, sin, the need for redemption, and a final judgment. I mentioned Jesus returning, and afterwards I was roundly chastised by some of the professors who said, "Look, we have got to get in our heads that Jesus is never coming back and things are always going to continue as they were from the beginning." Now, that man is in a seminary teaching other ministers, and they go out with that kind of unbelief. It shouldn't be surprising to anybody that knows the Bible because Peter said that in the last days, that's exactly what was going to happen. People would come along and say, "Where's the promise of His coming? All things continue as they were from the beginning." But here was this man seriously advocating that, and in that manner,

> unbelief really creeps into the Church.[22]

Although Christ may appear slow to us human beings with regard to His return, it's not as if He has somehow voided His promise of coming again. G. C. Berkouwer observes:

> "Delay" does not mean cancellation, but simply implies that what is expected has been postponed until some future date. Still, a delay, particularly a long one, can raise serious doubts about the actual fulfillment. . . . The whole direction of the Christian community has always been toward the future, based, not on some futuristic fantasy, but on the promise of the living God.[23]

A Major Source of Encouragement

While we can't be dogmatic about the details of Christ's return, we surely can take comfort in the certainty of it. One time a Mississippi pastor was preaching on the Second Coming, using Matthew 24 as his text. When he quoted verse 27, "for as the lightning cometh out of the west; so shall also the coming of the son of man be," suddenly a large light bulb fell from the ceiling and shattered on the ground, just by the pulpit. The pastor looked up and said to the stunned congregation, "His coming will be just as sudden and unexpected, and devastating to the dreams that are not Christ-centered."[24]

The Future Belongs to God

Sometimes as we look at the world, it's easy to get depressed about how the future looks. We see the rise of the occult. We see the rise of the cults. We see the increase of Islam. We see the rise of atheism and agnosticism. We see growing unbelief, it would seem, from many seminaries and liberal churches—to a sickening degree. We see all sorts of bad things coming out of Hollywood. We see homosexuality gaining an incredible foothold in our society. Foothold? In some cases, it seems more like a stranglehold. We see all these things. Yet consider for just a moment: The future belongs to God. Jesus Christ is coming back, and that makes all the difference in the world.

During the Civil War, a famous hymn was born—a hymn that reminds us that the future belongs to God because Jesus' return is the culmination of history. In 1864, General Sherman and his soldiers were marching to the sea, from Chattanooga through Atlanta to the ocean. Because of Sherman's success, the Confederate leadership replaced General Johnston with "the impetuous" General John Hood, who immediately proceeded to march near the rear of Sherman. This was a serious threat to Sherman's communications and his storehouse of supplies in the nearby town of Allattoona. Sherman made provisions to protect the garrison at Allattoona. Meanwhile, he sent them a now-famous message: "Hold the fort. I am coming." This word of encouragement kept the men steady, despite the onslaught of attack. And Sherman indeed came and rescued them.

One of the survivors—or should I say conquerors?—there at the fort in Allattoona told this story to evangelist P. P. Bliss, who became so inspired by it that he penned a hymn: "Hold the Fort, for I Am Coming."[25] And so it is that Jesus is coming. We are to occupy until He comes, not throw up our hands in despair because of all the evil that is around us.

Lay aside any controversial issues regarding the end times for a moment. Who else but a Christian can have a positive view of the future?

• Can the humanist?

Consider the fact that we're just ending the bloodiest century in humankind's history. Man has killed more of his own in the twentieth century than in all other centuries combined. Between the communists and the fascists, more than a hundred million human beings have been slaughtered during the 1900s, despite all human progress.

Who else but a Christian can have a positive view of the future?

• Can the Muslim?

Since the late 1970s, Islam has been spreading in many parts of the world, including Western Europe. The irony of Islam's view of future events is that it believes this about the future: Jesus (yes, Jesus) is coming back, and He will be the judge of all human beings.[26]

• Can the atheist or agnostic?

How can we tell? What guarantees, if any, does life give him or her?

• Can the secular scientist?

While there has been great progress in science and technology, humanity's basic nature hasn't changed. While we can split the atom to gain a cheap source of electricity, the same power can be harnessed to blow up the world several times over. While there are great advances in technology, there are also corresponding corruptions in their use. We have great industrial development—yet pollution at the same time. And look at all the fuss caused by the difference between two-digit year setting versus a four-digit year setting, a problem commonly known as Y2K. You name the group, and I guarantee that it has no logical basis for optimism about the future—except for Christians. As Billy Graham once put it: He's an optimist because he's read the last chapter, and he knows how it all ends.

I like the way the late Paul Little put it:

> One of the most fascinating features of the Bible is that it tells what is ahead. Both Old and New Testaments contend that history is moving to a climax and that the sovereign God is in control. Helmut Thielecke, in his book, *The Waiting Father,* sums up this truth in a magnificent way: "When the drama of history is over, Jesus Christ will stand alone upon the stage. All the great figures of history—Pharaoh, Alexander the Great, Charlemagne, Churchill, Stalin, Johnson, Mao Tse-Tung—will realize they have been bit actors in a drama produced by another."[27]

Little went on to write that the Second Coming is our great hope:

> The second coming of Christ is the great anticipation of the church. As Christians we should, with Paul, love to look for that "blessed hope and the glorious appearing of the great God and our savior Jesus Christ" (Titus 2:13). His coming is an incentive for holy living.[28]

Here again Little stressed the point that in the big picture of things, details about the Second Coming and how they will all work out are not nearly as important as the fact that He will return:

> Whatever point of view expositors take on the

Tribulation, the Rapture, and the Millennium, it is thrilling to realize that all agree on the great, glorious, and incontestable fact that *Jesus is coming again*. The details of his next appearance are interesting and important to study, but differences in interpreting these details should never obscure the central fact of His coming.

It is significant that neither our Lord nor the prophets and apostles mention the return of Christ for speculative purposes, but always as a motive for practical daily holiness. We could summarize the doctrine: "since all these things are to be destroyed in the way, what sort of people ought you to be in holy conduct and godliness" (2 Peter 3:11, NASB).[29]

Conclusion

The climax of all history is the return of Christ. Yet who can pretend to know it all when it comes to the end times? Whoever thinks he or she knows is deceived. We need to be humble and teachable, while we continue to search the Scriptures "to see if these things be so." This side of paradise there are some things about the last days that we just won't know until we (or some future generation) experience them. Meanwhile, there are things that are unambiguous that we do know, such as being ready for His coming.

I believe strongly that it was Jesus' intention that we all should watch and wait for Him (not idly out in some desert or on someone's ranch in the hills), while being busy about our Father's business. We all should be ready and live our lives so that we would not be embarrassed at His appearing. For every time the Lord talked about His return He would say, "Keep watch, because you do not know the day or the hour" (Matt. 25:13). Even so, come quickly, Lord Jesus.

21

Failed Predictions of Christ's Return

Don't ever prophesy; for if you prophesy wrong, nobody will forget it: and if you prophesy right, nobody will remember it.[1]

—Josh Billings

The young theologian-to-be entered seminary with all sorts of anticipations for what he was going to learn. It was during the 1960s, and like many evangelical Christians, he held the view that those days were the very, very end times. Of course, ours was the generation that would finally see Christ. Yet while doing research in the seminary library and studying church history, a significant discovery shocked him. Since the beginning of Christianity to the present, virtually *every* generation in church history thought its time was the last.[2]

Alas, this pattern has repeated itself, sometimes leading people astray. B. J. Oropeza, author of the book 99 *Reasons Why No One Knows When Christ Will Return* (named after the now-discredited 88 *Reasons Why the Rapture Is in 1988*), points out:

> No prophecy regarding the date of the Lord's return has ever come true. Centuries of date-setters have all proved mistaken. Charismatic Montanists who predicted the appearance of the New Jerusalem in the second century, Christians who believed the final century was A.D. 900-1000, Dominican monk Brother Arnold who hailed the dawning of a new era in A.D. 1260, Bohemian Father Martinek Hauska who predicted the Second Coming in 1420, German bookbinder Hans Nut who heralded the millennium in 1528, Nicholas of Cusa who predicted the end in 1734, Mother Ann Lee of the Shakers who claimed to be the incarnation of Christ in 1830—all have been wrong.[3]

There have been many times throughout church history that people were absolutely convinced that Jesus was coming back at a certain date, though Jesus said no one knows for sure when that date will be. We've seen this damaging pattern over and over. Been there. Done that.

Here we are at the turn of a new millennium—a significant shift in history in the minds of many. Apocalyptic fever is in the air. Many are convinced, like the young seminarian was before his studies, that this is it—that Christ will come back in *our* lifetime. Those who believe thusly maintain that the founding of Israel as a nation is the key to understanding why we are in the very last days. They also hold that every thousand years or every two thousand years, God does something significant in world history. They believe the creation of humankind was roughly six thousand years before Christ. The flood was roughly four thousand years before Christ. The call of Abraham was roughly two thousand years before Christ. Christ came two thousand years ago. And now we're at the turn of not only the next millennium but also the next bimillennium.

Jesus, however, said nobody knows when He will return. Therefore, we should be ready regardless of when it will be.

Regardless of one's views on the millennium and the return of Christ, we can all agree that there is a strong need for wisdom and for watching out for false prophets who would use the return of Christ for earthly gain. Date setting is extremely unprofitable and unhealthy. It has led many astray and causes the world to merely write off true Christianity.

Apocalyptic Fears

When I first worked on this chapter, I thought that this was uniquely a Christian problem—setting dates, predicting the end, and so on—but looking at the bigger picture, I found that it's actually universal. Down through the ages in all cultures and climes, apocalyptic fears have gripped humankind. Such concerns are not unique to Christians. Most of this chapter will focus on false predictions related to the second coming of *Christ*, but it's helpful to touch on a few non-Christian examples as well because they're symptomatic of the apocalyptic type of thinking.

The word "apocalypse" is another name for Revelation, the last book in the Bible. It records the vision of the Apostle John, describing how the world will end. Through usage, "apocalypse" has also come to mean "a catastrophe so enormous that it will bring about the end of the world."

Consider a pagan example—the Aztecs. Because they were afraid that the sun might go out, every fifty-two years they took a number of ritualistic precautions to keep this from happening: They put out all their cooking fires because they believed this would cause the sun to see their need for him to return. They held day-long prayer vigils and prayer processions. They offered a human sacrifice and used the heart of the victim to perform the New Fire Ceremony. The heart of the victim was cut out and burned in a ceremonial urn or on a special rock. From this fire, torches were lighted and the "new" fire was transported down to the temple, and then eventually to every home. If the Spaniards had not conquered them in the early 1500s, their next fifty-two-year cycle, which was calculated according to the star cluster Pleiades, would have taken place in 2019.[4]

Apocalyptic Ebb and Flow

Richard Kyle, professor of history and religion at Tabor College, contends that humankind's focus on doomsday, since the world began, has been in a state of ebb and flow. He believes "apocalyptic movements arise during times of social instability and transition."[5] In China, for example, long before any Christian influence appeared, messianic movements occurred when a reigning dynasty had lost its "Mandate of Heaven" and was on the decline.[6]

In 999 the Ecumenical Council announced the world was coming to an end

In the West, one of the most unstable times was the tenth century (just before the turn of the second millennium of the Christian era). It was a period filled with superstition and visions of mass destruction: Fire-breathing dragons were seen in the clouds, and blood seemed to rain from the sky. Wars were tearing Europe apart—besieged by fanatic Muslims, pagan Bulgars, Magyar horsemen, and axe-wielding Vikings. Corruption was rampant in high places. Popes and kings plotted each other's assassination. The strong oppressed the poor, who were helpless to resist. And in 989 Halley's Comet appeared.

No wonder in 999 the Ecumenical Council announced the world was coming to an end. For hadn't the Bible said in 2 Peter 3:8: "But do not forget this one thing, dear friends: With the Lord a day is like a thousand years, and a thousand years are like a day"? Hadn't it been a thousand years since Jesus was born? It was in this terrified mode that the faithful waited on New Year's Eve for God to end the world. Richard Erdoes described it this way:

> On the last day of the year 999, according to an ancient chronicle, the old basilica of St. Peter's at Rome was thronged with a mass of weeping and trembling worshipers awaiting the end of the world. This was the dreaded eve of the millennium, the Day of Wrath when the earth would dissolve into ashes. Many of those present had given away all of their possessions to the poor—lands, homes, and household goods—in order to assure for themselves forgiveness for their trespasses at the Last Judgment and a good place in heaven near the footstool of the Almighty. Many poor sinners—and who among them was not without sin?—had entered the church in sackcloth and ashes, having already spent weeks and months doing penance and mortifying the flesh. . . . The last day of the year 999 and the first day of the year 1000 had come and gone. Yet still the earth stood and people still lived.[7]

The Montanists

Looking backward from the tenth century to the time of Christ, we find that some of the people of His generation expected Him to return at any moment. In so doing they ignored His teaching found in Matthew 24:36, 44: "No one knows about that day or hour, not even the angels of heaven, nor the Son, but only the Father. . . . So you also must be ready, because the Son of Man will come at an hour when you do not expect him."

Reviewing early church history, we find that the most apocalyptic group was the Montanists, named for their founder Montanus of Phrygia (modern Turkey), who formed this group during the Roman persecution of Christians (about 156–172), a very dreadful and unstable time. Montanus believed he was the voice of the Holy Spirit and that his authority was second only to Christ's. Two prophetesses, Priscilla and Maximilla, ministered with him. Montanus believed Christ's return was imminent and at His return He would establish a New Jerusalem in Phrygia, and a thousand-year reign of peace on earth.

Montanists lived an exceedingly austere life. They banned marriage, fasted for long periods of time, and were urged to seek out persecution rather than flee it. Maximilla, who outlived Montanus and Priscilla and who died in 179, prophesied, "After me there will be no prophecy, but the End will come."[8] The church recognized that Montanus was teaching heresy and eventually excommunicated his followers.

Columbus and Nostradamus

During the Middle Ages, the Black Plague of the 1300s, which killed about one-third of the population of Europe, created a "medical" apocalypse. Because of the cataclysmic, apocalyptic conditions they were living through, seers predicted that the Antichrist would arrive in 1346, 1347, 1348, 1360, 1365, 1387, 1396, 1400, 1417, and 1418.[9]

Even an otherwise-godly man can sometimes make a false prediction about the Second Coming. Take the example of Christopher Columbus. He wrote this in his *Book of Prophecies*:

> St. Augustine says that the end of this world will occur in the seventh millennium following the Creation;[10] the sacred theologians accept his interpretation, in particular the cardinal Pierre d'Ailly in *Verbo* XI and in other places . . .
>
> From the creation of the world, or from Adam, until the Advent of our Lord Jesus Christ figure 5,343 years and 318 days, by the calculation of King Alfonso. . . . Adding these figures to the approximate 1,501 years [since the birth of Christ in Columbus' time], the total is an approximate 6,845 years.
>
> According to this calculation, there are but 155 years left for the fulfillment of the seven thousand, at which time I said above, by the authorities cited, that the world will come to an end.[11]

As a result, Christopher Columbus (based on his reading of St. Augustine and others) predicted the world was to come to an end in 1657.

The most famous end-time prophet of the Middle Ages was the non-Christian seer Nostradamus, a medical doctor from St. Remy, France.

Born in 1503, he became the favorite astrologer of Catherine de Medici because he wrote a verse that she believed predicted the untimely death of her husband, King Henry II, who was killed in a freak accident. During a friendly jousting match, a splinter from his opponent's lance pierced his helmet above his right eye, and he died ten days later.

Although Catherine had thirty thousand astrologers at her beck and call, she thought Nostradamus was the best. The verse she read was from a book he had just published in 1555 called *The Centuries*, because it was composed of quatrains divided into groups of one hundred. All of the verses were cryptic and obscure. To derive any meaning at all from them required enormous imagination: They included contortions, convolutions, word substitutions, and the ignoring of certain facts. Nevertheless, he developed a following of believers called Nostradamites who exist to this day. They believe he has predicted such things as the great fire of London, Napoleon's imprisoning two popes: Pius VI and Pius VII, Hitler's rise to power and his death, and the assassination of President Kennedy. Note that their interpretations of the quatrains keep changing as new historical events unfold, and they generally appear after the fact. For example, there is nothing written before 1963 about the assassination of a president.

Here is what Nostradamus said about the end of the world: "In the year 1999, and seven months, from the sky will come the great King of Terror."[12] Perhaps in the year 2000, they will tell us what it means, but beforehand, we can expect many of them to be quaking in terror.

"Mad Miller"

Jumping ahead to the nineteenth century, we see second-coming fever emerging in full force. A chief promoter of premillennialism during the 1800s in North America was a man named William Miller. Raised by a devout Baptist mother, he became a deist as an adult. Nevertheless, serving as a captain of the militia in the War of 1812 and observing miraculous victories for the Americans caused him to seek the Lord. After the war, he made a personal search of the Scriptures and determined that Jesus would return in 1843[13] to establish a thousand-year reign of peace.

Miller believed he should make his views public so he began preaching, and in 1836 published a book, *Evidence from Scripture and History of the Second Coming of Christ about A.D. 1843*. Several national newspapers also carried stories about him. As a result, his message spread like wildfire through the mainline denominations, and he soon had over fifty thousand followers, who were called Millerites or Adventists.

On January 1, 1843, Miller declared a definite time frame for Christ's return. It would be sometime between March 21, 1843, and March 21, 1844. The fever pitch of the Millerites increased as the year wore on. It was augmented by the appearance of a comet that blazed across the sky and was so bright it could be seen with the naked eye. Yet the whole year passed by, and nothing happened. As a result, some of the Millerites left the movement.

In August 1844, Samuel S. Snow, a committed Millerite who had been studying Jewish chronology, revised the prediction, making the date October 22, 1844. This day also came and went. It was called the Day of Disappointment. Miller admitted that he must have made some miscalculation, although he could not imagine what it was. After that, he faded into obscurity and died in 1849 a broken man.

Seventh-day Adventists

Miller's followers were not as defeated as Miller, however. Three small groups remained. They became the forerunners of the modern-day Seventh-day Adventists. One group, in western New York, led by Hiram Edson, declared that Jesus *had* cleansed the temple in 1844, except that the temple was not located on earth where they expected it to be, but in heaven. Their belief was based on a vision that Hiram Edson had in 1844, when he saw Christ entering the heavenly sanctuary. Christ was supposed to purify the heavenly sanctuary and then begin an "investigative judgment" as to those who were worthy of salvation. When He finished, He would come back to take the faithful to reign with Him in heaven for one thousand years, leaving Satan to destroy the earth. Christ would then return a third time to destroy Satan, purify the earth, and take 144,000 to live in heaven with him forever.

A second group in New Hampshire, led by Joseph Bates, emphasized worship on the seventh day. They believed that worship on the first day would make one liable to receive the mark of the beast and to drink the cup of God's anger. Bates began to promote his idea of seventh-day worship in 1844, and in 1846 he wrote a forty-eight-page tract entitled *The Seventh-Day Sabbath, a Perpetual Sign*.

A third group in Portland, Maine, was led by Mrs. Ellen G. White. She was a prophetess, who had thousands of visions over several decades and made interpretations of Scripture that were considered by her followers to be as authentic as the Bible itself. In February 1845, she had a vision of Christ entering the heavenly sanctuary and confirming Edson's vision of the preceding year, and in 1847 she had a vision of herself being taken up into the heavenly sanctuary, where she saw the ark, the Ten Commandments, and a halo of glory around the Sabbath commandment, thus confirming Bates' belief in worshiping on the seventh day.[14]

Note that none of these groups set any more dates for Christ's return, but a lesser-known group called the Second Adventists continued to do so, declaring it would be 1873/1874. Also note that well-known "cult watchers," such as the late Dr. Walter Martin and Eric Pement, view today's Seventh-day Adventists as generally being orthodox on the key doctrines of Christianity.

Jehovah's Witnesses

From the Second Adventists emerged the Jehovah's Witnesses. Richard Abanes, director of the Religious Information Center in Southern California, notes that the Jehovah's Witnesses is "one of the most deceptive and dangerous of today's apocalyptic cults."[15] The first president was Charles Taze Russell. Raised in the Reformed Faith in Allegheny, Pennsylvania, he disliked the doctrines of hell and predestination and found more of what he was looking for in the Second Adventist meetings. By 1884 he became their leader, and subsequently his followers were called Russellites. (Not until 1931, when the second president took over, was the name changed to Jehovah's Witnesses.) Russell seemed to believe he was the infallible interpreter of the infallible Word. He wrote a seven-volume interpretation of Scripture called *Studies in the Scriptures*. The late Dr. John Gerstner, professor of church history and government at Pittsburgh Theological Seminary, notes:

> According to *The Watch Tower and Herald of Christ's Presence*, May 25, 1925, Russell was the angel referred to in Ezekiel 9:11, or the seventh messenger of the church. That is clearly the notion of the infallible teacher. That Russell thought of himself in such a way, although he disclaimed "superiority or supernatural power," is appar-

> ent. How else can one explain his statement in *Studies in the Scriptures*, "it would be better to leave the Bible unread and read his *Studies* than to read the Bible and ignore his *Studies*."[16]

Although 1874 came and went without any visible sign of Christ, Russell took the position that Christ had returned *invisibly* and could be seen only by the those who had true faith. Note that this is contrary to Revelation 1:7: "Look, he is coming with the clouds, and *every eye* will see him, even those who pierced him" (emphasis mine). Nevertheless, as far as Russell was concerned, Christ had already come, and the only thing lacking before the end was the Battle of Armageddon, which he predicted would take place in 1914. It would be preceded by a "Time of Trouble," which would begin in 1874, the year of Christ's invisible return.

To arrive at the 1914 date, Russell used a patchwork of Scriptures, which scholarly exegetes have found appalling. He began with Luke 21:24: "Jerusalem will be trampled on by the Gentiles until the *times* of the Gentiles are fulfilled." He believed the *appointed times* began when Jehovah had no representative government on earth, that is, when Israel lost her sovereignty and was carried away into Babylonian captivity in 607 B.C.

Russell then turned to Daniel 7:14, which he interpreted as meaning that at the end of the *appointed times* Christ would receive a kingdom that would never be destroyed. From Daniel, Revelation, and Ezekiel, he determined when the *appointed times* would end. From Daniel 4:25-26, where King Nebuchadnezzar was reduced to the state of a beast, he said the *seven times* equaled the *times of the nations*. For Nebuchadnezzar, this meant seven years, but it had to be something else for the nations because the time would already have passed.

In Revelation 12:14, he found that "a time, and times and half a time," that is, a total of three and a half times, equaled 1,260 days. Therefore, seven times would equal 2,520 days. From Ezekiel 4:6 he determined that a day equals a year. So there you have it: 607 B.C. plus 2,520 equals 1914.[17] Later he started studying pyramidology and came up with the same 1914—a double proof that he was correct.[18] Talk about a jigsaw puzzle approach to the prophetic Scriptures.

Russell and his group evangelized with great zeal because they believed no one who was killed at the Battle of Armageddon would be raised from the dead during the Millennium, and the only way to survive Armageddon was to join the Watchtower organization.[19] When World War I began in 1914, Russell thought it was the beginning of Armageddon. He died in 1916, still believing the end was near.

Russell's mantle of infallibility was passed down to succeeding presidents of the organization: Judge Franklin Rutherford, 1917; Nathan Knorr, 1942; Frederick Franz, 1977, and so on. Russell himself, as well as his successors, continuously rewrote predicted dates for Armageddon without ever saying they had made a mistake and without ever giving any reasons for doing so.

Here is how some of the predictions were changed:

1874—the Time of Trouble begins; the world to end in 1914.
1915—the world will end as a result of World War I.
1914—the Time of Trouble begins; the world to end in 1925.
1929—Armageddon is near.
1940—Armageddon is just ahead as a result of World War II.
1975—this is the year for Armageddon.
Yada-yada-yada.

By 1943, Russell's *Studies in Scripture* (1886), originally entitled *Millennial Dawn*, was so outdated that it had to be completely rewritten and all his calculations omitted.

The leaders of the Jehovah's Witnesses ruined many young people's lives by advising them not to get married or not to go on for further schooling. With Armageddon so near, it would be better for them to spend their time witnessing.[20] It's tragic that they still are out there—still leading people astray.

When Prophecies Fail

Why do leaders of apocalyptic groups keep recruiting when their prophecies fail? Do their followers do the same? These questions were asked and answered in a study made at the University of Montana and published in an essay, "Fifteen Years of Failed Prophecy."[21] The study tested the cognitive dissonance theory of Festinger, Riecken, and Schachter. In 1956 they asserted that when a prophecy fails, the result will be an increase in recruiting if five conditions are present:

(1) Belief in the prediction must be held with deep conviction.

(2) Members must have committed themselves to the prediction by

engaging in important actions that are difficult to undo.

(3) The prediction must be specific enough that it can be clearly disconfirmed.

(4) There must be undeniable evidence that the prediction was wrong.

(5) Members must have social support from fellow believers.

The subject of the study was a Baha'i sect in Montana—the Baha'is Under the Provisions of the Covenant (BUPC). Although this research was conducted in relation to a non-Christian sect, the findings are still instructive for pseudo-Christian sects. Their leader, Leland Jensen, over a fifteen-year period, 1980–1995, had made twenty failed prophecies about a nuclear holocaust that would usher in the Millennium. Over the fifteen-year period, he made seven types of explanations for prophecy failures:

Isn't it tragic that the great news has been perverted by those who cause others to stray from God?

(1) The prediction was fulfilled spiritually rather than physically.

(2) The prophecy was fulfilled physically, but not in the manner expected.

(3) The date was off because of a miscalculation.

(4) The date was a prediction, not a prophecy.

(5) The leaders had a moral responsibility to warn the public despite the date's uncertainty.

(6) God had given the world a reprieve.

(7) The predictions had been tests of the members' faith.

The results of the study indicated that the members were disheartened and stopped recruiting after the first failure, but the leaders kept on. Eventually, however, the leaders became less enthusiastic, the organization became more bureaucratic, and the members paid little or no attention to the prophecies.

In the Christian or pseudo-Christian sects, when prophecies fail, leaders take the Scriptures and twist them to try to rationalize some sort of explanation, like the example with the Jehovah's Witnesses: Christ *did* come back in 1874, but *spiritually*.

Isn't it tragic that the great news that Jesus is coming and will right every wrong has been perverted by those who cause others to stray from God?

The Ones Who Couldn't Wait

Waiting. So far we have been looking at groups of people who were waiting for the Second Coming, the end, the Millennium, Armageddon. Tragically, however, there have been those in history who could not wait. Taking prophecy into their own hands, they calmly or frantically, but always misguidedly, forced a confrontation with doomsday with poison, gun, or fire. Some of those apocalyptic cults ended in horrifying ways, such as the Jim Jones mass murder–suicide of more than nine hundred people in 1978, the Armageddon shoot out at Mt. Carmel [Ranch Apocalypse] in Waco, Texas, in 1993, and the fiery deaths of the members of the Solar Temple in 1994. Thankfully, most false predictions about the end don't result in such violence.

Failed Predictions

The dustbin of history, to borrow a phrase from Ronald Reagan, is filled with would-be prophets who have falsely predicted Christ's return in their time. Nevertheless, these false prophets still speak today . . . even though Jesus said no one knows the hour of His return.

Let's chart out some of those false predictions, some of which are in the text of this book and some of which are not. When we put them on paper we realize how wrong it is to set dates. Some of these people are orthodox. Some were heretics. All had one thing in common. They believed Jesus was coming back at a specific date.

In our own time, some are putting the return of the Jews to Israel (1948) or their regaining Jerusalem (1967) as the gauge to the prophetic clock. Yet many Christians have been wrong before. Our Lord Himself said we should be ready and we will *not* know the time of His return. Premillennialist Tim LaHaye sums up this excellent warning in a sentence: "Any time a person sets a specific date we know he is wrong."[22]

False Predictions [By no means an exhaustive list]		
Predictor	**Year or Era of Prediction**	**Prediction**
Some members of Thessalonian church	First century	Thought His return so soon they quit their work. Paul rebuked them and told them to get back to work (2 Thess. 2:2; 3:10-12)
Ignatius, Bishop of Antioch	Early 2nd century	"The last times are come upon us"[23]
Montanus	c. 156 A.D.	Predicted return of Jesus and establishment of New Jerusalem in a town of Phrygia[24]
Maximilla	died 179	"After me there will be no prophecy, but the End will come"[25]
Ecumenical Council	999	Christ would return to Jerusalem on Jan. 1, 1000
Joachim of Floris	Middle Ages	Christ would return in 1260[26]
Melitz	?	Predicts end of the world between 1365 and 1367[27]
Miscellaneous	Early 1300s	The Antichrist will come in 1346, 1347, 1348, 1360, 1365, 1387, 1400, 1417, 1418[28]
Christopher Columbus	1502	A better sailor than a prophet, he predicts the end to come on 1657[29]
Nostradamus	1555	"The King of Terror" will come from the sky in 1999
Mother Shipton	Early 16th century	"The world to an end will come, in eighteen hundred eighty-one"[30]

Cotton Mather Puritan divine	1600s	Jesus will come in 1697. When that failed to happen, he quietly reset the date to 1736, then to 1726. Believed that New England would be the location of New Jerusalem[31]
Isaac Newton	1700s	Great scientist, poor theologian, sets the date at 1715[32]
William Miller	1831	Christ will return by the end of the Jewish year 1843
William Miller	1843	After this failure, his followers revised it to October 22, 1844
Irvingites	Early 1800s	Christ will return in 1864[33]
Joanna Southcott	1800s	Has vision that He will return on October 19, 1884[34]
Second Adventists	1800s	This Millerite offshoot said Christ will return 1873/1874
Charles Taze Russell	1800s	Founder of Jehovah's Witnesses predicts Christ will return in 1874. When nothing seemed to happen, he declared that Jesus came back "spiritually"
Charles Taze Russell	1874	In 1914, Armageddon will take place
Lewis S. Chafer	1952	Jesus' return is so close that He is "at the door"[35]
Hal Lindsey	1970	It could happen in 1988. Since a generation is roughly forty years and since Israel became a nation in 1948 "all these things could take place."[36] Later revises it to 2007 [implied] since that's 40 years after Jerusalem fully returned to Israel.

Charles Taylor	1970s	The editor of *Bible Prophecy News* predicts the Rapture to take place in September 1984[37]
Edgar Whisenant	1988	Published *88 Reasons Why the Rapture Will Be in 1988*[38] (2 million copies sold). Set the date between September 11 and 13
Edgar Whisenant	1989	After the 1988 fiasco, readjusted his prediction by one year
Dami Sect in Korea	1992	Convinced Christ will return October 20 or 28. Many quit their jobs, sell their homes, etc. Leader of the group is later convicted of fraud[39]
Harold Camping	1992	After thirty years of study on the matter, concluded that 1994 was the year, and September 6 the day[40]
Marilyn J. Agee	1990s	The Rapture will take place in 1998[41]

The moral of the story is don't set dates for the Second Coming. Date setting is unscriptural, dangerous, and can lead many astray.

I'm tempted to say to these people: What part of "no" as in "no man knows the hour" don't you understand?

B. J. Oropeza, the author of *99 Reasons Why No One Knows When Christ Will Return*, says we should not only avoid date-setting, but we should also avoid date-*suggesting*.[42] He points out, "No one knows the time of the end, but we can certainly play a lot of guessing games."[43] Giving one recent example of such a failed prediction, he says, "Harold Camping suggests that the phrase 'no one knows' in Mark 13:32 really means that no one has yet experienced Judgment Day. In Camping's view, Jesus did not know the time of his own return only in the sense that he had not yet experienced the coming judgment. He did know the date, however, and so can we."[44]

Oropeza cautions that many in our day are setting themselves up for a big letdown: "With all the date-setting of the 1990s, we are fast approaching another Great Disappointment: A.D. 2000. Instead of learning from history, Christian soothsayers seem doomed to repeat it."[45]

People have been often wrong throughout church history. Why do we keep repeating this same mistake? I'm reminded of the little poem by British poet Steve Turner: "History repeats itself. It has to. No one is listening." Yet Jesus told us His Second Coming would catch us unawares.

Meanwhile, we should occupy until He comes. I doubt Christ would be pleased with all the wild speculation that goes on these days, trying to chart and pinpoint the Second Coming. All this does is waste time, and it can even lead people astray. History is strewn with would-be prophets of the Second Coming who have predicted that they knew the date of the end of the world or the Rapture and so on. All this does is invite the world to ridicule the church, and it sidetracks us from obeying what He has clearly commanded us to do.

The writer of Deuteronomy said, "The secret things belong to the Lord our God, but the things revealed belong to us and to our children forever, that we may follow all the words of this law" (Deut. 29:29). In other words, there are some secrets known only to God. When Christ will return is one of those. The date has not been revealed to us, and it won't be. It's one of the "secret things of God." It wasn't even known to the Son of God when He was here on earth. Meanwhile, there are many things in God's Word we know about clearly: Things we are to obey.

Conclusion

If people tell you that Christ is coming back on such and such a date and they say they can prove it with a patchwork of various Scripture verses, don't you believe it. Consider the words of our Lord Himself: "No one knows about that day or hour, not even the angels in heaven, nor the Son, but only the Father. . . . Therefore keep watch, because you do not know on what day your Lord will come" (Matt. 24:36, 42).

22

Practical Applications to the Return of Christ

There are two ways of looking at the Lord's coming: a looking for it and a looking at it.[1]

—A. B. Simpson

So what does the Second Coming mean in terms of our daily lives? How we view the return of Christ can have profound implications on how we live our lives, especially in terms of our Christian impact on our culture and in our planning for the future. For example, why start a Christian college if Jesus is returning this year? Martin Luther said if he knew Christ were coming back tomorrow, he would still plant his apple tree today. Some nonmillenarians feel that the reason many modern evangelicals are not salt in our decaying culture is because they're so wrapped up in the Second Coming and end-times prophecies that doing anything to clean up the culture is a waste of time in light of the urgency of the hour.

Let's consider some practical steps to which I would think most Christians could agree. . . .

Stop Asking "When"

The New Testament speaks some three hundred times about the return of Christ,[2] but nowhere in the Old or New Testaments does God indicate exactly "when" Christ will come.

The first thing we must do is to stop looking for the "when" answer. We must stop trying to patchwork together Scriptures to come up with a formula for a specific date. As we just saw, all those who have done so in the past have failed miserably. They have brought credibility problems on themselves, and worse, possibly on the Gospel—at least in the minds of some.

If would-be prophets have missed it so badly in the past, why should we be any different? No one has been able to calculate the date because God does not want us to know it. When God wants us to know something, He makes it clear. The return of Christ is not one of those things. In his intriguing book *Last Days Madness*, nonmillenarian Gary DeMar writes:

> There is nothing complicated in all of this. All one has to do is follow the words and themes throughout Scripture. There is no need for complicated mathematical schemes to determine hidden timetables that are not self-evident for all to see and understand. When God wants to set a timetable, He sets a timetable: 7 years (Genesis 45:6), 40 years (Numbers 14:34), 70 years (Jeremiah 25:11), 400 years (Genesis 15:13).[3]

One writer disputed DeMar's point. The problem was she lost her credibility because she predicted the Rapture was to occur in 1992.[4]

We must learn to trust God the way Abraham did. God told Abraham "I will make you into a great nation" (Gen. 12:2). It did not happen during Abraham's lifetime. When Abraham died, he had only two sons. Nevertheless, Abraham died believing God (Heb. 11:8-12). And in God's time, He fulfilled His promise.

Paul said God sent Jesus into the world "when the time had fully come" (Gal. 4:4). That means at exactly the right time. We must have faith that when God sends Jesus again, it will also be in the fullness of time. Jesus said, "No one knows about that day or hour, not even the angels in heaven, nor the Son, but only the Father" (Mark 13:32).

Curiosity Killed the Cat

The problem is we can't stop wondering. We keep asking ourselves, "Is the time getting full? It looks pretty full to me." We allow world events—floods, hurricanes, famines, wars, earthquakes, plagues, and the new millennium—to affect our thinking. Bible scholar Gary DeMar calls this "newspaper exegesis." He defines "newspaper exegesis" as "reading the Bible through the lens of today's newsprint." He continues, "When current events change, somehow the clear teaching of the Bible on these subjects changes."[5] For example, some people believe the Cobra helicopters used in the Vietnam War are the locusts described in Revelation 9:7. The helicopters are an invention of this century. In the preceding 1900 years, no believer could have come up with this interpretation. Bottom line: We must stop using "newspaper exegesis." Of course, we should still try to discern the times and apply the Bible to our lives in general. We just to need to be guided by a little "sanctified common sense."

Prepare Your Heart

After we have made a decision to give up the "dating game," what is the next step? To repeat the question asked by Ezekiel and popularized by Francis Schaeffer, "How shall we then live?" Jesus' teaching on this is very clear. Matthew 25 gives us some answers. Remember, that chapter contains the continuation and conclusion of the Olivet Discourse; the break between chapters 24 and 25 is arbitrary. Jesus gives three parables to illustrate what He expects of us: The parable of the wise and foolish virgins, the parable of the talents, and the parable of the sheep and goats.

The parable of the wise and foolish virgins teaches us to prepare our hearts. We must be completely and continuously ready at all times, watching with a joyful hope.

> At that time the kingdom of heaven will be like ten virgins who took their lamps and went out to meet the bridegroom. Five of them were foolish and five were wise. The foolish ones took their lamps but did not take any oil with them. The wise, however, took oil in jars along with their lamps. The bridegroom was a long time in coming, and they all became drowsy and fell asleep.
>
> At midnight the cry rang out: "Here's the bridegroom! Come out to meet him!"
>
> Then all the virgins woke up and trimmed their lamps. The foolish ones said to the wise, "Give us some of your oil; our lamps are going out."
>
> "No," they replied, "there may not be enough for both us and you. Instead, go to those who sell oil and buy some for yourselves."
>
> But while they were on their way to buy the oil, the

> bridegroom arrived. The virgins who were ready went in with him to the wedding banquet. And the door was shut.
>
> Later the others also came. "Sir! Sir!" they said. "Open the door for us!"
>
> But he replied, "I tell you the truth, I don't know you."
>
> Therefore keep watch, because you do not know the day or the hour (Matt. 25:1-13).

I don't see how the Lord could be more clear about being ready at all times. Here are some things we can learn from this parable.

- We need to be prepared for a long delay. We must have extra oil, that is, a deep faith, so our zeal will not flag and so we will not become weary of watching and waiting. Note that all of the virgins, both the wise and the foolish, fell asleep. So did the disciples in the Garden of Gethsemane.
- We need to keep watch *constantly* because Jesus will come when we least expect Him. Jesus said, "Be dressed ready for service and keep your lamps burning" (Luke 12:35). We tend to think Jesus will come only in times of great turmoil: social, political, economic, or ecological. When things seem peaceful, and when we can perceive no danger, we forget that He might come then. We slack off. We fall asleep at the switch. Yet we are admonished to be alert at all times. "Therefore keep watch because you do not know when the owner of the house will come back—whether in the evening, or at midnight, or when the rooster crows, or at dawn. If he comes suddenly, do not let him find you sleeping. What I say to you, I say to everyone: 'Watch!'" (Mark 13:35-37).

Watch and be ready. Jesus repeated that theme over and over. He didn't say, Watch your prophecy charts. He said, Watch for My return. In short, be on your guard. Don't let Him catch you unprepared.

I'll never forget when I once interviewed a former homosexual for his televised testimony. He said he was a lapsed Christian, and one time during the act, the thought occurred to him, "How would you like it, John, if Christ came back now, or you died right now and met Him while you're doing this?"[6] Personal holiness should be a natural by-product of being ready for Christ's return. Joel Green says, ". . . our hope in Christ['s return] spurs us on to *daily faithfulness*."[7]

Personal Holiness should be a natural by-product of being ready for Christ's return

- We must be ready *now*. Someday it will be too late to go out and get the faith we pretend to have or deceived ourselves into thinking we had. When the foolish virgins finally realized they had to get their own oil—that no one could lend it to them—and went out to buy it, it was too late. Before they returned, the bridegroom had already shut the door and would not open it again. Spiritually, there is a point of no return.
- We must watch *expectantly* with a joyful heart. Jesus is the bridegroom who comes for us with a glad shout so we can enter into his victory celebration. "For the Lord Himself will descend from heaven with a shout, with the voice of the archangel, and with the trumpet of God" (1 Thess. 4:16, NASB).

Work Diligently

While the parable of the wise and foolish virgins teaches us how to prepare our hearts—we are to be fully prepared, constantly watching, and full of joy—the second parable in Matthew 25, the parable of the talents, teaches us how to work. We are to work diligently, making the most of the talents God has given us.

In this well-known parable (Matt. 25:14-30), several points stand out:

- All the servants recognized that the talents they had received were not their own, but their lord had entrusted the talents to them. This made the faithful servants grateful and thankful to have such an honor, but it made the unfaithful servant afraid.
- None of the servants knew when the lord would return. The parable says the lord was gone "a long time." The faithful servants were not concerned about the time frame. They set out immediately to make the most of their talents, and they doubled them. The man who had five talents made five more, and the man who had two talents made two more. But the unfaithful servant, who was afraid, did nothing with his talent except to hide it in the ground.
- When the lord returned, he rewarded each faithful servant for his diligence by giving him more. He said, "Well done, good and faithful servant; you were faithful over a few things, I will make you ruler over

many things, enter into the joy of your lord." The lord, however, refused to accept "fear" as an excuse from the unfaithful servant for having done nothing. The servant's explanation of why he was afraid served only to make the lord more angry and disgusted. He called the servant "wicked and lazy." He took away the one talent he had entrusted to the servant and cast him into outer darkness.

The lesson to be learned here is that we must never be so paralyzed with fear about the Lord's coming that we cannot work. Starting today, we must work diligently to double the talent or talents He has so graciously entrusted to us. Then, whenever He returns "to settle His accounts," He will say to us, "Well done, good and faithful servant. Enter into the joy of your Lord."

Nor do you find any of these servants sitting around trying to figure out when the master will return. Listen to the wise words of premillennialist Chuck Swindoll on this subject:

> No matter how much we may love the Lord Jesus Christ and believe in His Word, we need to remember that there is still a life to be lived and responsibilities to be faced. And to cop out because Christ is coming is not only poor practically, it's abominable theology. Never once in Scripture is irresponsibility excused on the basis of one's confidence in Christ's return. Anticipation is one thing. Blind fanaticism is quite another. . . . There's something about Christ's soon return that stirs up our urgency and keeps us involved. God planned it that way. Anticipating the Savior activates our involvement in today's needs. . . . What we need is balance. We need to be informed and aware, thinking it could occur at any moment, but carrying out our lives as responsibly as if His return would not be for another two or three generations.[8]

What great insight . . . for living!

The third parable is that of the sheep and the goats. Christ calls us to serve the needy and poor in His name (Matt. 25:31-46). This parable concludes with the great judgment of believers and nonbelievers alike.

Let's Be About Our Father's Business

The parable of the talents certainly discourages laziness. It teaches us to be ready and active. When Jesus returns, how will He find us? Sitting under a tree and shooting the breeze while waiting for His return? Should we sell all we have, flee to the desert, and there wait for the Rapture, as some have mistakenly and foolishly done? Jesus clearly tells us we don't know when He's going to come and to *occupy* until He does. How do we get this simple truth so distorted so often? Similar to the parable of the talents is the parable of the minas, found in Luke 19. It is instructive to look at it because it sheds additional light on the parable of the talents.

> Now as they heard these things, He spoke another parable, because He was near Jerusalem and because they thought the kingdom of God would appear immediately. Therefore He said: "A certain nobleman went into a far country to receive for himself a kingdom and to return. So he called ten of his servants, delivered to them ten minas [worth about three months' salary], and said to them, 'Do business till I come.' But the citizens hated him, and sent a delegation after him, saying, 'We will not have this man to reign over us.'
>
> "And so it was when he returned, having received the kingdom, then he commanded these servants, to whom he had given the money, to be called to him, that he might know how much every man had gained by trading. Then came the first, saying, 'Master, your mina has earned ten minas.' And he said to him, 'Well done, good servant; because you were faithful in a very little, have authority over ten cities.' And the second came, saying, 'Master, your mina has earned five minas.' Likewise he said to him, 'You also be over five cities.'
>
> "Then another came, saying, 'Master, here is your mina, which I have kept put away in a handkerchief. For I feared you, because you are an austere man. You collect what you did not deposit, and reap what you did not sow.' And he said to him, 'Out of your own mouth I will judge you, you wicked servant. You knew that I was an

> austere man, collecting what I did not deposit and reaping what I did not sow. Then why did you not put my money in the bank, that at my coming I might have collected it with interest?
>
> "And he said to those who stood by, 'Take the mina from him, and give it to him who has ten minas.' (But they said to him, 'Master, he has ten minas.') 'For I say to you, that to everyone who has will be given; and from him who does not have, even what he has will be taken away from him. But bring here those enemies of mine, who did not want me to reign over them, and slay them before me'" (Luke 19:11- 26, NKJV).

Notice that unlike the other parable, this one begins with Jesus' reason for telling it: "Because He [Jesus] was near Jerusalem and because they [the disciples] thought the kingdom of God would appear immediately" (Luke 19:11). Jesus wanted to let the disciples know that the kingdom would be a *long time* in coming and know what they should be doing until it arrived.

The disciples had the mistaken idea that Jesus would soon be crowned king and they would be ruling as "princes and peers."[9] The parable plainly teaches that they were to receive no high positions, but they were to play the part of ordinary tradesmen. The nobleman in the parable told his servants, "*Do business until I come*" or, as the King James puts it, "Occupy till I come." Matthew Henry explains, "A true Christian is a spiritual tradesman. A tradesman is someone who, having made his trade his choice, and taken pains to learn it makes it his business to follow it, makes all other affairs bend to it, and lives on the gain of it."[10]

If we are to be tradesmen, we must also be wise, using our time in the most effective way possible. A wise tradesman knows the best time to buy and sell his wares. This is called "redeeming the time." In Ephesians 5:15-16, we read, "Therefore be careful how you walk, not as unwise men, but as wise, making the most of your time" (NASB). Elsewhere Paul wrote, "Be wise in the way you act toward outsiders; make the most of every opportunity" (Col. 4:5). Matthew Henry explains that "redeeming the time" literally means *buying the opportunity*. He continues:

> It is a metaphor taken from merchants and traders who diligently observe and improve the seasons for merchandise and trade. Good Christians must be good husbands of their time. They should make the best use they can of the present seasons of grace. Our time is a talent given to us by God for some good end, and it is misspent and lost when it is not employed according to His design. If we have lost our time heretofore, we must endeavor to redeem it by doubling our diligence in the future.[11]

The idea of being a "religious tradesman" may be new to you, but it inspired a seventeenth-century British pastor, Rev. Richard Steele, to write an entire book on the subject. The full title of his work is *The Religious Tradesman or Plain and Serious Hints of Advice for the Tradesman's Prudent and Pious Conduct: From His Entrance into Business, to His Leaving of It*. It covers the ethics and principles of living the Christian life in one's work. Though written in the 1600s, its principles are timeless. It is full of Scripture and has a foreword by Isaac Watts. In 1997, the 1747 version of *The Religious Tradesman* was revised and is currently being used in a course on Reformed Evangelism.[12]

Avoid Laziness

These parables Christ told not only encourage us to be ready and be about our Father's business, but they also contain a direct or indirect condemnation of laziness. Years ago when Art Linkletter hosted a talk show with little children, they used to come up with some great candid comments, proving that out of the mouths of babes come truths. The following dialogue shows that the parents being spoken about are not exactly paradigms of diligence:

There was the little girl who told the whole world about her doctor dad.

> Little girl: "My dad's a doctor, and he sure hates to be bothered by all the calls from sick people, especially at dinnertime and everything gets cold."
> Art Linkletter: "What can he do about it? After all he's a doctor."

> Little girl: "He changes the phone number and doesn't tell them, so they can't find him."[13]

And then there was the little boy who told the whole world about his father, who liked everything about his job, except . . . the job.

> Little boy: "My dad's a fireman and he sure likes his job."
> Art Linkletter: "What's he like best about it?"
> Little boy: "All the big fires happen on his day off."[14]

All joking aside, about a year ago a friend of mine told me he stepped onto a car-rental shuttle bus at an airport. Only the driver was there, and the driver had one of the modern "Jesus is coming by midnight tomorrow" type of prophecy books, and he struck up a conversation with my friend. The driver said he was really ready for the Lord's return. By that, however, he meant that he was tired of life. He was ready to just escape from his responsibilities and be raptured. This is wrong thinking. As Chuck Swindoll says of fanatics who shirk their responsibility under the guise of awaiting the Second Coming: "They don't worry too much about today's assignments, either, because they are so caught up in the tomorrow of God's plan."[15]

Joel Green says this about the Thessalonians, whom Paul rebuked for their dereliction of duty: "It could have been their emphatic belief in the imminence of Jesus' return that was leading them to idleness. However, the coming lordship of Christ Jesus cannot be only hoped for and awaited. The expectation of the Day of the Lord sets its stamp on our present calling and mission."[16]

A Meaningful Life

Not only are we not to be lazy, but also consider the good news that God has allowed us the joy of working with Him. David Breese, speaker on "Pause for Good News," writes:

> Consider the millions of citizens of the city of man grinding their days away in futility. Even those who think of themselves as purposeful are accomplishing things of no lasting value. Most of the people on earth

> travel about in little circles going nowhere. When they die their lives will show no eternal consequence. How different are the accomplishments of those committed to the eternal purposes of God. To live a godly life is not easy. But is abundantly possible.[17]

David C. Needham points out, "Out of all the eternal ages of our existence as God's children, these tiny years here on earth have a destiny that can never be repeated."[18] How's that a motive for being ready for His return or death, whichever comes first?

Be Prepared

Preparation is an important part of life. Consider how many years we spend in school. First, there's preschool or kindergarten just to prepare for grade school. Elementary school prepares us for junior high. Junior high school prepares us for high school, which in turn prepares us for college. If we go on to graduate school, college prepared us. If we become a doctor, we were prepared by rigorous training in medical school and through internships. If we become a lawyer, we were prepared in law school. If we're in a different type of field, for example, a carpenter, again we need preparation. We don't just become a master carpenter . . . we were trained and prepared for it. Whatever the profession, there is preparation.

When it comes to marriage, there is preparation. Part of the reason so many marriages are failing in our time is the lack of preparation. Couples are about to embark on one of the most important endeavors of their lives (marriage), and they are woefully unprepared.

Even before we're born, there's preparation. Nine vital months in the womb of development, preparing for a lifetime. Little things that go wrong in that time of preparation can affect a person for a lifetime. If a pregnant woman is drinking, she's often affecting that baby for a lifetime. So there's preparation in the womb.

There's preparation through *years* of schooling. Then, there's preparation for specific professions. Next, there's preparation for retirement. Thus, in a sense, all of life is preparation.

Many projects and tasks require preparation, sometimes quite elaborate steps to get ready. Before surgery, the nurses and doctors have to prepare the operating table. A writer has to prepare by doing extensive research before he or she puts the first sentence on paper. Before construction workers make a building, they have to prepare the ground. Preparation, preparation, preparation.

When it comes to the state of our souls, we must be *ready* now for whichever comes first—the second coming of Christ or our deaths.

D. L. Moody used to tell a rather convicting story on the need to get ready:

> One day, a little girl said to her mother, "Mamma, my Sunday school teacher tells me that this world is only a place in which God lets us live a while, so that we may prepare for a better world. But, Mother, I do not see anybody *preparing*. I see you preparing to go into the country, and Aunt Eliza is preparing to come here. But I do not see anyone preparing to go there. Why don't they try to get ready?"[19]

Indeed, many people seem to prepare elaborately for their vacations or their retirement. Yet they neglect to prepare for what really counts—eternity. People did not prepare for Christ's first coming, and alas, people seem not to be preparing for His Second Coming.

Polishing the Brass on the Titanic?

D. James Kennedy makes an interesting observation about the Christians in our culture who are so caught up in the imminent return of Christ that they neglect their social responsibility. They assume that since Jesus is coming any year now, why waste time dealing with the burning political issues we face? He writes:

> This second advent of Christ is the great hope of the Christian. It will climax history, being the final exclamation point to the last page of the last volume of history that will have been written. When Jesus Christ appears again in all His glory in the sky, the drama of the ages will be brought to a glorious conclusion.
>
> How will it be? How will He come? Unfortunately, it is true many fanatics have labored over their charts to set

their dates and hours and seasons for Christ's return. Others have divided the people of God endlessly on all the minutiae connected to the second coming. And often they are woefully wrong in these details.

Meanwhile, some Christians do nothing to fight back against the onslaught against the faith because they think that it's all just a part of fulfilled prophecy. Things will just get worse and worse and then Christ will come. They feel like we should do nothing to preserve our culture from sliding away from Christ and deeper and deeper into the sewer—despite the call of Jesus for us to be *salt* as well as light.

Why should we fight against abortion, pornography, the worldwide persecution of Christians or fight to preserve religious liberty in America, wonder these people, since it's all going to get worse and worse anyway? Why polish the brass on the *Titanic*, since it's sinking anyway? I don't agree with the analogy that we're on a sinking ship; but even if I did, I'd like to say to such people, "we might not want to polish the brass, but at least we should unclog the toilets! The stench in our culture stinks to high heaven."[20]

Are Our Efforts Foreordained to Doom?

Earlier this century, postmillennialist James Snowden said:

> Premillenarians say that Christ the King is absent and tell us what great things He will do when He comes again. But Christ Himself assures us He is present and is even now with us in our work. . . . To reduce this great commission to the premillenarian program of preaching the gospel as a witness to a world that is to grow worse and worse until it plunges into its doom of destruction, is to emasculate the gospel of Christ and wither it into pitiful impotency. This is to send the gospel out into the world as a futile thing, foreordained to failure from the start. No, the gospel is the power of God unto salvation, and Jesus Christ, marching in the greatness of His

> strength, sends us on no empty errand of uttering a message that will die away in the air on an unheeding and hostile world, gathering only a few out of its innumerable multitudes and consigning the vast majority to destruction, but He sends us to "make disciples of all the nations" and thereby win the world itself.[21]

We must be ready now for whichever comes first—the second coming of Christ or our death

Au contraire! cry the premillennialists. Haven't there been more missionaries in the last hundred years or so in part because of the strong revived interest in the soon return of our Lord? Ideas have consequences. Ideas move the world. Many people believe today that the energy in worldwide evangelism, the zeal to get the message out in radio, television, print, is often the work of premillennialists. Dr. Adolf Harnack, a respected scholar from earlier this century who was also somewhat liberal,[22] said this:

> In the history of Christianity three main forces are found to have acted as auxiliaries of the gospel. They have elicited the ardent enthusiasm of many whom the bare preaching of the gospel would never have made decided converts. These are . . . a belief in the speedy return of Christ and in His glorious reign on earth. . . . First in point of time came the faith in the nearness of Christ's second advent and the establishing of His reign of glory on the earth. Indeed it appears so early that it might be questioned whether it ought not to be regarded as an essential part of the Christian religion.[23]

I suppose the postmillennialists might counter, Yeah, but are they doomed to failure? Not necessarily. Besides, remember D. L. Moody's famous reply to a high-brow critic of his evangelistic methods? He rejoined, "I like how I'm evangelizing better than you're not evangelizing."

Political Involvement

One of the criticisms I've heard levied against dispensationalism is the idea that it teaches withdrawal from the world, including withdrawal from the political process, to the point that we lose our role as *salt* as well as light in our culture. Darby himself declared in 1840 while visiting Geneva (John Calvin's old stomping ground):

> What we are about to consider will tend to show that, instead of permitting ourselves to hope for continued progress of good, we must expect a progress of evil; and that the hope of the earth being filled with the knowledge of the Lord before the exercise of His judgment, and the consummation of this judgment on the earth, is delusive. . . . Truly Christendom has become completely corrupted, the dispensation of the Gentiles has been found unfaithful: can it be restored? No! Impossible.[24]

Critics would argue, you get what you expect. If you expect everything to get worse, it will.

Recently, I read an interesting critique of the conservative party in the United States. The main point of the writer was that too many of the Christians in that party had essentially resigned themselves to losing, believing everything will get worse thus fulfilling Bible prophecy anyway. Colonel V. Doner played an important role in motivating the Christian right in the 1970s and 1980s. He was the CEO of Christian Voice and cofounded the American Coalition for Traditional Values with Tim LaHaye and Jerry Falwell. Around that time, he was on all the major network news and talk shows. He has had extensive experience with the Republican Party and is disillusioned with the way he feels we let it take advantage of us. Colonel Doner says that Christians somehow think that if we were to create our own political party, "it would be doomed" from the outset. Why?

> Because our dispensationally driven eschatology dictates the Devil cleaning up—and soon! We are not only *not* going to win the culture wars—we're not even supposed to—'cause the earth is not the Lord's, it's the Devil's!
>
> While this Gnostic-Dualist-Dispensational model of "the End Times" has been largely abandoned by most evangelical churches in terms of teaching, defending, or

> even strict adherence, it's perfidious residue after a century of permeating almost every denomination, continues to subconsciously (at the very least) inform our world-view. The practical consequences of this particularly abominable and destructive heresy have discouraged long-term planning, strategic thinking, or even the forming of a rudimentary "Christian world-view." Thus, investing massive resources in the scholarly "heavy-lifting" necessary to develop a full-orbed world-view that comprehensively applies Biblical truth to all areas of life (as the Protestant Reformers and Puritans did) is nonsensical when viewed from the currently dominant evangelical-pietist dispensational paradigm.
>
> For those who haven't caught on yet, in this novel scheme cooked up by British layman, John Nelson Darby—and institutionalized by convicted felon turned Bible commentator, C. I. Scofield—1800 years of church theology, history and Biblical scholarship are disregarded, the church doomed to defeat, and the Devil inherits God's earth, making a lie of Matthew 28:19-20.[25]

Doner goes on to say that we no longer "engage the culture" as we ought.[26]

Here's an interesting thought to ponder: How is it that evangelicals represent some 36 percent of American society,[27] while gays, lesbians, and bisexuals comprise only 4.2 percent of the population,[28] yet they seem to have more political clout than we do? Could it be an underlying assumption that "it's all going to get worse any way since prophecy dictates that"?

Meanwhile, let's hear a rebuttal from a premillennialist, who would likely agree with much of the above analysis (but not the part about dispensationalism). This comes from Ed Hindson and his book *Is the Antichrist Alive and Well?*

> Concerned about the unprecedented advance of secularism in our society, we cry out against it—but can we really stop it? Evangelical social involvement has brought many issues to the forefront of the public policy debate.

> Some progress has been made by groups like Focus on the Family, the Christian Coalition, and the Liberty Alliance. But there has been little legislative change that could not be undone by a different administration. . . . We cannot give up on society merely with the excuse that these are the "last days" so it doesn't matter. We don't know for sure how much time we have left; therefore, we dare not presume on God's timetable.[29]

That's well put. I would hope we could all agree with that. Before we leave the subject of politics, there's one area where lives hang in the balance depending on what we do or don't do.

Why Get Involved? It's All Fulfilling Biblical Prophecy

Let's look at an example where apathy can arise from the idea that prophecy is fatalistic. Is the prophecy that everything is going to get increasingly worse being fulfilled anyway, or should we fight for justice? One of the worst evils of our time is the international persecution of Christians. It is a dangerous time to be a Christian for some two-hundred million people in several different countries—primarily the radical Islamic regimes (e.g., Sudan, Saudi Arabia, etc.) and the remaining communist countries (e.g., China, Vietnam, etc.). According to Dr. David Barrett, the greatest church statistician alive, the number of martyrs per year (specifically murdered/martyred for their faith) is 163,000. Broken down to a daily number, that equals 446 martyred a day. That's a number bigger than many of our churches in North America, and for a long time, many U.S. government officials have not seemed to care. If you have HIV or AIDS or are a homosexual and you may face persecution in your country, come on over to the United States—the "Golden Door" is wide open. But if you're a persecuted Christian, you need not apply. This is the message we've been sending to the persecuted church.

Nina Shea, who is a human rights attorney and the director of the Puebla Institute, says this about the church in China: "With hundreds of house churches demolished or shut, their pastors sent to labor camps to be beaten and tortured, and several Catholic bishops behind bars, the Chinese government has systematically set out to crush this affront to its power—waging a battle that affects millions of underground Chinese

Christians."[30] The reason I mention this as an example of the global persecution of Christians is because I hear every once in a while the sentiment that we should just let the persecuted church be since Christianity grows under torture. Besides, this persecution is just the fulfilling of prophecy. Kismet. This is simply a distorted, fatalistic view of prophecy. As long as the United States is the world's sole superpower, we can have a hand in curbing these human rights abuses. We certainly have leverage in those cases of abuse where the United States gives money to the nation in question.

Nina Shea says since the end of the Cold War, the global persecution of Christians is the number one human rights abuse in the world today. Even some Jews have helped sound the alarm on these atrocities, including Michael Horowitz of the Hudson Institute and Abe Rosenthal of the *New York Times*. It is criminal for us to do nothing about the torture, rape, false imprisonment, and murder of our fellow believers when it is in our power to do something. It is wrong to turn a deaf ear to the cries of the persecuted church because, after all, "it fulfills biblical prophecy." That's a wrong view of prophecy!

Home Is Where the Heart Is

Where your treasure lies, said our Lord, there will your heart be also. Home is where the heart is. Sadly many professing Christians are making this earth their home to the exclusion of their heavenly home. Their affairs, hearts, and minds are focused on this world and not the next. Yet this ought not to be. The Negro spiritual says well what our attitude should be: "Swing low, sweet chariot, coming for to carry me *home*" [emphasis mine]. It's almost as if the return of Christ would be an interruption to our earthly plans. That's not right. We should be ready at any given moment, whether He comes tonight, next year, next century, or next millennium.

Some Thoughts on Missions

The worldwide spread of the Gospel is very important. Taking the return of Christ very seriously, we cannot neglect either our role as salt (including, for example, political involvement) and light (including evangelism and missions). Listen to these great nuggets on missions that put its urgency in a new light:

- "People who do not know the Lord ask why in the world we waste our lives as missionaries. They forget that they too are expending their lives and when the bubble has burst they will have nothing of eternal significance to show for the years they have wasted."
  —Nate Saint (He was one of the five killed by the Auca Indians in Ecuador in 1956. His surviving sister labored among his murderers for the rest of her life until her recent death in the 1990s.)
- "O Lord, save us from any more diversions. Pour out a revival of love for all nations. Mark this decade with a new Pentecost. Prevent another generation from wasting tens of millions of man hours arguing about the future while forgetting the needs of the lost today."
  —John Gilman
- "World evangelization requires the whole Church to take the whole gospel to the whole world."
  — The Lausanne Covenant (1974)
- "What is the need of the hour? It is to believe that our God controls the universe and that when He said, 'The earth shall be filled with the glory of the Lord as the waters cover the sea,' He meant it."
  —Dawson Trotman (founder of The Navigators)[31]
- "We work for a glorious future which we are not destined to see. . . . Missionaries do not live before their time. Their great idea of converting the world to Christ is no chimera: it is Divine. Christianity will triumph. It is equal to all it has to perform."
  —David Livingstone[32]

Conclusion

The Bible gives specific and practical ways to behave until Christ returns. If we follow them—that is, if we stop asking when—if we prepare our hearts, and if we work diligently, we will be joyfully fruitful all the days of our lives. We should never stand gazing wistfully up into heaven as the disciples did when Jesus left. The angels admonished them to get to work (Acts 1:11). Whatsoever our hand finds to do, we should do it with all our might (Ecc. 9:10).

23

Be Ready for His Coming

Salvation is free for you because someone else paid. [1]

—Anonymous

During one of the most exciting games in the history of baseball, one of the players made a classic mistake—the kind that will forever be remembered in the history books. It was the seventh game of the 1924 World Series between New York and Washington. In the bottom of the ninth, with two outs and two strikes, Goose Goslin, batting for Washington, hit a home run. The fans went wild. This would win the game for Washington. Excitement was in the air. But wait a minute! Something was wrong. The umpire motioned with his thumb, "Out!" The fans were going nuts: *How could he be out? Was the ump blind?* Nervously, the Washington crowd watched as the coaches, the umpire, and a few of the players consulted on the field. And then the sad conclusion was reached: He *was* out. For in the excitement of the moment, Goslin had actually neglected to *touch first base*! All was lost that day because of this tragic oversight. Unbelievable.

Do you realize the same can be true in the spiritual realm? We can seemingly do many things for our church, for our community, and for our country, but if we don't tag first base—that is, if we don't accept God's salvation on His terms—then all is in vain. Jesus said:

> Not everyone who says to me, "Lord, Lord," will enter the kingdom of heaven, but only he who does the will of my Father who is in heaven. Many will say to me on that day, "Lord, Lord, did we not prophesy in your name, and in your name drive out demons and perform many miracles?" Then I will tell them plainly, "I never knew you. Away from me, you evildoers!" (Matt. 7:21-23).

In short, some people think they are on their way to heaven, but they will be in for a surprise on Judgment Day. They have never touched first base spiritually. Have you? Are you *ready* for His coming?

It's one thing to be cognizant of the Second Coming and filled with facts about it. It's another thing to make sure we're prepared on a personal level. Will Jesus' return be good news or bad news for you? The purpose of this final chapter is to make sure you are ready to meet Him if you're not already. For we will all meet Jesus Christ one day—either as Savior or as Judge.

The Bad News

As a starting point, we must recognize that in our natural state, there is a breakdown between us and God. In the last century, a famous non-believer was dying. Even though he was a minister, he wasn't a Christian by his own admission. I'm talking about Ralph Waldo Emerson. He may have been a great philosopher and had some insights into the human condition, but in the big picture of things, he was lost . . . and worst of all, he didn't know it. When he was on his deathbed, his Christian aunt came to him and asked him if he had made his peace with God. Emerson replied, "I didn't know we had quarreled." We may chuckle at his response, but we shall meet the aunt one day in heaven, and I don't think we can say the same about him (unless there was some miracle in his heart before he died).

What has caused the separation between God and man? The Hebrew prophet Isaiah proclaimed 750 years before Christ: "Surely the arm of the Lord is not too short to save, nor his ear too dull to hear. But your iniquities [sins] have separated you from your God; your sins have hidden his face from you, so that he will not hear" (Isa. 59:1-2). In other words, God is so holy that our sins keep us from directly approaching Him. We need to grasp that in our race toward first base, or we'll never tag it. We need to recognize and acknowledge that we're lost before we can become found. There are tragic consequences if we don't, and yet your average person seems oblivious to his or her lostness.

One undying myth I find in our culture is the idea that most people go to heaven when they die. If you ask people where they think they'll go when they die, usually they'll respond that we can't know that for sure. Yet God says (through the Apostle John): "I write these things to you who believe in the name of the Son of God so that you may *know that you have eternal life*." (1 John 5:13, emphasis mine). We can know that for sure.

Meanwhile, ask the average person what the entrance requirement for heaven is,[2] and amazingly they will answer virtually always the same . . . with some sort of "works" answer:

- "I go to church."
- "I keep the ten commandments."
- "I never hurt anyone."
- "I'm not as bad as Ted Bundy."

The person who says these things is essentially trusting his or her own good works as being good enough for him or her to make it into heaven. Yet it doesn't work that way.

In Paul's letter to the Romans, especially chapter 3, he made it absolutely clear that in our natural state, we are all sinners and deserving of God's wrath:

> As it is written, "There is none righteous, no, not one; there is none who understands; there is none who seeks after God. They have all gone out of the way; they have together become unprofitable; there is none who does good, no, not one" (Rom. 3:10-12, NKJV).

But the gift of God is eternal life in Jesus Christ our Lord

The Good News

Later in the same book, Paul said, "the wages of sin is death, *but the gift of God* is eternal life in Jesus Christ our Lord" (Rom. 6:23, emphasis mine). Again, this is contrary to what the average person thinks. They think that the wages of a good life is heaven. But how good do you have to be? That answer is in the Sermon on the Mount. You have to be perfect: "Be ye therefore perfect," said Jesus, "even as your Father which is in heaven is perfect" (Matt. 5:48, KJV). Well, now wait a minute! If only perfect people are going to make it to heaven, then who's going to heaven? None of us are perfect except Jesus.

Who can make it? "For all have sinned and fall short of the glory of God" (Rom. 3:23). Answer: No one can make it to heaven apart from Christ's shed blood on the cross.

The Centrality of the Cross

There is only one Savior, and there is only one source of salvation, and that is His death. The only reason anybody is saved is because Jesus died for sinners.

Because of Jesus' death on the cross—and only because of His death on the cross—there is full and absolute forgiveness available. All we have to do is come to Him and ask, and as we do, we have to humble ourselves before Him. We have to acknowledge our sins and turn from them. We have to give God our lives, our hearts, and our souls—through faith in Jesus Christ. He in turn gives it all back to us to make us free and whole and perfect in His sight. What an exchange: We give Him our sin; He gives us forgiveness, the cleansing of our hearts, and eternal life.

Accept the Gift of Eternal Life

Have you ever received the free gift of eternal life, which is made available to us through Christ's death on the cross? Let's reiterate a few key points:

- God loves us, but He is holy and our sins separate us from Him.
- Therefore, God sent His only Son, Jesus Christ, who lived a perfect life and then sacrificed His life on the cross in order to appease the wrath of God for our sins.
- We need to repent of our sins—to turn away from them.
- The gift of God is eternal life. We need only reach out and take Jesus as our personal Savior and Lord, and heaven is ours.

If you haven't done so already, I urge you to repent and to ask Jesus into your heart. I recommend that you pray something like this, in your own words if you wish:

> Dear God, I know that I have sinned against You in word, thought, and deed. I'm sorry for all my sins. But I thank You for Your mercy. I thank You that You forgive me based on Christ's death on the cross in our place. I thank You, Jesus, for dying for me in my place. I receive You right now, Lord Jesus, as my Savior and Lord. Please, cleanse me from the sin in my life and make me new again. Thank You for Your forgiveness. In Jesus' name. Amen.

If you prayed that sincerely, then that is an important first step toward eternity.

Here are a few key basics to growth in Christ:

(1) Read your Bible and meditate on it. I recommend a wonderful book that, if you use daily, by the end of three years, you will have studied every passage of the Bible. It is called *Search the Scriptures*.[3] If you need to get a more modern translation to help you understand the Bible better, then by all means get one, such as the *New International Version* (NIV).

(2) Join a Christ-centered, Bible-believing church and get involved there. Join a Bible group within that church and cultivate good relationships with other believers, including those you can trust and to whom you can be accountable.

(3) Tell others about your decision for Christ. Learn how to graciously share your faith with others. It's my understanding that we literally hasten the day of His return as we continue to proclaim His Gospel and to convert and disciple people.

Once we know Jesus as our personal Lord and Savior, our "thank You" to Him for His gift of salvation will be to serve Him in every area of our lives. Good works will naturally flow from our lives, as good oranges grow naturally on a good orange tree. We are not saved *by* good works (Eph. 2:8-9), but we are saved *unto* good works (Eph. 2:10).

Conclusion

To be saved is the best single way anyone can prepare for Christ's return. This way if He comes, we won't shrink back at His appearing. Instead, we welcome Him with great anticipation. This is why to the Christian the Second Coming fills us with such hope. I am reminded of the ending of the classic novel *Jane Eyre*, by Charlotte Brontë. She closes with one of the characters uttering a prayer familiar to the readers of the New Testament:

> "My master," he says, "has forewarned me. Daily he announces more distinctly,— 'Surely I come quickly!' and hourly I more eagerly respond,—'Amen; even so come, Lord Jesus!'"[4]

And so, just as with Christians throughout the ages, we declare the same words: Even so, come quickly, Lord Jesus! Amen.

Endnotes

Preface

1 T. Norton Sterrett, *How to Understand Your Bible* (Downers Grove, IL: InterVarsity Press, 1974), 139.

2 Ben Franklin, *Poor Richard's Almanack*, "BEING the choicest Morsels of *Wisdom*, written during the Years of the Almanack's Publication, By that well-known *Savant*, Dr. Benjamin Franklin of Philadelphia" (Mt. Vernon, NY: Peter Pauper Press, originally published 1743, reprint not dated).

3 Charles Caldwell Ryrie, *The Basis of the Premillennial Faith* (New York: Loizeaux Brothers, 1954), 47.

4 Edger C. Whisenant, *88 Reasons Why the Rapture Is in 1988* (Nashville: World Bible Society, 1988), "On Borrowed Time," 5.

Chapter 1

1 Richard Erdoes, *A.D. 2000: Living on the Brink of Apocalypse* (San Francisco: Harper & Row, 1988), x.

2 Hal Lindsey, *The 1980's: Countdown to Armageddon* (New York: Bantam, 1980), back cover.

3 William T. James, ed., *Foreshocks of Antichrist* (Eugene, OR: Harvest House, 1997), 382.

4 Salem Kirban, *Countdown to Rapture* (Irvine, CA: Harvest House, 1977), 188.

5 George Gallup Jr., and Sarah Jones, *100 Questions and Answers: Religion in America* (Princeton, NJ: Princeton Religion Research Center, 1989), 21. This Gallup survey was conducted for Robert Schuller Ministries. The survey itself was taken December 1982.

6 Ibid.

7 Jeffrey Sheler, "The Christmas Covenant," *U.S. News and World Report*, 19 December 1994, 62.

8 Robert Payne, *The History of Islam* (New York: Dorset Press, 1959), xi.

9 *National Survey of Religion and Politics 1992*, University of Akron Survey Research Center. Reported in *Time*, 30 January 1995, 75.

10 Ibid.

11 Adrian Rogers, *Revelation: Volume 2* (Memphis, TN: Love Worth Finding, 1995), 9.

12 D. James Kennedy, *Messiah: Prophecies Fulfilled* (Fort Lauderdale, FL: Coral Ridge Ministries, 1985).

13 A mathematician, Peter Stoner, had his graduate students calculate what the odds would be of any one person fulfilling just eight of these prophecies. He found the chance was one in 10^{17}—one in 100,000,000,000,000,000! Consider this illustration from Stoner. If we were to:

> take 10^{17} silver dollars and lay them on the face of Texas. They would cover all of the state two feet deep. Now mark one of these silver dollars and stir the whole mass thoroughly, all over the state. Blindfold a man and tell him that he can travel as far as he wishes, but he must pick up one silver dollar and say that this is the right one. What chance would he have of getting the right one? Just the same chance that the prophets would have had of writing these eight prophecies and having them all come true in any one man, from their day to the present time. [Source: Peter Stoner, *Science Speaks* (Chicago: Moody Press, 1963), 109.]

In short, God has inspired the writing of the Bible, and prophecies that Jesus fulfilled in His first coming provide ample evidence for that fact.

14 Lee Strobel, *Inside the Mind of Unchurched Harry and Mary* (Grand Rapids, MI: Zondervan, 1993), 36.

15 Paul Little, *Know What You Believe* (Wheaton, IL: Victor Books, 1987), 124-125.

16 Sproul, *The Last Days According to Jesus*, (Grand Rapids: Baker Book House, 1998), 203.

17 Charles R. Swindoll, "The Scripture Anticipates His Coming," in *Ten Reasons Why Jesus Is Coming Soon: Ten Christian Leaders Share Their Insights*, ed. John Van Diest (Sisters, OR:

Multnomah Books, 1998), 11.

18 J. Marcellus Kik, *An Eschatology of Victory* (Philadelphia: Presbyterian and Reformed, 1971), 160.

19 St. Augustine, *The City of God* (New York: Image Books, 1950, 1958), 492.

20 D. James Kennedy with Jerry Newcombe, *The Gates of Hell Shall Not Prevail* (Nashville: Thomas Nelson, 1996), 238.

21 David Moore, interviewed by the author, *The Coral Ridge Hour*, (Fort Lauderdale, FL: Coral Ridge Ministries-TV), March 1998.

22 Rousas John Rushdoony, introduction to *An Eschatology of Victory*, by J. Marcellus Kik (Philadelphia: Presbyterian and Reformed, 1971), ix.

23 Paul Lee Tan, *The Interpretation of Prophecy* (Winona Lakes, IN: BMH Books, Inc., 1974), 117.

24 Charles R. Swindoll, "The Scripture Anticipates His Coming," John Van Diest, gen. ed., *Ten Reasons Why Jesus Is Coming Soon: Ten Christian Leaders Share Their Insights* (Sisters, OR: Multnomah Books, 1998), 12-13.

Chapter 2

1 Edgar Allan Poe, "The Rationale of Verse," *The Pioneer*, March 1843.

2 Donald Grey Barnhouse, *Revelation: An Expository Commentary* (Grand Rapids, MI: Zondervan, 1971, 1974), 422.

3 *Noah Webster's First Edition of an American Dictionary of the English Language* (San Francisco: Foundation for American Christian Education, 1828, 1995), definition of "millennium."

4 C. S. Lewis, "Prudery and Philology" (written in 1955) in *Present Concerns: Essays by C. S. Lewis* ed. Walter Hooper (New York: Harcourt Brace Jovanovich, 1986), 88.

5 Thomas Ice and Timothy Demy, *Fast Facts on Bible Prophecy* (Eugene, OR: Harvest House, 1997), 164. (I'm indebted to *Fast Facts on Bible Prophecy* for much of the information in this list.)

6 M. R. DeHaan, *The Second Coming of Jesus* (Grand Rapids, MI: Zondervan, 1944, 1971), 46.

7 C. I. Scofield, ed., *Scofield Reference Bible* (New York: Oxford University Press, 1909, 1917), note to Genesis 1:28.

8 Lewis Sherry Chafer, *Dispensationalism* (Dallas: Dallas Seminary Press, 1951), 39.

9 Charles Ryrie, *Dispensationalism Today* (Chicago: Moody Press, 1965), 47.

10 C. Marvin Pate, ed., *Four Views on the Book of Revelation* (Grand Rapids, MI: Zondervan, 1998), 29.

11 Sproul, *The Last Days According to Jesus*, 158.

12 Ice and Demy, 217-222.

Chapter 3

1 DeHaan, *The Second Coming of Jesus*, 46.

2. Sproul, *The Last Days According to Jesus*, 153.

3 Sproul, citing Gentry, 154.

4 Ibid., 153.

5 Richard Kyle, *The Last Days Are Here Again: A History of the End Times* (Grand Rapids, MI: Baker Book House, 1998), 20.

6 Joel B. Green, *How to Read Prophecy* (Downers Grove, IL: InterVarsity Press, 1984), 102.

7 Ibid., 103.

8 G. C. Berkouwer, *The Return of Christ* (Grand Rapids, MI: Eerdmans, 1972), 424.

9 David Barrett and Todd Johnson, *Our Globe and How to Reach It* (Birmingham, AL: New Hope, 1990), 57.

10 Loraine Boettner, *The Millennium*, rev. ed. (Phillipsburg, NJ: Presbyterian & Reformed, 1957, 1984), 18.

11 Routine by comedian Emo Philips, transcribed from video, reproduced in Michael J. Hostetler, *Illustrating the Sermon* (Grand Rapids: Ministry Resource Library, Zondervan, 1989), 78-79.

Chapter 4

1 Little, *Know What You Believe*, 128.

2 Scofield, ed., *Scofield Reference Bible*, 1,252.

3 Hal Lindsey with C. C. Carlson, *The Late Great Planet Earth* (Grand Rapids, MI: Zondervan, 1970, 1972), 14-15.
4 DeHaan, *The Second Coming of Jesus*, 86.
5 Scofield, 989.
6 Ibid., 1,000.
7 DeHaan, 17.
8 Ice and Demy, *Fast Facts on Bible Prophecy*, 30.
9 DeHaan, 16.
10 Ibid., 17.
11 Scofield, 1,337.
12 Lindsey, 111.
13 Ice and Demy, 24.
14 Kenneth Barker, gen. ed., *The NIV Study Bible* (Grand Rapids, MI: Zondervan, 1985), 1,318.
15 Ice and Demy, 135.
16 Isaac Watts, "Joy to the World!" *Choice Hymns of the Faith* (Fort Dodge, IA: Gospel Perpetuating Fund, 1945), 522.
17 Scofield, 1,227.
18 Dave Hunt, *Global Peace and the Rise of Antichrist* (Eugene, OR: Harvest House, 1990), 5.
19 Grant R. Jeffrey, *Armageddon: Appointment with Destiny* (Toronto: Frontier Research, 1988), 193.
20 Ron Rhodes, "Millennial Madness," *Christian Research Journal* (Fall 1990), 39.
21 Boettner, *The Millennium*, 142-43.
22 George Eldon Ladd, *The Presence of the Future: The Eschatology of Biblical Realism* (Grand Rapids, MI: Eerdmans, 1964, 1996), 336-37.
23 George Eldon Ladd, *The Blessed Hope* (Grand Rapids, MI: Eerdmans, 1956), 148.
24 Barnhouse, *Revelation: An Expository Commentary*, 427.
25 Ibid., 428.
26 Alexander Reese, *The Approaching Advent of Christ* (Grand Rapids, MI: Grand Rapids Intern Publications, a division of Kregel, 1937), 17-18.
27 Ibid., 227.
28 Lindsey, 80.

Chapter 5

1 Kik, *An Eschatology of Victory*, 205.
2 Green, *How to Read Prophecy*, 117.
3 Berkouwer, *The Return of Christ*, 87.
4 D. Martyn Lloyd-Jones, *The Church and the Last Things*, vol. 3, Great Doctrines of the Bible (Wheaton, IL: Crossway Books, 1998), 4.
5 Green, 118.
6 Jay Adams, *The Time Is at Hand* (Phillipsburg, NJ: Presbyterian & Reformed, 1966, 1970), 29.
7 Scofield, ed., *Scofield Reference Bible*, 901.
8 Will Durant, *Caesar and Christ: A History of Roman Civilization and of Christianity from Their Beginnings to A.D. 325* (New York: Simon and Schuster, 1944; renewed 1972), 652.
9 Joseph Mede, quoted in *Christ's Second Coming: Will It Be Premillennial?*, by David Brown (Grand Rapids, MI: Baker Book House, 1876, 1983), 336 [emphasis his].
10 Ibid., 337.
11 Scofield, 634.
12 Adams, 89.
13 Ibid., 86.
14 Ibid., 28, 38.
15 Boettner, *The Millennium*, 136.
16 Scofield, 275.
17 Adams, 96-97.
18 Kenneth Scott Latourette, *A History of the Expansion of Christianity*, vol. 1: *First Five Centuries*

(Grand Rapids, MI: Zondervan, 1970), 214.

19 David Barrett lists 1.758 billion Christians as of 1990 in the world. He describes three potential scenarios as we reach 2000. One gives a figure of 1.9 billion Christians; another 2.1 billion; the third (which apparently has not happened) 3.2 billion. Source: Barrett and Johnson, *Our Globe and How to Reach It*, 56.

20 Philip Schaff, *Person of Christ: The Miracle of History*, (Boston: The American Tract Society, undated), 323, 328.

21 James Allan Francis, *The Real Jesus and Other Sermons* (Philadelphia: The Judson Press, 1926), 123.

22 Adams, 7.

23 John Jefferson Davis, *Christ's Victorious Kingdom: Postmillennialism Reconsidered* (Grand Rapids: Baker Book House, 1986), 10-11.

24 Berkouwer, 74.

Chapter 6

1 Charles Feinberg, *Premillennialism or Amillennialism?* (Wheaton, IL: Van Kampen Press, 1954), 32.

2 Erwin Lutzer, *Exploding the Myths that Could Destroy America* (Chicago: Moody Press, 1986), 27.

3 Green, *How to Read Prophecy*, 98.

4 Ibid., 81.

5 Ibid., 99.

6 John Walvoord, *Major Bible Prophecies: 37 Crucial Prophecies That Affect You Today* (Grand Rapids, MI: Zondervan, 1991), 16.

7 Sterrett, *How to Understand Your Bible*, 142.

8 Hal Lindsey, *Planet Earth: The Final Chapter* (Beverly Hills, CA: Western Front, Ltd., 1998), 24.

9 Tan, *The Interpretation of Prophecy*, 49.

10 Ibid., 50.

11 J. Dwight Pentecost, *Things to Come* (Findlay, OH: Dunham, 1958), 23-24.

12 Boettner, *The Millennium*, 82.

13 James H. Snowden, *The Coming of the Lord* (New York: Macmillan, 1919), 198-99.

14 Robert Van Kampen, *The Rapture Question Answered* (Grand Rapids, MI: Fleming H. Revell, 1997), 32 [emphasis his].

15 Quoted in Tan, 54.

16 Kik, *An Eschatology of Victory*, 131.

17 Ibid., 132.

18 Feinberg, 18.

19 Robert Anderson, *The Coming Prince* (Grand Rapids, MI: Kregel, 1954), 147.

20 Kik, 135.

21 Ibid., 156.

22 Tan, 30-31.

23 Kik, 192.

24 Tan, 36.

25 Quoted in Feinberg, 51.

26 Whisenant, *88 Reasons Why the Rapture Is in 1988*, 5 [emphasis mine].

27 J. D. Douglas, gen. ed., *The New International Dictionary of the Christian Church* (Grand Rapids, MI: Regency Reference Library, a division of Zondervan, 1974, 1978), 733.

28 George L. Murray, *Millennial Studies* (Grand Rapids, MI: Baker Book House, 1948), 40.

29 Philip Edgcumbe Hughes, *Interpreting Prophecy* (Grand Rapids: William B. Eerdmans, 1976), 123.

30 Green, 88.

Chapter 7

1 Quoted in Sterrett, *How to Understand Your Bible*, 85.

2 Boettner, *The Millennium*, 19.

3 Barnhouse, *Revelation: An Expository Commentary*, 431.

4 Kik, *An Eschatology of Victory*, 205.

5 B. B. Warfield, "The Millennium and the Apocalypse," article reprinted in *Biblical Doctrines*, quoted in Boettner, 31-32.
6 Walvoord, *Major Bible Prophecies: 37 Crucial Prophecies That Affect You Today*, 375.
7 George Eldon Ladd, *Crucial Questions About the Kingdom of God* (Grand Rapids: Eerdmans, 1952), 137.
8 Boettner, 45.
9 Hughes, *Interpreting Prophecy*, 110.
10 Quoted in Kik, 205.
11 Ibid., 196.
12 Walvoord, 383.
13 Boettner, 15.
14 Ibid., 68.
15 Quoted in Boettner, 71.
16 J. Barton Payne, *Encyclopedia of Biblical Prophecy* (Grand Rapids, MI: Baker Book House, 1980), 625.
17 Quoted in Payne.
18 Ibid.
19 Ibid.
20 Adams, *The Time Is at Hand*, 85.
21 J. Stuart Russell, *The Parousia: A Critical Inquiry into the New Testament Doctrine of Our Lord's Second Coming* (Grand Rapids, MI: Baker Book House, 1887, 1985), 80.
22 Feinberg, *Premillennialism or Amillennialism?*, 27.
23 Kik, 129.
24 Gary DeMar, *Last Days Madness: The Folly of Trying to Predict When Christ Will Return* (Atlanta: American Vision, 1997), 96.
25 Kik, 137.
26 Ibid.
27 Ibid., 138.
28 Ibid., 141.
29 Walvoord, 262.
30 Green, *How to Read Prophecy*, 79.
31 Boettner, 63.
32 Ibid.
33 Tan, *The Interpretation of Prophecy*, 268.
34 Ibid., 269.
35 Ibid., 160-161.
36 Ibid., 201.

Chapter 8

1 Quoted in *Revelation: Four Views: A Parallel Commentary*, ed. Steve Gregg (Nashville: Thomas Nelson, 1997), front jacket cover.
2 Pate, gen. ed., *Four Views on the Book of Revelation*, 11.
3 I'm partially indebted to the NIV's subtitles for these highlights.
4 Barker, gen. ed., *The NIV Study Bible*, 1923.
5 David Chilton, *Days of Vengeance* (Tyler, TX: Institute for Christian Economics, 1987), 39.
6 Ibid., 19.
7 Adams, *The Time Is at Hand*, 49.
8 Robert L. Thomas, "A Classical Dispensationalist View of Revelation," in *Four Views on the Book of Revelation*, gen. ed. C. Marvin Pate, 191.
9 Eusebius, *Church History*, Book III, Chapter 5, "The Last Siege of the Jews after Christ." Reproduced in *A Select Library of Nicene and Post-Nicene Fathers of the Christian Church*, second series, translated into English with Prolegomena and Explanatory Notes under the editorial supervision of Philip Schaff and Henry Wace, Volume I. *Eusebius: Church History, Life of Constantine the*

Great, and Oration in Praise of Constantine. Eusebius notes by Arthur Cushman McGiffert (Grand Rapids, MI: Eerdmans, 1890, 1986), 148, footnote 1.
10 Sproul, *The Last Days According to Jesus*, 132.
11 Kenneth Gentry, *Before Jerusalem Fell: Dating the Book of Revelation: An Exegetical and Historical Argument for a Pre-A.D. 70 Composition* (Tyler, TX: Institute for Christian Economics, 1989), 336.
12 Lloyd-Jones, *The Church and the Last Things*, vol. 3, 152.
13 Adams, 51.
14 Ibid., 53.
15 Ibid., 87.
16 Thomas in Pate, 225.
17 Kyle, *The Last Days Are Here Again: A History of the End Times*, 33.
18 Lloyd-Jones, 148-49.
19 Henry H. Halley, *Halley's Bible Handbook: An Abbreviated Bible Commentary* (Grand Rapids, MI: Zondervan, 1927, 1962), 594.
20 Ibid., 595.
21 Ibid.
22 C. Marvin Pate, "Introduction to Revelation," in *Four Views on the Book of Revelation*, gen. ed. C. Marvin Pate, 18.
23 Tim LaHaye, *Revelation: Illustrated and Made Plain* (Grand Rapids, MI: Zondervan, 1976), 1.
24 Lloyd-Jones, 145-46.
25 LaHaye, 4.
26 Thomas in Pate, 182, 224.
27 D. L. Moody, quoted in *The Theocratic Kingdom*, 3 Volumes by George N. H. Peters, (Grand Rapids, MI: Kregel, 1952), I, 174.
28 Keith Mathison, *Dispensationalism: Rightly Dividing the People of God?* (Phillipsburg, NJ: Presbyterian and Reformed, 1995), 7.
29 Jack Van Impe, *Revelation Revealed: A Verse-by-Verse Study* (Dallas: Word Books, 1982, 1996), 7.
30 Kenneth L. Gentry Jr., "A Preterist View of Revelation," *Four Views on the Book of Revelation*, gen. ed. C. Marvin Pate, 37.
31 Lloyd-Jones, 144-48.
32 Pate, 18.
33 Sam Hamstra Jr., "Apocalypse Now," *Four Views on the Book of Revelation*, gen. ed. C. Marvin Pate, 131.
34 Ibid.
35 Lindsey, *The Late Great Planet Earth*, 122.
36 Sproul, 45.
37 Green, *How to Read Prophecy*, 77.
38 Adams, 103.
39 LaHaye, foreword (n.p.).
40 Ibid.
41 Joseph A. Seiss, *The Apocalypse* (Grand Rapids: Zondervan Publishing House, 1957), 527.

Chapter 9

1 Hughes, *Interpreting Prophecy*, 33.
2 Feinberg, *Premillennialism or Amillennialism?*, 27.
3 John Walvoord, *The Rapture Question* (Grand Rapids, MI: Zondervan, 1957), 52.
4 Ryrie, *The Basis of the Premillennial Faith*, 33.
5 George L. Murray, *Millennial Studies* (Grand Rapids, MI: Baker Book House, 1948), 192.
6 Philip Schaff, *History of the Christian Church*, vol. 2, (New York: Charles Scribner's Sons, 1882-1910), 614.
7 Felician A. Foy, ed., *The 1988 Catholic Almanac* (Huntington, IN: Our Sunday Visitor Publishing Division, 1987), 199-200.
8 I refer to the separation of church and state as "the separation of the institution of the church from

the institution of the state" because it's a very different concept than the rabid type of separation of God and state that legal groups like the American Civil Liberties Union promote through their endless litigious battle to remove any remaining vestige of our nation's Christian heritage.

9 Hal Lindsey, talk at Christian Booksellers Association Convention, 14 July 1998, Dallas, TX.

10 Kyle, *The Last Days Are Here Again: A History of the End Times*, 74.

11 Ibid.

12 William B. Neatby, A *History of the Plymouth Brethren* (London: Hodder and Stoughton, 1901), 339.

13 Adams, *The Time Is at Hand*, 1.

14 Ed Hindson, *Is the Antichrist Alive and Well?: 10 Keys to His Identity* (Eugene, OR: Harvest House, 1998), 182.

15 Kyle, 115.

16 W. E. Blackstone, *Jesus Is Coming* (New York: Fleming H. Revell, 1878, 1932), 36.

17 LaHaye, *Revelation: Illustrated and Made Plain*, 288.

18 Gerald B. Stanton, *Kept from the Hour* (Grand Rapids, MI: Zondervan, 1956), 226.

19 Keith Mathison, *Dispensationalism: Rightly Dividing the People of God?* (Phillipsburg, NJ: Presbyterian and Reformed, 1995), 12.

20 John F. Walvoord, *The Blessed Hope and the Tribulation: A Biblical and Historical Study of Posttribulationism* (Grand Rapids: Zondervan Publishing House, 1976), 15.

Chapter 10

1 Bertrand Russell, *Why I Am Not a Christian and Other Essays on Religion and Related Subjects*, Paul Edwards, ed. (New York: A Clarion Book, a division of Simon and Schuster, 1957), 16-17.

2 Sproul, *The Last Days According to Jesus*, 13.

3 Ibid., 14.

4 Lloyd-Jones, *The Church and the Last Things*, vol. 3, Great Doctrines of the Bible, 99.

5 Lindsey, *Planet Earth: The Final Chapter*, 67.

Chapter 11

1 Sproul, *The Last Days According to Jesus*, 26.

2 Ibid., 45.

3 Gary North, publisher's preface to *The Great Tribulation* by David Chilten (Fort Worth: Dominion Press, 1987), xi.

4 Norman, "Eusebius of Caesarea," in *The New International Dictionary of the Christian Church*, gen. ed. J.D. Douglas, (Grand Rapids, MI: Regency Reference Library, a division of Zondervan, 1974, 1978), 356.

5 Quoted in Douglas, 356.

6 Eusebius, *Church History*, Book III, Chapter 9, "Josephus and the Works Which He Has Left," 143.

7 Lindsey, *Planet Earth: The Final Chapter*, 21-22.

8 Eusebius, *Church History*, Book III, Chapter 5, "The Last Siege of the Jews after Christ," 138.

9 Ibid.

10 Ibid.

11 Ibid., 138-39.

12 Ibid., 139.

13 Ibid.

14 Quoted in Kik, *An Eschatology of Victory*, 122-23 [emphasis mine].

15 Ibid., 92.

16. Josephus, *The Antiquity of the Jews*, book V, chapter 13, section 6, book VI, chapter 3, sections 3 and 4. Quoted in Eusebius, *Church History*, chapter 6, 140.

17 Ibid., 141.

18 Ibid.

19 Eusebius, *Church History*, 141.

20 Quoted in Kik, 119.

21 Eusebius, *Church History*, Book III, Chapter 7, 141.
22 Josephus, *The Antiquity of the Jews*, Book VI, Chapter 5, section 3. Quoted in Eusebius, *Church History*, Book III, Chapter 8, "The Signs Which Preceded the War," 142-43 [emphasis and bracketed comments mine].
23 Eusebius, Book III, Chapter 8, 143.
24 Gaalya Cornfield, gen. ed., *Josephus: The Jewish War* (Grand Rapids, MI: Zondervan, 1982), 427 [bracketed comment mine].
25 Eusebius, *Church History*, 142 [bracketed comment mine].

Chapter 12

1 DeMar, *Last Days Madness: The Folly of Trying to Predict When Christ Will Return*, 20.
2 Kik, *An Eschatology of Victory*, 30.
3 Sproul, *The Last Days According to Jesus*, 16.
4 Quoted in Kik, 61.
5 DeMar, 33.
6 Ibid.
7 DeMar, 34.
8 Sproul, 98.
9 Lindsey, *The Late Great Planet Earth*, 54.
10 Charles Haddon Spurgeon, *The Gospel of the Kingdom*, 218, quoted in Kik, 31.
11 John Calvin, *Commentary on a Harmony of the Evangelists, Matthew, Mark, and Luke*, vol. 3, trans. by William Pringle (Grand Rapids, MI: Eerdmans, 1949), 151.
12 Ibid., 152.
13 Term cited by R. C. Sproul, interviewed in "The Bible: Fable, Fraud, or Fact?" *The Coral Ridge Hour*, Fort Lauderdale, FL: Coral Ridge Ministries-TV, 4 December 1994.
14 The Jesus Seminar, a project of the Westar Institute, is a group of trendy, theological liberals (approximately 80) who voted secretly on the authenticity of the sayings of Jesus. They concluded that He said only 18 percent of what is attributed to Him in the Gospels. Conservatives counter that their conclusions were based on their antisupernaturalistic biases and extrabiblical writings, not on the text of the passages in question. Their findings can be found in Robert Funk, Roy Hoover, and the Jesus Seminar, *The Five Gospels; What Did Jesus Really Say?* (New York: Macmillan, 1993).
15 "Scholars Doubt Jesus Vowed Second Coming," *Miami Herald*, 6 March 1989, 1A.
16 Gallup and Jones, *100 Questions and Answers: Religion in America*, 21.
17 See Benjamin Breckinridge Warfield, *The Inspiration and Authority of the Bible* (Philadelphia: Presbyterian and Reformed, 1948); Norman L. Geisler and William E. Nix, *A General Introduction to the Bible* (Chicago: Moody Press, 1968, 1988); F. F. Bruce, *The New Testament Documents: Are They Reliable?* (Downers Grove, IL: InterVarsity Press, 1943, 1974); Erwin Lutzer, *Seven Reasons We Can Trust the Bible* (Chicago: Moody Press, 1998); John R. W. Stott, *The Authority of the Bible* (Downers Grove, IL: InterVarsity Press, 1974).
18 Matthew Henry, *Commentary in One Volume*, ed. Leslie F. Church (Grand Rapids, MI: Regency Reference Library, a division of Zondervan, 1961), 1,325 (commentary on Matt. 24:1-3).
19 DeMar, 29.
20 Sproul, 13.
21 Mansel, *The Gnostic Heresies*, quoted in Kik, 82.
22 Kik, 92.
23 Calvin, 120-21.
24 DeMar, 45.
25 Eusebius, Book II, Chapter 8, 110.
26 Kik, 93.
27 *Seneca Ad Lucilium Epistulae Morales*, trans. Richard M. Gummere, vol. 2, 437. Quoted in DeMar, 188.
28 DeMar, 51.

29 From the Parthians through Armenia, see John Foxe, *Foxe's Book of Martyrs*, updated into modern English in "The Deaths of the Apostles," Jerry Newcombe, ed., *The Moral of the Story: Timeless Tales to Cherish and Share* (Nashville: Broadman & Holman, 1996), 57-65.
30 For Syria through Gaul, see Philip Doddridge, quoted in Thomas Scott, *The Holy Bible Containing the Old and New Testaments, According to the Authorized Version; with Explanatory Notes, Practical Observations, and Copious Marginal References* (New York: Collins and Hannay, 1832), vol. 3, 109.
31 For Pontus through Asia, see Eusebius, *Church History from* A.D. *1-324*, Book III, Chapter 1, 132.
32 DeMar, 43.
33 Sproul, 85, 87.
34 Kik, 96.
35 A. T. Pierson, *Many Infallible Proofs*, 67, quoted in Dave MacPherson, *The Incredible Cover-Up* (Medford, OR: Omega, 1975, 1980), 128.
36 MacPherson, 128.
37 Ibid., 48.
38 Isaac Asimov, *Asimov's Guide to Halley's Comet: The Awesome Story of Comets* (New York: Walker and Company, 1985), 6.
39 Tan, *The Interpretation of Prophecy*, 332.
40 Sproul, 114.
41 Kik, 102.
42 Ibid., 103.
43 Josephus, quoted in Kik, 103.
44 Kik, 104.
45 Ibid., 113.
46 Van Kampen, *The Rapture Question Answered*, 77.
47 Charles Spurgeon, quoted in Kik, 158.
48 Kik, 159.
49 Ibid., 162 [bracketed inserts are mine].
50 Ibid., 165.
51 Ibid., 163.
52 Sproul, 127.
53 Green, *How to Read Prophecy*, 74.

Chapter 13

1 Ed Hindson, *Final Times* (Eugene, OR: Harvest House, 1996), 11.
2 William T. James, "Bridge over the Abyss," in *Foreshocks of Antichrist*, gen. ed. William T. James (Eugene, OR: Harvest House, 1997), 381.
3 Van Kampen, *The Rapture Question Answered*, 38.
4 Ibid., 38-40.
5 Robert Jamieson, A. R. Fausset, and David Brown, *Commentary, Practical and Explanatory on the Whole Bible* (Grand Rapids, MI: Zondervan, 1800s, 1976), 979 (Commentary on Mark 13:30).
6 Scofield, ed., *Scofield Reference Bible*, 1,106.
7 Lindsey, *The Late Great Planet Earth*, 62.
8 Lindsey, *Planet Earth: The Final Chapter*, 6.
9 Ibid., 21-22 [bracketed notes are his].
10 James, 7.
11 LaHaye, "The Signs of the Times Imply His Coming," gen. ed. John Van Diest, *Ten Reasons Why Jesus Is Coming Soon: Ten Christian Leaders Share Their Insights*, 196.
12 Ibid., 197.
13 Ibid., 227.
14 Ralph Reed, *Politically Incorrect: The Emerging Faith Factor in American Politics* (Waco, TX: Word, 1994), 5.
15 David Barrett, guest on *The Coral Ridge Hour*, Fort Lauderdale, FL: Coral Ridge Ministries, 8 November 1998.

16 Paul Lee Tan, *Encyclopedia of 7,700 Illustrations: Signs of the Times*, (Rockville, MD: Assurance Publishers, 1984), 408.
17 D. James Kennedy, *The Wolves Among Us: The Cults* (Fort Lauderdale: Coral Ridge Ministries, 1985).
18 *Action Sheet* for Truths That Transform: interview with Dr. Walter Martin of the Christian Research Institute (Fort Lauderdale, FL: Coral Ridge Ministries, 17 October, 1988).
19 LaHaye, 195.
20 Lindsey, *The Late Great Planet* Earth, 101.
21 Tan, *Encyclopedia of 7,700 Illustrations*, 1571.
22 Paul Johnson, *Modern Times* (New York: Harper and Row, 1983), 729.
23 John F. Kennedy, Address to the United Nations, 25 September 1961.
24 LaHaye, 198.
25 Tan, *Encyclopedia of 7,700 Illustrations*, 420.
26 David Wallechinsky, Irving Wallace, and Amy Wallace, *The People's Almanac™ Presents The Book of Lists* (New York: Bantam Books, 1978), 97. See numbers 1 and 5.
27 J. R. Church, "Riders of Revelation 6, Mount Up!" in *Foreshocks of Antichrist*, gen. ed. William T. James, 333.
28 DeMar, *Last Days Madness: The Folly of Trying to Predict When Christ Will Return*, 188.
29 Grant R. Jeffrey, *Armageddon: Appointment with Destiny* (Toronto: Frontier Research, 1988), 278.
30 Ibid.
31 James, 16.
32 Ibid., 9, 18, 20.
33 Jeffrey, 267-68.
34 Ibid., 268-69. Based on Zephaniah 3:9.
35 Ibid., 269-72. Based on Genesis 16:11-12; Psalm 82:2-8; Ezekiel 35:1-5, 10.
36 Ibid., 272-73. Based on Isaiah 43:6; Zephaniah 3:10.
37 Ibid., 273. Based on Isaiah 27:6; 35:7; Joel 2:23.
38 Ibid., 274. Based on Isaiah 2:2; Ezekiel 43:19; 2 Thessalonians 2:3-4; Revelation 11:1-2.
39 Ibid., 274-75. Based on Exodus 30:25-26. The plants needed to produce a special type of oil God commanded the priests in Exodus to use were seemingly lost forever. But now a flask has been found so a temple yet to be built can be consecrated after all in the exact way God prescribed. This is important because of Daniel 9:24 (which most preterists believe was already fulfilled).
40 Ibid., 275-76. Jeffrey writes, "Ezekiel foretold that the sacred vessels and linen robes would be prepared for use in the future Temple in the Millennium." (Based on Ezek. 44:16-17). He adds, "It is significant that the Temple Institute in the Old City of Jerusalem has prepared over eighty of the special sacred objects, vessels, and linen priestly garments required for future Temple services."
41 Ibid., 276-77. Based on Daniel 2:40-41.
42 Ibid., 277-78.
43 Ibid., 278-83. Based on Daniel 7:14; Revelation 13:7-8.
44 Ibid., 283-84. Based on Revelation 13:16-18.
45 Ibid., 284-85. Based on Revelation 11:9-10, where the whole world witnesses the resurrection of God's two witnesses. How could the whole world learn of it instantaneously without our modern communications?
46 Ibid., 285-86. Based on Daniel 12:4.
47 Ibid., 286-87.
48 Ibid., 287. Based on Revelation 11:18.
49 Ibid., 287-88. Based on Revelation 16:12.
50 Ibid., 290.
51 Ibid.
52 Ibid.
53 Ibid. [emphasis mine].
54 James, 392.

55 Van Kampen, 68.
56 Green, *How to Read Prophecy*, 107.

Chapter 14
1 Adams, *The Time Is at Hand*, 87.
2 Hughes, *Interpreting Prophecy*, 97.
3 Boettner, *The Millennium*, 265.
4 Van Impe, *Revelation Revealed: A Verse-by-Verse Study*, 233.
5 He cites Isaiah 32:1 by mistake; it should be Daniel 2:44.
6 Ibid., 233-36.
7 Ibid., 236.
8 Adams, 3.
9 Boettner, 20.
10 Ibid., 198.
11 John Calvin, *Institutes of the Christian Religion*, Henry Beveridge, trans. (Grand Rapids, MI: Eerdmans, 1989), book 3, chapter 25, section 5, 265 [bracketed comments mine].
12 Tan, *The Interpretation of Prophecy*, 58 [bracketed comment mine].
13 Sproul, *The Last Days According to Jesus*, 198.
14 Ibid.
15 Ice and Demy, *Fast Facts on Bible Prophecy*, 12.
16 J. D. Douglas, gen. ed., *The New International Dictionary of the Christian Church*, 794.
17 Ibid.
18 Gary North, publisher's preface in *The Great Tribulation* by David Chilton, xiii.
19 Ibid.
20 Boettner, 14.
21 Douglas, 659.
22 Ibid.
23 Sproul, 198.
24 Ibid.
25 Boettner, 17.
26 Kyle, *The Last Days Are Here Again: A History of the End Times*, 21.
27 Ice and Demy, 134.
28 Tan, 58.
29 Barnhouse, *Revelation: An Expository Commentary*, 424.
30 Feinberg, *Premillennialism or Amillennialism?*, 41.
31 John Walvoord, "Escape from Planet Earth," in *Foreshocks of Antichrist*, ed. William T. James, 356.
32 Tan, 26.
33 Lindsey, *The Late Great Planet Earth*, 176.
34 Ibid., 181.
35 Van Impe, 237.
36 Ibid.
37 Ibid., 239.
38 Boettner, 80.
39 Oswald Allis, *Prophecy and the Church* (Philadelphia: Presbyterian and Reformed, 1964), 241.
40 Adams, 5.
41 B. B. Warfield, *Calvin and Augustine* (Philadelphia: Presbyterian and Reformed, 1956), 309.
42 *Compton's Pictured Encyclopedia*, s,v. "Augustine, St."
43 St. Augustine, *The City of God*, 719-20.
44 Ibid., 720.
45 Ibid., 723.
46 Ice and Demy, 12-13.
47 Bruce L. Shelley, entry on "Hodge, Charles," J. D. Douglas, gen. ed., *The New International Dictionary of the Christian Church*, 473.

48 Charles Hodge, *Systematic Theology*, vol. 2 (New York: Charles Scribner's Sons, 1872), 94.
49 A. A. Hodge, *Outlines of Theology* (New York: Hodder and Stoughton, 1878), 568.
50 Harold Lindsell, entry on "Warfield, B. B.," J. D. Douglas, ed., *The New International Dictionary of the Christian Church*, 1,030.
51 B. B. Warfield, *The Saviour of the World*, 129. Quoted in An *Eschatology of Victory*, Kik, 5.
52 B.B. Warfield, "The Gospel of the Second Coming," in *The Bible Magazine*, April 1915.
53 J. G. Vos, *Reformed Presbyterian Testimony* (Belfast, 1901), 137.
54 Quoted in Philip Schaff, Savoy Confession, *Creeds of Christendom*, 723, cited in Kik, 13.
55. Westminister Confession.
56 Kik, 14.
57 Boettner, 45.
58 Ibid.
59 M. R. DeHaan, *The Second Coming of Jesus* (Grand Rapids, MI: Zondervan, 1944, 1971), 110.
60 Boettner, 46-47.
61 Ibid., 52.
62 Ibid., 53.
63 Ibid., 38.
64 Ibid., 39.
65 Ibid., 40.
66 Snowden.
67 Boettner, 33.
68 Samuel L. Blumenfeld, *Is Public Education Necessary?* (Boise, ID: The Paradigm Company, 1985), p. 10.
69 Quoted in Ferdinand S. Schenck, *Christian Evidences and Ethics* (New York: Young Men's Christian Association Press, 1910), 85.
70 For more details on this see D. James Kennedy and Jerry Newcombe, *What If Jesus Had Never Been Born?* (Nashville: Thomas Nelson, 1994) and D. James Kennedy and Jerry Newcombe, *What If the Bible Had Never Been Written?* (Nashville: Thomas Nelson, 1998).
71. Boettner, *The Millennium*, 59.
72 Quoted in Ibid., 33-34.
73 Quoted in Ibid., 35.

Chapter 15

1 R. B. Girdlestone, *The Grammar of Prophecy*, 1, quoted in *Encyclopedia of Biblical Prophecy* by J. Barton Payne, 38.
2 Barker, gen. ed., *The NIV Study Bible*, 1,298.
3 Walvoord, *Major Bible Prophecies: 37 Crucial Prophecies That Affect You Today*, 166.
4 Ibid., 155.
5 Ibid.
6. The discerning reader may notice a discrepancy in that 445+33=478, not 483.
7 Ibid., 170.
8 Payne, 667.
9 E. B. Pusey, *Daniel the Prophet* (New York: Funk and Wagnalls, 1891), quoted in Payne, 667.
10 Oskar Skarsaune, *Endtimes* (Oslo, Norway: Credo Forlag, 1992).
11 Walvoord, 149-59.
12 Ibid., 154.
13 Kik, *An Eschatology of Victory*, 102.
14 Ibid., 106-7.
15 Scofield, ed., *Scofield Reference Bible*, 914.
16 Kik, 107.
17 Ibid., 108.
18 Ibid., 109-10.
19 Ibid., 110.

20 Ibid.
21 Hindson, *Is the Antichrist Alive and Well?: 10 Keys to His Identity*, 135.
22 DeMar, *Last Days Madness: The Folly of Trying to Predict When Christ Will Return*, 175.
23 Ibid., 38-40 [emphasis in first instance his; all the rest mine].
24 Van Impe, *Revelation Revealed: A Verse-by-Verse Study*, 124-25 [emphasis mine].
25 DeMar, 171 [emphasis his].
26 Ibid., 172.
27 Hindson, 130.
28 Boettner, *The Millennium*, 221.
29 Ibid., 221-22.
30 George M. Marsden, *Fundamentalism and American Culture: The Shaping of Twentieth-Century Evangelicalism: 1870–1925* (Oxford: Oxford University Press, 1980), 60-61.
31 Ibid., 58.
32 Feinberg, *Premillennialism or Amillennialism?*, 18.
33 Anderson, *The Coming Prince*, 147.

Chapter 16
1 Jeffrey, *Armageddon: Appointment with Destiny*, 159.
2 Lindsey calls the Rapture "Project Disappearance." Lindsey, *The Late Great Planet Earth*, 135. He also calls it "the ultimate trip" and "the living end" (p. 137).
3 DeHaan, *The Second Coming of Jesus*, 16.
4 Ibid., 66.
5 MacPherson, *The Incredible Cover-Up*, 3.
6 Van Impe, *Revelation Revealed: A Verse-by-Verse Study*, 82.
7 St. Augustine, *The Confessions, The City of God, On Christian Doctrine* (Chicago: Encyclopedia Britannica, 1952), 534-35.
8 John Calvin, *Commentaries on the Epistles of Paul the Apostle to the Philippians, Colossians, and Thessalonians* (Grand Rapids, MI: Eerdmans, 1948), 283 [emphasis his].
9 Ibid.
10 Dave MacPherson, *The Great Rapture Hoax* (Fletcher: New Puritan Library, 1983), 137.
11 Ibid., 125.
12 Van Kampen, *The Rapture Question Answered*, 47-48 [emphasis his].
13 Ibid., 79.
14 Ibid., 131.
15 Ibid., 64.
16 Oswald J. Smith, *Tribulation or Rapture—Which?* (London: The Sovereign Grace Advent Testimony, undated).
17 Lloyd-Jones, *The Church and the Last Things*, vol. 3, 147.
18 Wallechinsky, Wallace, and Wallace, *The People's Almanac™ Presents The Book of Lists*, 469.
19 Elisabeth Kubler-Ross, *On Death and Dying* (New York: Macmillan, 1969), 7.
20 Herbert Lee Williams, *A Man You Can Trust* (Memphis: Kirbilee Books, 1977), 111.
21 Robert Ervin Hough, *The Christian After Death* (Chicago: Moody Press, 1974), 9.
22 John E. Zoller, *Heaven* (Windsor, ON: Babington, 1965), 5-6.
23 Quoted in "Death Whispers," by Philip Yancey, *Christianity Today*, 13 May 1988.
24 Williams, *A Man You Can Trust*, 111.
25 Hough, *The Christian After Death*, 16.

Chapter 17
1 DeHaan, *The Second Coming of Jesus*, 86.
2 Lindsey, *The Late Great Planet Earth*, 80.
3 Hindson, *Is the Antichrist Alive and Well?: 10 Keys to His Identity*, 164.
4 Ice and Demy, *Fast Facts on Bible Prophecy*, 107.
5 Lloyd-Jones, *The Church and the Last Things*, vol. 3, 113.

6 Jeffrey, *Armageddon: Appointment with Destiny*, 10.
7 Green, *How to Read Prophecy*, 117.
8 Hughes, *Interpreting Prophecy*, 108.
9 Ibid., 104.
10 Scofield, ed., *Scofield Reference Bible*, 1,147.
11 Ibid., 1,151.
12 Hughes, 104-5.
13 Ibid., 105.
14 Ibid., 107.
15 Jeffrey, 12.
16 Van Kampen, *The Rapture Question Answered*, 92.
17 John Wilmot, *Inspired Principles of Prophetic Interpretation* (Swengel, PA: Reiner, 1967), 94.
18 Boettner, *The Millennium*, rev. ed., 310.
19 Lloyd-Jones, 109.
20 Hindson, 168.
21 Benjamin Disraeli, *Beaconsfield's Life of Lord Bentinck*, quoted in Lawson, *Greatest Thoughts About Jesus Christ*, 131.
22 Jeffrey, 77.
23 Ibid.
24 Ibid., 79.
25 Lindsey, *Planet Earth: The Final Chapter*, 25.
26 A whole book devoted to this point is written by a messianic Jew: Michael L. Brown, *Our Hands Are Stained with Blood: The Tragic Story of the "Church" and the Jewish People* (Shippensburg, PA: Destiny Image® Publishers, 1992, 1997).
27 DeMar, *Last Days Madness: The Folly of Trying to Predict When Christ Will Return*, 83-84.
28 Grace Halsell, *Prophecy and Politics: Militant Evangelists on the Road to Nuclear War* (Westport, CT: Lawrence Hill and Co., 1986), 195.
29 DeMar, 84.
30 Dwight Wilson, *Armageddon Now!: The Premillenarian Response to Russia and Israel Since 1917* (Tyler, TX: Institute for Christian Economics, 1977, 1991), 95.
31 Ibid., 96-97.
32 DeMar, 184.
33 Ibid., 126.
34 Lindsey, *Planet Earth: The Final Chapter*, 15.
35 For more on a Christian condemnation of anti-Semitism, see D. James Kennedy and Jerry Newcombe, *What If Jesus Had Never Been Born?*, 212-214.
36 Hughes, *Interpreting Prophecy*,94.
37 Ibid., 85.

Chapter 18

1 St. Polycarp, *Epistle to the Philippians*, quoted in *Encyclopedia of Religious Quotations*, ed. Frank S. Meade, (Old Tappan, NJ: Fleming H. Revell, 1965), 9.
2 Robinson, *The Ten Commandments*, xii-xiii.
3 Ed Hindson writes, "Anti-Catholic fundamentalists were convinced that Kennedy was going to form an alliance with the pope and the communists and take over the world." *Is the Antichrist Alive and Well?: 10 Keys to His Identity*, 20.
4 This list is comprised from different sources, but primarily from Hindson, *Is the Antichrist Alive and Well?* 19-21, and Richard Kyle, *The Last Days Are Here Again: A History of the End Times*, 131-32.
5 Associated Press, 19 January 1995, 6:40 EST, V0463.
6 St. Augustine, *The Confessions, The City of God, On Christian Doctrine*, 546.
7 Green, *How to Read Prophecy*, 76-77.
8 Ibid., 108.
9 DeMar, *Last Days Madness: The Folly of Trying to Predict When Christ Will Return*, 157.

10 G. C. Berkouwer, *The Return of Christ*, 279.
11 John Foxe, *Foxe's Book of Martyrs* (Springdale, PA: Whitaker House, 1563, 1981), 18, 26.
12 D. James Kennedy and Jerry Newcombe, *What If Jesus Had Never Been Born?*, 160.
13 St. Augustine, 546.
14 David Barrett, comments on D. James Kennedy, *The Coral Ridge Hour*, Fort Lauderdale, FL, 8 November 1998.
15 Little, *Know What You Believe*, 125.

Chapter 19

1 Michael Reagan and Bob Phillips, *The All American Quote Book* (Eugene, OR: Harvest House, 1995), 256.
2 Laurie Copans, "Temple Rebuilding Goes Mainstream," Associated Press, 18 October 1998.
3 Randall Price, *Jerusalem in Prophecy* (Eugene, OR: Harvest House, 1998), 253.
4 Ibid., 255.
5 Lindsey, *The Late Great Planet Earth*, 56.
6 David Brown, *Christ's Second Coming: Will It Be Premillennial?* (Grand Rapids, MI: Baker Book House, 1876, 1983), 375.
7 Ibid., 379.
8 DeMar, *Last Days Madness: The Folly of Trying to Predict When Christ Will Return*, 29 [bracketed comment is mine].
9 Ibid., 59.
10 Kik, *An Eschatology of Victory*, 138.
11 Tan, *The Interpretation of Prophecy*, 296.
12 Lloyd-Jones, *The Church and the Last Things*, Great Doctrines of the Bible, vol. 3, 109 [bracketed comment is mine].
13 Mathison, *Dispensationalism: Rightly Dividing the People of God?*, 8.
14 Tan, 349.
15 Brown, 53.
16 Ibid., 54.
17 To clarify his point, we also added the end of verse 22 and the beginning of 24.
18 Ibid., 55.
19 DeHaan, *The Second Coming of Jesus*, 66.
20 Felician A. Foy, ed., *The 1988 Catholic Almanac*, 199.
21 Boettner, *The Millennium*, 275.
22 Blackstone, *Jesus Is Coming*, 103-6.
23 Brown, 260, 290.
24 Ibid., 218.
25 Ice and Demy, *Fast Facts on Bible Prophecy*, 116.
26 Adams, *The Time Is at Hand*, 38.
27 Kik, 167.
28 Ibid.
29 Ibid., 171.
30 Tan, 273-74.
31 Thomas Aquinas, *A Tour of the Summa [Summa Theological]*, Paul J. Glenn, ed., (St. Louis: B. Herder Book, 1960), The Last Things, Question 88, "Time and Place of the General Judgment," 445.
32 Ibid., Question 89, "Persons to be Present at the Last Judgment," 446.
33 Scofield, ed., *Scofield Reference Bible*, 1,147.
34 Ibid., 1,151.
35 Brown, 310.
36 Hughes, *Interpreting Prophecy*, 105.
37 Scofield, 1,341.
38 Mark Twain, cable to Associated Press on 2 June 1897.

39 Chafer, quoted in Feinberg, *Premillennialism or Amillennialism?*, foreword.
40 Lindsey, 176.
41 DeMar, 6.
42 Brown, 17.

Chapter 20

1 Lloyd-Jones, *The Church and the Last Things*, Great Doctrines of the Bible, vol. 3, 83.
2 *Parade* magazine, 2 December 1984, 17.
3 *Dialogue with Trypho*, 80f. Quoted in Hughes, *Interpreting Prophecy*, 100-1.
4 Mathison, *Dispensationalism: Rightly Dividing the People of God?*, 122.
5 E. Schuyler English, *Re-Thinking the Rapture: An Examination of What the Scriptures Teach as to the Time of the Translation of the Church in Relation to the Tribulation* (Neptune, NJ: Loizeaux Brothers, 1954), 26.
6 DeMar, *Last Days Madness: The Folly of Trying to Predict When Christ Will Return*, 24.
7 DeHaan, *The Second Coming of Jesus*, 17.
8 Joey Adams, *The God Bit* (New York: Mason & Lipscomb Publishers, 1974), 183.
9 Van Kampen, *The Rapture Question Answered*, 77.
10 Quoted in DeMar, 142.
11 Ibid., 20.
12 Gary North, publisher's preface in *The Great Tribulation* by David Chilton, xi.
13 Van Impe, *Revelation Revealed: A Verse-by-Verse Study*, 233.
14 Alexander Reese, *The Approaching Advent of Christ* (Grand Rapids, MI: Kregel, 1975), 240.
15 C. S. Lewis, *Mere Christianity* (New York: Macmillan, 1960), 51 [bracketed comment is mine].
16 Lindsey, *Planet Earth: The Final Chapter*, 26.
17 Hindson, *Is the Antichrist Alive and Well?: 10 Keys to His Identity*, 182.
18 Charles Spurgeon, *The Quotable Spurgeon* (Wheaton, IL: Harold Shaw, 1870, 1990), 37.
19 For further details, see D. James Kennedy with Jerry Newcombe, *The Gates of Hell Shall Not Prevail* (Nashville: Thomas Nelson, 1996), Chapter 11.
20 Tim LaHaye, "The Signs of the Times Imply His Coming," Van Diest, gen. ed., *Ten Reasons Why Jesus Is Coming Soon: Ten Christian Leaders Share Their Insights*, 193.
21 Payne, *Encyclopedia of Biblical Prophecy*, 583.
22 Transcript from interview with James Montgomery Boice (Fort Lauderdale, FL: CRM-TV, June 1994), 2-3.
23 Berkouwer, *The Return of Christ*, 66.
24 Tan, *Encyclopedia of 7,700 Illustrations: Signs of the Time*, 1,239-40.
25 Walter B. Knight, *Knight's Master Book of New Illustrations* (Grand Rapids, MI: Eerdmans, 1956), 604.
26 Payne, *The History of Islam*, xi.
27 Little, *Know What You Believe*, 124.
28 Ibid., 126.
29 Ibid., 128.

Chapter 21

1 Quoted in *The Encyclopedia of Religious Quotations* ed. Frank S. Mead, (Old Tappan, NJ: Fleming H. Revell, 1965), 358.
2 Comment to author by Rev. Ron Kilpatrick, chief librarian at Knox Theological Seminary, Fort Lauderdale, Florida, 1997.
3 B. J. Oropeza, *99 Reasons Why No One Knows When Christ Will Return* (Downers Grove, IL: InterVarsity Press, 1994), 175-76.
4 Eva Shaw, *Eve of Destruction: Prophecies, Theories, and Preparations for the End of the World* (Los Angeles: Lowell House, 1947), 11-14.
5 Kyle, *The Last Days Are Here Again: A History of the End Times*, 24.
6 Jonathan Z. Smith and William S. Green, eds., *The Harper Collins Dictionary of Religion* (San

Francisco: Harper, 1995), 221-22.

7 Erdoes, *A.D. 2000: Living on the Brink of Apocalypse*, 1, 194.

8 Quoted by Tim Dowley, organizing editor, in *Eerdmans Handbook to the History of Christianity* (Grand Rapids, MI: Eerdmans, 1977), 74.

9 Bernard McGinn, *Antichrist* (San Francisco: Harper, 1994), 173.

10 St. Augustine, *The City of God*, XXII, 30.

11 Christopher Columbus, *Book of Prophecies*, Kay Brigham, trans. (Fort Lauderdale, FL: TSELF, 1991, originally written 1502), 181.

12 Nostradamus, Century 10, Quatrain 72, quoted in Erika Cheetham, *The Final Prophecies of Nostradamus* (New York: Pedigree Books, 1989), 424.

13 This becomes confusing, but this is how William Miller arrived at the 1843 date. In making his calculations, he used one day to equal one year (Ezek. 4:6) and relied on two passages in Daniel. The first, Daniel 9:24-27, says that after seventy weeks (or 490 days), the Messiah will come to save Israel. Using as a starting date 457 B.C., the year that King Artaxerxes decreed the temple should be rebuilt in Jerusalem, he arrived at 33/34 A.D., which was the year Christ was crucified. Therefore, he believed this prophecy had already been fulfilled. The other passage, Daniel 8:14, says that the sanctuary will be cleansed in 2,300 days. For this calculation, he also used the same starting date of 457 B.C. He then arrived at A.D. 1843 Note that in order for his calculations to work, both the seventy weeks and the 2,300 days must run concurrently.

14 Anthony A. Hoekema, *The Four Major Cults* (Grand Rapids, MI: Eerdmans, 1963), 92-98.

15 Richard Abanes, *End-Time Visions: The Road to Armageddon?* (Nashville: Broadman & Holman Publishers, 1998), 229.

16 John H. Gerstner, *The Theology of the Major Sects* (Grand Rapids, MI: Baker Book House, 1963), 34.

17 Hoekema, 252-54.

18 Abanes, 69-74, 235.

19 Hoekema, 308.

20 Abanes, 243, 397.

21 Robert W. Balch, John Domirovitch, Barbara Mahnke, Vanessa Morrison, "Fifteen Years of Failed Prophecy: Coping with Cognitive Dissonance in a Baha'i Sect," in *Millennium, Messiahs, and Mayhem*, eds. Thomas Robbins and Susan J. Palmer, (New York: Routledge, 1997), 73-90.

22 LaHaye, "The Signs of the Times Imply His Coming," 193.

23 Quoted in Kyle, 27.

24 Boettner, *The Millennium*, 364.

25 Dowley, 74.

26 Boettner, 335-36.

27 Ibid., 336.

28 McGinn, 173.

29 Columbus, 181.

30 Quoted in Boettner, 336.

31 Oropeza, 79.

32 Ibid.

33 Ibid.

34 Ibid.

35 Quoted in ibid., 340. L. S. Chafer, *Bibliotheca Sacra*, July-September 1952.

36 Lindsey, *The Late Great Planet Earth*, 54.

37 Oropeza, 175.

38 Whisenant, *88 Reasons Why the Rapture Will Be in 1988*.

39 Kyle, 139.

40 Harold Camping, *1994?* (New York: Vantage, 1992).

41 Oropeza, *99 Reasons Why No One Knows When Christ Will Return*, 22.

42 Ibid., 33.

43 Ibid., 34.

44 Ibid., 43.
45 Ibid., 62.

Chapter 22

1 Eleanor Doan, *Speakers Sourcebook II* (Grand Rapids: Ministry Resources Library, a division of Zondervan, 1968), 77 [emphasis hers].
2 *Nelson's Illustrated Bible Dictionary* (Nashville: Thomas Nelson, 1986), 960.
3 DeMar, *Last Days Madness: The Folly of Trying to Predict When Christ Will Return*, 16.
4 D. A. Miller, *Watch and Be Ready! 1992 Millions Disappear,* cited in Oropeza, *99 Reasons Why No One Knows When Christ Will Return*, 46.
5 DeMar, 4.
6 "Coming Out: Breaking Free from Homosexuality," Fort Lauderdale, FL: Coral Ridge Ministries, 11 October 1998.
7 Green, *How to Read Prophecy*, 130.
8 Charles R. Swindoll, "The Scripture Anticipates His Coming," John Van Diest, ed., *Ten Reasons Why Jesus Is Coming Soon: Ten Christian Leaders Share Their Insights*, 12-13.
9 Matthew Henry, *Matthew Henry's Commentary* (Grand Rapids, MI: Zondervan, 1960), 1,485.
10 Ibid., 1,335.
11 Ibid., 1,856.
12 The 1997 version is available from Reformation Christian Ministries, 13950 122nd Street, Felsmere, FL 32948-6411; phone: 561-571-8833; e-mail: rcm@ask.net.
13 Art Linkletter, *Kids Say the Darndest Things* (Caroline House, 1978), 81.
14 Ibid., 73.
15 Swindoll, 11.
16 Green, 132.
17 David Breese, *Living for Eternity* (Chicago: Moody Press, 1988), 102.
18 Quoted in ibid., 16-17.
19 D. L. Moody, *Heaven How to Get There* (Springdale, PA: Whitaker House, 1982), 76.
20 D. James Kennedy with Jerry Newcombe, *The Gates of Hell Shall Not Prevail*, 238 (quote slightly adapted).
21 Quoted in Boettner, *The Millennium*, 29.
22 Douglas, gen. ed., *The New International Dictionary of the Christian Church*, 452.
23 Adolf Harnack quoted in Feinberg, *Premillennialism or Amillennialism?*, 28.
24 John Nelson Darby, speech in Geneva, 1840, in William Kelly, ed., *The Collected Writings of J. N. Darby*, Prophetic no. 1, vol. 1 (Kingston-on-Thames: Stow Hill Bible and Tract Depot, undated), 471, 486.
25 Colonel V. Doner, *The Late Great GOP and the Coming Realignment* (Vallecito, CA: Chalcedon Foundation, 1998), 41-42 [emphasis his].
26 Ibid.
27 George Barna, *Absolute Confusion: How Our Moral and Spiritual Foundations Are Eroding in This Age of Change* (Ventura, CA: Regal Books, 1993), 86-87.
28 The most scientific study on sex in America to date was conducted under the auspices of the University of Chicago and released in 1993. It found: "About 1.4 percent of the women said they thought of themselves as homosexual or bisexual and about 2.8 percent of the men identified themselves in this way." Source: Robert T. Michael, John H. Gagnon, Edward O. Laumann, and Gina Kolata, *Sex in America: A Definitive Study* (Boston: Little, Brown and Company, 1993), 176.
29 Hindson, *Is the Antichrist Alive and Well?: 10 Keys to His Identity*, 157-58.
30 "Center for Religious Freedom," Washington, DC: Puebla Institute, 20 February 1998, 33.
31 David Shibley, ed., *Challenging Quotes for World Changers* (Green Forest, AR: New Leaf Press, 1995).
32 W. G. Blaikie, *The Personal Life of David Livingstone*, 162, 478, quoted in Iain H. Murray, *The Puritan Hope: A Study in Revival and the Interpretation of Prophecy* (Edinburgh: The Banner of Truth Trust, 1971), 182, 183.

Chapter 23

1 Quoted in *The Encyclopedia of Religious Quotations* ed. Frank S. Mead, 394.

2 The discerning reader may recognize a paraphrased version of the two diagnostic questions used in Dr. D. James Kennedy's Evangelism Explosion program, based in Fort Lauderdale, Florida.

3 Alan Stibbs, ed., *Search the Scriptures* (Downers Grove, IL: InterVarsity Press, 1949, 1974).

4 Charlotte Brontë, *Jane Eyre* (New York: A Signet Classic, The New American Library, Inc., 1960), 456.

Index

A

B

C

D

I

J

K

L

M

Scripture Index

Joel

Amos

Micah

Zechariah

Malachi

Matthew

Mark

2 Thessalonians

2 Timothy

Titus

Hebrews

1 Peter

2 Peter

1 John

Jude

Revelation

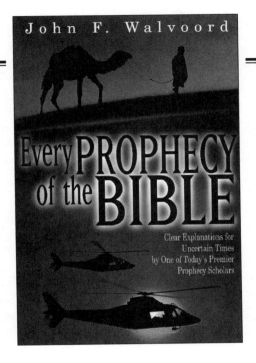

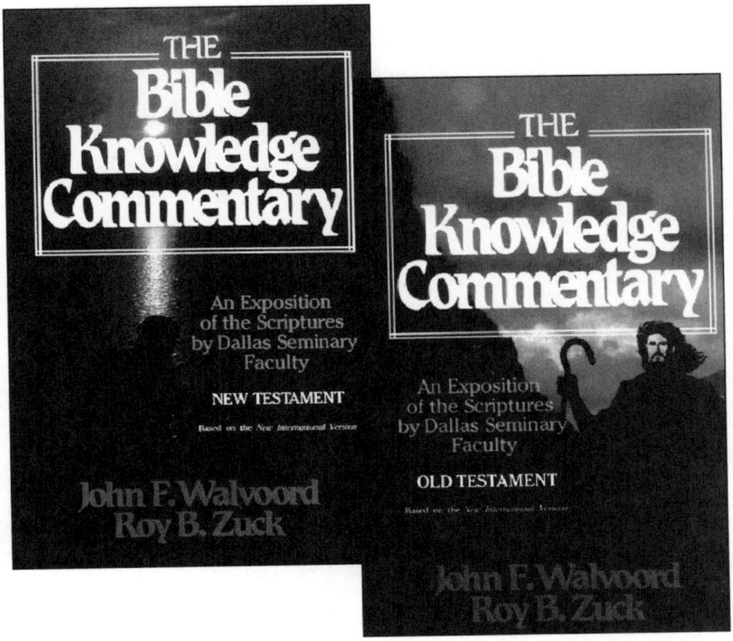

THE BIBLE KNOWLEDGE COMMENTARY

by John F. Walvoord & Roy Zuck

Old Testament ISBN: 0-88207-813-5

New Testament ISBN: 0-88207-812-7

"How do Bible-time customs help me understand the meaning of this passage?" "How can this alledged contradiction be explained?" *The Bible Knowledge Commentary* answers these and other questions about the Scriptures, discussing the Bible verse by verse and often phrase by phrase. In addition, maps, charts, and diagrams help you grasp the meanings of the biblical text. Unlike most others this commentary is by authors from one school—Dallas Theological Seminary. *The Bible Knowledge Commentary*—popular in style and scholarly in content—will deepen your understanding of God's written Word.